Beyond Political Independence
Zambia's Development Predicament in the 1980s

BEYOND
POLITICAL INDEPENDENCE

Zambia's Development Predicament
in the 1980s

Edited by

KLAAS WOLDRING

with special assistance from
CHIBWE CHIBAYE

Mouton Publishers
Berlin · New York · Amsterdam

CIP-Kurztitelaufnahme der Deutschen Bibliothek

Beyond political independence: Zambia's development
predicament in the 1980s / ed. by Klaas Woldring with
special assistance from Chibwe Chibaye.
– Berlin; New York; Amsterdam: Mouton, 1984.
   ISBN 3–11–009951–9

Library of Congress Cataloging in Publication Data

1. Zambia--Economic conditions--1964-   --Addresses,
essays, lectures. 2. Zambia--Social conditions--
1964-   --Addresses, essays, lectures. 3. Zambia--
Politics and government--1964-   --Addresses, essays,
lectures. I. Woldring, Klaas, 1934-   · II. Chibaye,
Chibwe.
HC915.B48 1984   330.96894'04   84-20715
ISBN 3-11-009951-9

To Aafke,
whose name means *African*,
a wife with courage, compassion and loyalty.

Contents

Notes on the Contributors

Dr. Peter Meyns was Head of the Department of African Development Studies, University of Zambia (UNZA) in the period 1979 to 1982 and now lectures at the Universität-Gesamthochschule, Duisburg, West Germany. He has published previously on development problems in Mozambique, Tanzania and Zimbabwe.

Dr. Marcia Burdette is a Professor in Political Science at Fordham University, New York. She was a Research Affiliate with the Institute for African Studies (UNZA) in 1981 — her second stint in Zambia — and is now working for CUSO in Lusaka.

Dr. Mulenga Bwalya is a Lecturer in the Department of Political and Administrative Studies at UNZA who has specialised in rural development and politics.

Professor David Evans was formerly Director of UNZA's Rural Development Studies Bureau. He retired in 1981.

Professor Roger Tangri was Head of the Department of Political and Administrative Studies at UNZA until mid-1982. Previously he worked as an academic in Sierra Leone and Malawi.

Gilbert Mudenda, M.Soc.Sc. (The Hague), is a Lecturer in the Department of African Development Studies at UNZA.

Dr. Raj Bardouille is Head of the Manpower Research Unit of the Institute for African Studies at UNZA.

Francis Kasoma, M.A. is Head of the Department of Mass Communications at UNZA.

Fred Roos is a former First Secretary of the Royal Dutch Embassy in Lusaka. He returned to the Dutch Foreign Affairs Department in 1982.

Dr. Klaas Woldring was a Senior Lecturer in the Department of Political and Adminstrative Studies at UNZA from 1979 to 1981 and then returned to the Northern Rivers College of Advanced Education, Lismore, NSW, Australia.

Dr. Chibwe Chibaye, formerly Head of the Department of Political and Administrative Studies, University of Zambia, now Principal, President's Citizens College, Kabwe.

INTRODUCTION
by Klaas Woldring

Zambia is a vast and in many ways a beautiful country with ample resources for its five million inhabitants. It gained political independence in October 1964 when it ceased to exist as Northern Rhodesia; formerly, it was a component of the colonial Federation of Rhodesia and Nyasaland which was dissolved in 1963 after a precarious ten-year existence. I had the privilege to live and work in Northern Rhodesia from 1962 to 1964 and again, in Zambia, from 1979 to 1981 which enabled me to compare and contrast two quite different political situations.

It is my conviction that Zambia has come a long way since Independence Day. With some exceptions the mind of the older generation of Zambians has been well-nigh decolonised and, furthermore, the youthfulness of the Zambian population (46 % under 15 in 1980) suggests that the direct colonial experience, psychologically speaking, is virtually forgotten. Gone is the subservience or apparent subservience to whites in the colonial period that I remembered as the then migrant from Holland. Returning to Zambia in 1979, now as an Australian citizen, I at once noticed an omnipresent sense of racial equality, clearly no longer an issue except perhaps in relation to the activities of white Rhodesian infiltrators during the bush war which was still raging then.

In many areas there is evidence of growth and economic progress as compared to 1964. Yet, the realities of neo-colonialism soon revealed themselves to me. It proved to be quite a depressing, though important, learning process to be back in Zambia that can only be explained with great difficulty to citizens of affluent Western nations who have never lived in a Third World country.

In 1983 Zambia, viewed from both political and economic perspectives, stands at a crossroads. The first post-independence phase is behind her. The ageing nationalist leadership, heroes of yesteryear, have found the involvement in the liberation wars and the mounting economic problems of the 1970s as much as they could take. President Kaunda and some of his able lieutenants have taken the challenges on the chin and continue to do so, but many other party faithfuls have fallen by the wayside. The younger leadership, spread very thinly, thus far has not lived up to expectations. Austerity measures are the order of the day. Foreign exchange problems on and off bedevil development plans at every level. Educational reforms, long contemplated, don't get off the ground. Real wages have fallen steadily, the oil price went up 12fold and unemployment has risen dramatically during the 1970s. Whither Zambia? What happened to the promise of the late sixties? Zambia is not lacking in natural resources but it it clear even to casual visitors that the Government appears to be increasingly unable to tap these resources fully. Zambia is not without friends however. The President and his Cabinet Ministers have knocked on many doors in their search for development aid and assistance to overcome the ravages of the wars of liberation in Zimbabwe, Angola, Namibia and South Africa. They have usually been given a sympathetic hearing both in Western and Socialist capitals and although the terms may sometimes have been harsh Zambia has been bailed out throughout the post-independence period. There has always been adequate confidence in the recovery of the economy and the stability of the political system and, in the longer term, the solution of the liberation struggles in adjacent lands. This confidence is now at a low ebb. Negotiations with the International Monetary Fund during 1981 and 1982 have been lengthy and tough, resulting in a 20% devaluation of the Kwacha in January 1983 — this in spite of a greater flexibility and sense of North-South realism on the part of the Fund in recent months. The President frequently appeals to the people, urging them to attain self-sufficiency in food production to counter dependence on imported foods which has increased considerably in recent years. It is hopeful that the Government has launched a multimillion dollar wheat production programme in the course of 1982, aimed at making the country self-sufficient in wheat by the end of this decade. Critics of such efforts argue that Zambia should instead concentrate on stimulating the production of indigenous crops because it would be both cheaper and more relevant to the majority of her population.

The Canadian International Development Agency (CIDA) is convinced however "given better farm management techniques" that Zambia could rapidly increase her wheat-growing capacity by launching new and expanding existing rain-fed programmes with yields well above the world average. If the 1980s were to prove this claim, a change in the Zambian diet may be preferable to malnutrition or, worse, starvation.

This text aims to analyse the various aspects of Zambia's political economy as well as her foreign relations. All contributions are original. With the exception of the editor's chapter on foreign policy, part of which was published in the December 1980 issue of *Australian Outlook*, none has been published before. Nearly all were written specifically for this volume which was planned first in late-1980. Most chapters were completed during 1982, though some date back to late 1981. All authors have an intimate knowledge of Zambian political and economic conditions. All except one have been associated with the University of Zambia for several years.

Peter Meyns opens the volume with a perceptive overview of Zambia's political economy. This is followed by an in-depth study of the copper mining industry by Marcia Burdette. Mrs Burdette's chapter is a fairly long one but has been included because it must rank as one of the most thorough and helpful analyses of that industry in recent years. The rural sector is covered by three chapters: Mulenga Bwalya highlights the powerlessness of the peasants in that sector which suggests that their values and economic opportunities are likely to remain in limbo for the foreseeable future, however undesirable this may be; Bwalya argues furthermore that the essence of official efforts at "decentralisation" and "participatory democracy" is to achieve more effective control by the national elite over the peasantry rather than their free and independent mobilisation; and David Evans' short chapter reinforces this thesis by emphasising the unfavourable pricing policies for small-scale producers and their transport and marketing problems. Evans makes a plea for much greater encouragement of small-scale producers on economic grounds rather than pushing cooperative ventures or gigantic schemes like the new State Farms Project.

I review some of the recommendations by the French agronomist, René Dumont, who visited Zambia for the second time in October 1979 — again invited by President Kaunda. The very limited circulation of Dumont's frank report and his critical remarks outside Zambia after his research visit suggest that the Government didn't like his findings and recommendations this time. Nevertheless, some of his ideas were in fact incorporated subsequently in the multi-strategy Operation Food Production. Roger Tangri presents a case study of the Industrial Development Corporation of Zambia (INDECO), a Holding Parastatal which, since independence, has been the Government's principal instrument for the implementation of its industrial policies. Gilbert Mudenda discusses the process of class formation in contemporary Zambia. His Marxist analysis of social reality is an essential ingredient of this text though it should not be assumed that all other contributions are necessarily based on strictly Marxist interpretations. Raj Bardouille introduces the reader to a study of Lusaka's growing Informal Sector and particularly provides insights into the role of women in that fringe market situation. I undertook the thorny and no doubt controversial task of delving into emerging corruption patterns that have surfaced in Zambia in recent years. In addition, glaring cases of inefficiency, mismanagement, tribalism and nepotism, revealed by several public inquiries but not always acted upon, are discussed. It needs to be stated at the outset that the President has relentlessly urged his senior officials to perform their tasks diligently and honestly and to set the right example. A new Anti-Corruption Act (1980) and an extensive inquiry into the Civil Service in 1981 and 1982 were the result of such official concern. The 1980s should reveal how effective these measures may prove to be. By 1982 it was obvious that there was considerable distrust, even contempt, for party officialdom and senior bureaucrats in the cities and, even more so, in rural areas. The misuse of political power for private gain is perhaps still not widespread and therefore containable in Zambia. But swift and quite drastic action is needed if respect for authority is not to be undermined further or, better still, to be restored. Francis Kasoma presents an interesting chapter on the rôle of the press and its nature in Zambia. Emphasising its education function, Kasoma also believes that the Western-orientated news reporting tradition is likely to continue throughout the 1980s. We can only speculate as to the effects of the Press Bill still before Parliament and the proposed takeover from the multi-national Lonrho of the *Times of Zambia* by the Zambian Government announced recently. The final section comprises two chapters, one by Klaas Woldring on foreign policy, with special reference to the Southern African geopolitical context, and one most innovative chapter by Fred Roos on external aid agencies. Roos' chapter, based on much practical experience, contains several policy recommendations which should be of interest to aid experts working on the ground in developing countries. While it is quite true, as Dr. Leonard Chivuno, Director of Zambia's National Planning and Development Commission has said, that foreign experts are expensive and sometimes quite wasteful to Zambia, Roos tries to show how existing programmes and foreign expertise could be integrated and coordinated much better to achieve greater effectiveness and continuity.

This text should appeal to the general reader interested in development problems, students at tertiary institutions in Zambia and elsewhere as well as to specialist officials working in the areas of foreign affairs and development aid.

Acknowledgements

The welcome contribution of the Northern Rivers College of Advanced Education, Lismore, N.S.W., Australia, towards the preparation of the manuscript is gratefully acknowledged. Special thanks is extended to Mrs Norma Hawkins for greatly improving the style and grammar of chapters 7 and 9A. The responsibility for those chapters, naturally, remains the editor's in every respect.

K.W.

CHAPTER 1

The Political Economy of Zambia
by Peter Meyns

This chapter looks at the political economy of Zambia. The analysis will be limited to the main features of Zambia's development since independence, leaving more detailed discussion of specific issues to other contributions in this volume.

The material conditions of production and reproduction are fundamental for an understanding of the structure of a given society. In the case of Zambia's political economy this inevitably means focusing on the rôle of copper as the centrepiece of the analysis. The first section looks at the socioeconomic structure of Zambia's development, drawing lines from colonial to post-colonial features. The second section identifies three phases of development since independence – boom, economic nationalism and crisis – and seeks to characterize each of them. Zambia's predicament is specific with regard to its dependence on copper, but far from unique among Third World countries in many respects. The purpose of this chapter is to analyse the situation in Zambia as it is and as it has evolved under the influence of international and national factors, not to discuss possible alternative strategies of development.

1. The Structure of Zambia's Development

The main feature of Zambia's political economy is its dependence on copper. In 1891 when Rhodes' British South Africa Company (BSAC) secured, by dubious means, a Royal Charter over much of what is today Zambia, its aim was to exploit the territory's mineral riches. It was not until the 1930s, however, that the copper boom in Northern Rhodesia started. By the time Zambia achieved independence the structure of its economy as a copper mono-economy was fully established.

Government policy since 1964 has not drawn into question the predominance of copper in the national economy. Rather it has sought to expand the mining industry in order to accumulate surpluses to develop other sectors of the economy. As a result, Zambia's dependence on copper was further consolidated, as was its integration into the world market with its uncertainties. The critical situation of its economy as a whole at the beginning of the 1980s is a reflection of changes on the world market but also of government policy; neither of these two factors should be neglected.

As Table 1 shows, the contribution of Zambia's copper industry to national development has been a highly unreliable factor. The ups and downs of export earnings from copper and cobald, small quantities of which are extracted from the same ore as copper, in the '70s, and the reduction of government revenue from the copper industry to zero after 1976 are the most drastic indicators. The fluctuations in export income are due to the prices paid for copper wire bars on the London Metal Exchange. After increasing steadily from K 395 per ton in 1964 to K 1,010 in 1970, thereby allowing Zambia to more than double its export earnings, the price stagnated throughout the '70s and slumped to K 765 in 1971/72 and again in 1975, when it dropped from K 1,326 (1974) to K 794 per ton. In 1979 and 1980, characterised by a new burst of inflation worldwide, the price did increase to K 1,571 and K 1,718 per ton only to drop again subsequently.

Table 1 Contribution of Copper to GDP, revenue, exports and employment

Year	Contribution to GDP		Contribution to Govt. revenue		Copper + Value of exports	Cobalt Contribution to exports	Employment Contribution in employment	
	Km.	%	Km.	%		%	'000	%
1964			57	53	302	92	46.7	17.7
1965	290	40	134	71	347	93	47.9	15.9
1966	379	44	163	64	465	95	48.9	15.7
1967	379	39	146	53	440	94	48	15.1
1968	411	38	183	60	520	96	48.2	14.7
1969	637	48	237	59	729	97	49.7	14.1
1970	457	36	218	52	688	97	49.7	13.6
1971	268	23	114	36	454	95	50.8	13.8
1972	317	23	56	19	500	93	52.8	14.1
1973	506	32	108	29	703	95	56.1	14.6
1974	607	32	341	53	846	94	57.5	14.6
1975	204	13	59	13	479	93	57.1	15.5
1976	330	18	12	3	705	94	59.1	15.9
1977	223	11	−1	—	661	94	56.7	15.4
1978	272	12	—	—	634	92	55.5	14.9
1979	470	18	-10	−2	926	86	57.7	15
1980	520	17	41	6	960	96		

Source: *Zambia Mining Year Book,* 1969-1980.

Due to the adverse price situation the copper mining companies in Zambia throttled their investments.[1] As a result the peak of 805,000 tons of copper exported in 1969 has not been touched again since. The amount exported annually was around 600,000 tons at the beginning of the '80s.

For a country which depends on foreign trade and external economic relations as much as Zambia does, the stagnation and fluctuation of world market prices for its major export product were bound to have far reaching effects. The most immediate one relates to the purchasing power of the country's export earnings to pay for its imports, its "terms of trade". While copper prices were stagnating, import prices soared after 1973 in the wake of economic crises in the leading industrial countries and world-wide inflation. This is shown in Figure 1. As a result Zambia's "terms of trade" went down from 100 in 1970 to 35 in 1978; 50 in 1979; and 31 in 1981; severely limiting its capacity to import goods as the purchasing power of its export earnings was, in 1981, less than a third of what it was in 1970. Inevitably this led to cutbacks of imports needed for industrial production, i.e. machines, spare parts, raw materials, as well as of consumer goods, and to serious shortages which in turn, together with the higher costs of imports anyway, increased inflation within the country.

Lack of foreign exchange became the most frequently cited reason for Zambia's economic problems in the 1970s. The overall balance of payments development is summarized in Table 2. It shows that Zambia has generally recorded a surplus on external trade, but that since 1969 the trade balance has experienced extreme oscillations between K 527.3 m. in 1969 and -K91.6 m. in 1975, the year of the greatest slump in world market prices for copper. The service accounts (items 4-6) have always been deficitary, reflecting Zambia's external dependence in two respects. Firstly, the main component of nonfactor services are transport and insurance charges. Being a land-locked country and strongly foreign trade-oriented, Zambia has to spend a lot of money to freight its goods to and from the ports in neighbouring countries, in addition to shipment overseas. These costs represent a heavy drain on foreign exchange. Secondly, payments regarding investment income and unrequited transfers reflect Zambia's dependence on foreign capital and expatriate manpower respectively, leading to high remittances of profits and dividends as well as salaries and gratuities. As a result, the current account, combining goods and services, has, since 1971, generally shown a deficit, as has the overall balance. To offset this deficit Zambia has had to draw on its foreign exchange reserves, increase its international borrowing, and introduce strict controls on foreign exchange spending. The annual changes in foreign exchange holdings are given in the bottom row of Table 2, mirroring the respective balance of the current and capital accounts.[2] What the Table does not show is the overall level of foreign exchange holdings. These had increased

Table 2 Balance of Payments 1964-1980 ('000,000 Kwacha)

	1964	1965	1966	1967	1968	1969	1970	1971	1972	1973	1974	1975	1976	1977	1978*	1979*	1980*
1 Exports	315.5	329.5	431.4	450.4	534	852.6	673.2	479.2	543.2	733.5	898.2	518	748.8	706.4	673.8	1091	1104.3
2 Imports	124.2	185.9	250.5	315.8	371.1	325.3	347.7	401.3	404.5	349.3	509.1	609.6	482.3	538.7	496.1	598	860
3 Trade balance	191.3	143.6	180.9	134.5	162.9	527.3	325.5	77.9	138.7	384.1	389.1	-91.6	266.5	167.7	177.7	493	244.3
4 Non-factor services	-50.2	-37.9	-60.6	-75.7	100.6	-96	-110.6	-103	-117.3	-132.6	-210.7	-215.4	-166.7	-170.2	-187.2	-288	-309
5 Investment income	-59.2	-30.6	-58	-50.6	-52.1	-47.5	-33.4	-43.6	-74.1	-77.3	-86.9	-75.1	-108.9	-104.8	-109.5	-99	-133
6 Unrequited transfers	-12.8	-22.6	-9.6	-0.1	-24.9	-51	-104.5	-107.8	-96.1	-80.2	-18.2	-79.9	-79.7	-64.6	-65	-60	-69
7 Current account (3-6)	69.1	52.5	52.7	8.4	-7.9	332.8	77	-176.5	-148.8	93.4	10.3	-462	-88.8	-171.9	-184	46	-316.7
8 Capital account	-51	-3.3	43.3	-32.1	14.3	-206.5	30.8	-37.9	33.8	-101.5	8.3	212	-47.4	-51.6	-74	97.8	82.4
9 SDR allocations	–	–	–	–	–	–	6	5.8	7.3	–	–	–	–	–	–	14.6	14.6
10 Overall Balance (7-9)	18.1	49.2	9.4	-23.7	6.4	126.3	113.8	-208.6	-107.7	-8.1	18.6	-250	-136.2	-223.5	-258.8	158.4	-219.7
11 Reserves and related items	-18.1	-49.2	-9.4	23.7	-6.4	-126.3	-113.8	208.6	107.7	8.1	-18.6	250	136.2	223.5	258.8	-158.4	219.7

* Provisional

Source: Bank of Zambia

in the first years of independence from K 153 m. in 1965 to an all time high of K 385 m. 1970. Subsequently, they dropped to K 116 m in 1980. A more drastic decrease was avoided by international borrowing. In addition Zambia piled up payment arrears to the extent of more than K 500 m. by the end of 1980.[3]

The prime importance of the copper mining industry has conditioned the overall structure of socioeconomic development in Zambia. Capital investment was concentrated in the Copperbelt and other urban centres. Colonial legislation was geared to the provision of labour power for the mines, recruited from the rural areas. Settler farmers established themselves in commercial agriculture along the line-of-rail to provide for the needs of the urban population. Agricultural improvement of the thousands of peasant households in the remoter parts of the country was largely neglected.

Since independence the pattern of extremely uneven development established under the colonial administration has in some respects been accentuated. Migration to the towns, attracted by the prospect of wage employment, has led to the growth of the urban population from 700,000 in 1963 to 2.4 million in 1930, which raised their proportion of the total population from 20 to over 40 %. As Table 1 shows, employment in the mines has not increased much since independence, nor has wage employment generally. Therefore, the influx of people to the towns was absorbed principally by the inpoverished squatter compounds, raising the number of unemployed, but also leading to an impressive spread of the informal economic sector on the fringes of established urban society. On the other hand, out-migration from the rural areas led to a disruption of the labour force there with an over-proportionate number of men away in the towns. Agricultural production in those areas, in particular of cash crops, apart from lacking government encouragement and incentives, suffered, and their marginal role in the national economy was enhanced as a result.

The build-up of manufacturing industries has followed the existing pattern. Comparing the location of industries in 1975 with that in 1966, it was noted that there was very little change. "10 towns along the line of rail together account for 98.3 % of all industrial enterprises."[4] In the towns along the line-of-rail they benefit from the proximity of developed infrastructural facilities. Furthermore, their market is along the line-of-rail, the urban population generally, and in particular the privileged strata in government and parastatal functions and in private business as well as the expatriates. It is for these strata that the import substitution industries geared to high income demand cater essentially. There are, in other words, good economic reasons to locate these industries along the line-of-rail.

The urban bias must also be seen in political terms. Given the crucial importance of the copper mining industry for the continuance of the existing

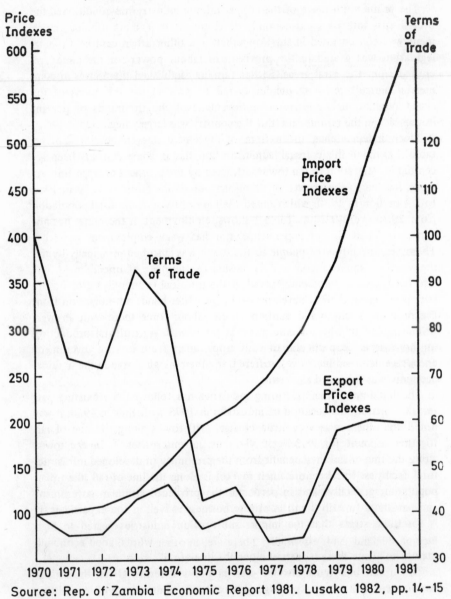

Zambia's Terms of Trade, 1970 - 1981
(1970 = 100)

Source: Rep. of Zambia Economic Report 1981. Lusaka 1982, pp. 14-15

system, the government sees a need to provide the mineworkers with material incentives. At the same time, however, as the wage conflicts in the '70s showed clearly, it seeks to keep their wages at a level in line with the mining companies and the state's interests. To keep the mines going is notably in the interest of the national elite. The foreign exchange earned by exporting copper is needed for business enterprises and to maintain the living standards of the privileged strata most strongly influenced by Western consumption patterns. As they hold a dominating rôle in Zambia's political economy, their interests carry considerable weight in government policy making. Lacking such power, the small peasants in the rural areas have been unable to counter the urban bias of Zambia's political economy.

In sum, the predominance of copper, the extremely uneven development between the line-of-rail and the remote rural areas, and the strong urban bias, principally reflecting the interests of the privileged national elite, can be seen as the main structural features of Zambia's political economy.

2. Phases of Development

a) *Postindependence Economic Boom*

The first years of independence in Zambia were years of unprecedented economic growth. This development was facilitated by an external factor: the increase of the world market price for copper by over 250 % between 1965 and 1970, which allowed Zambia to increase its export earnings by a similar margin. But the achievement of political independence was equally significant as it allowed the Zambian government to decide on the use of the revenue from the mining industry in the national interest. Until 1963 Zambia, then still Northern Rhodesia, had been part of the Central African Federation. In that period the settler-dominated Federal administration had syphoned off much of the money earned by the copper industry in Northern Rhodesia to finance development programmes in Southern Rhodesia. On the eve of independence Zambia also bought back the mineral rights of its own sub-soil riches, which the British South Africa Company had owned since 1891 and from which it had reaped bountiful profits, for a nominal amount of K 4 million, half of which the British government paid.[5]

Southern Rhodesia's Unilateral Declaration of Independence in 1965 was a further event which influenced Zambia's postindependence development. It precipitated efforts to create alternative outlets to the sea, in particular the road and rail connection to Dar es Salaam. Moreover, because of the sanctions policy against the illegal Smith-regime, Zambia was cut off from a major source of its import supplies, Southern Rhodesia having established itself as the regional industrial centre during the days of the Central African Federation. This represented a strong incentive to expand the hitherto neglected national manufacturing industries sector.

The industrialisation strategy Zambia embarked upon was essentially geared towards import substitution to reduce the amount of consumer goods and, to a lesser extent, industrial inputs it was importing, as well as to reduce the transport costs related to such imports. High growth rates averaging above 10 % p. a. were achieved in manufacturing industry between 1966 and 1974 as private enterprises sought to establish themselves on the Zambian market, and government initiated industrial projects in cooperation with foreign capital. As a result, the contribution of manufacturing to GDP doubled from 6.7 % in 1965 to 13 % in 1974. The most dynamic branch was beverages and tobacco, which by 1972 had increased its contribution to manufacturing value-added from 25 to 40 %. Large-scale enterprises, such as Livingstone Motor Assemblers, Nitrogen Chemicals of Zambia, Kafue Textiles and Nakambala Sugar Estates and refinery, were launched as joint ventures between INDECO, the parastatal holding company, and foreign partners, FIAT, Kobe Steel, Amenital and Textileconsult (Liechtenstein), and Tate & Lyle respectively. The foreign partners usually took out a minority shareholding and provided the technical and/or managerial expertise. Such cooperation with international capital and advisers as well as the principal focus on satisfying the demands of the high-income urban elite led to the production techniques adopted in manufacturing industry being generally "capital-intensive, and reliant on imports of parts and materials".[6] The case of the FIAT plant in Livingstone, putting together intermediary parts imported from Italy, is most striking. In short, imports of machinery, parts and materials were being substituted for imports of end-products. However, up to 1970 Zambia's foreign exchange reserves were increasing steadily; in this phase of its development there was no foreign exchange problem. Indeed, it can be argued that it was during these years of economic boom that the lavish spending habits were entrenched, which Zambia failed to discard in the following decade when the world copper market took a turn for the worse.

It must also be mentioned that these first years of independence also saw substantial improvements in the wage levels of urban workers. They had been notoriously underpaid under colonial rule. Following the report of the "Brown Commission" in 1966[7] the mineworkers led the way to real wage increases of over 35 % between 1966 and 1969. This also contributed to the increase of urban demand during the '60s.

In agriculture cash crop production was dominated by the line-of-rail provinces in general and the commercial farmers in particular. Even though adequate potential for self-sufficiency in food crops, especially the national staple, maize, existed, erratic government pricing policies led to a first serious shortfall of marketed maize in 1970.[8] For the improvement of small peasants a cooperativisation programme was launched, offering loans and other services to newly-formed cooperatives. The ill-conceived loans policy, administered by the short-lived Credit Organization of Zambia, involved a long-term loan of K 15 per acre of land cleared. Calculated on the basis of capital-intensive clearing methods, this was easy money for the peasants, which many pocketed after clearing land which they never put into production. Therefore, they were unable to repay the loans. Indeed, some thought anyway the loans were a gift for their part in the independence struggle.[9] As a result, much money was squandered, cooperatives and peasants were corrupted rather than encouraged to become self-reliant. Production was not enhanced, and many of the cooperatives were short-lived.

b) *Economic Nationalism and State Capitalism*

The Mulungushi Reforms of 1968 marked the beginning of a phase of development in which Zambia sought to increase its share of the burgeoning economy as part of its policy of achieving economic independence. This phase of economic nationalism drew its rationale from two features of the continuing postindependence economic boom.

In the introduction to the published version of President Kaunda's Mulungushi speech it was noted that the boom had brought considerable financial benefits and profits to expatriate enterprise. However, instead of investing this money into the expansion of their businesses the foreign capitalists had "expatriated increasingly large portions of their profits".[10] On the other hand, because of the inherited socioeconomic structure of Zambian society hardly any local businessmen were active in private enterprise.

The Mulungushi and subsequent reforms, therefore, set out to establish state control over crucial areas of economic activity, including mining, manufacturing, commerce and finance, and to strengthen the nascent Zambian business class. Support for Zambian private entrepreneurs took the form of government protective measures. They were to have privileged access to credit from financial institutions. Business licenses for retail trading throughout Zambia, with the exception of central trading areas in the main line-of-rail towns, were reserved to Zambians; and in the other locations new licenses had to go to Zambians, too. Similar protection was provided in the area of road transport and building minerals. Furthermore, government contracts from the Public Works Department worth less than K 100,000 were to be given to Zambians only.[11] Foreigners who owned businesses in the specified areas had to sell them to Zambians before their current licenses expired, or take out Zambian citizenship themselves.

The business areas covered by these protective measures fall into the realm of small and medium size enterprise. It was not Kaunda's intention "to create capitalism" in Zambia. Were Zambian companies to grow beyond a certain size, they would be taken over by the state. The dominant position in the national economy was reserved for state capital. In his Mulungushi speech Kaunda invited over 20 foreign-owned companies, essentially from the building material and construction industry, the road transport sector, retail and wholesale commerce and the breweries, to sell 51 % of their shares to the state. They were incorporated into the INDECO group of companies.

Kaunda had also deplored "the virtual lack of mining development since Independence" (p. 49) in 1968, and hoped to influence the copper mines' investment policy by limiting the amount of company profits remittable abroad to 50 %. Zambia's lack of the know-how and the manpower required to run the mines made a take-over a particularly sensitive issue. However, in 1969, it was thought necessary to secure state control over the copper mines, the king-pin of the Zambian economy, in order to increase copper output.

As a result of the Matero Reforms[12] Zambia took over 51 % of the shares of the two newly-created copper companies, Nchanga Consolidated Copper Mines (NCCM) and Roan Consolidated Mines (RCM), while the South African mining giant Anglo American held 49 % of NCCM and 12.25 % of RCM, and the US transnational American Metal Climax (AMAX) held 20 % of RCM. 16.75 % of RCM were in the hand of small shareholders, mainly in the USA. Following the increase of share capital in NCCM in 1978 and in RCM in 1979 Zambia's share in both companies increased to 60 %. In 1981 NCCM and RCM were amalgamated to form the Zambia Consolidated Copper Mines (ZCCM), one of the biggest copper companies in the world.. As in all other take-overs Zambia negotiated compensation payments. Given the high costs involved in the copper mines takeover, government bonds were issued to the former shareholders, to be repaid over 12 years in the case of NCCM (until 1982) and over 8 years in the case of RCM.[13] In addition, Anglo American and AMAX signed comprehensive management and marketing contracts involving lucrative fee payments with NCCM and RCM respectively.

By 1973 Zambia had discovered that mining investment and output had not increased after the take-over, and it was concluded that state control over the copper companies was still inadequate. Using the opportunity apparently provided by the fast recovery of the world market price for copper after the 1971/72 slump, President Kaunda announced in 1973 that Zambia would redeem the bonds issued to finance the 1969 take-over immediately. It also terminated the management and marketing agreements prematurely, as a result of which NCCM and RCM had to provide their own management and technical services rather than on secondment from Anglo or AMAX. Both transactions cost Zambia a lot of money, part of which had to be raised on the international market[14], as by the end of 1974 the copper price was on its way down in another, more serious and prolonged slump. Though Zambia as major shareholder now appointed the managing directors and, in principle, had more direct control of the companies' affairs, the dependence on expatriate technical staff remained unchanged under the new arrangements. Since 1980 technical services have been provided by the wholly Zambian-owned Zambia Engineering Services (ZES), based in England and overwhelmingly foreign-staffed. For the marketing of copper a new wholly Zambian-owned parastatal, the Metal Marketing Company (MEMACO), was established in 1974.

The years of the economic reforms were also years of political turmoil within Zambia's ruling party and the nation. The timing of the economic nationalist measures was not unrelated to the power struggle within the national elite. Certainly, the issue of establishing state control over the economy in the face of Zambia's external dependence and sharpening contradictions at its frontiers in southern Africa was only one of several conflicts in this power struggle.[15] But where the local business class is in an embryonic stage, political power is the most direct path to economic benefits. When Zambia's internal political conflict found a resolution with the establishment of a one-party state in late-1972, the predominance of state capital was also politically secured, and with it the economic advancement of the ruling elite and the state sector managers.

Indeed, by then state capitalism was already well on its way, so much so that in 1974 President Kaunda found reason to castigate certain of its more conspicuous consequences:

> The reforms have created a form of state capitalism where tremendous power is concentrated in the hands of a small managerial group who have their hands on the important switches and whose elitist attitudes set social patterns far beyond their immediate realm of command".[16]

c) *Copper slump and Economic Crisis*

Since 1975 the Zambian economy has been in a state of persistent crisis. Two factors heralded the beginning of this phase. The first resulted from Zambia's land-locked geographical situation and the political turmoil in Southern Africa. In January 1973 the border to Smith's Rhodesia was closed, shutting down what had been Zambia's main rail link to South African ports. In 1975 the main alternative outlet, the Benguela Railway, was also interrupted due to the civil war in Angola, further exacerbating Zambia's transport problems for its external trade. Great hope was placed on the

Tanzania-Zambia-Railway (TAZARA) which was opened in 1976,[17] but though it has catered for substantial amounts of Zambian trade its performance for various technical reasons did not come up to expectations and copper exports piled up. Therefore, in 1978 Zambia decided to go it alone (against its more radical fellow Front Line States), and re-opened its southern rail link. Since then this has again become Zambia's main trade outlet, making it more vulnerable to South African economic pressure.

Secondly and more fundamentally, the world market price for copper took a nose-dive in 1975. The world economy had gone into a recession which carried over into the '80s and has adversely affected the economies of many Third World countries.[18] Copper prices did recover in 1979/80, only to relapse again in 1981/82. In any case, price inflation of industrial products on the world market outpaced copper prices by far so that the purchasing power of Zambia's copper earnings was reduced substantially (Figure 1). In this phase the structural defects of Zambia's political economy surfaced with a vengeance. It was not merely a matter of having lived beyond its means, but more precisely of having relied on copper earnings without reducing the structural dependence of the national economy on the world market.

The high import component of the copper industry for qualified manpower as well as for machine inputs and spares led to considerable increases of the cost of production in face of world inflation. Similarly, manufacturing industry, to a large extent based on imported products and technical processes, suffered. Foreign exchange shortages and import restrictions led to the frequent lack of raw materials, spare parts and so on, bringing production to a standstill or down to uneconomic, below-capacity levels. As a result, many state enterprises were running at a loss, and were unable to satisfy the national demand for their products — therefore necessitating additional imports of consumer goods. These problems occur characteristically where advanced industrial technology is adopted by societies with less capital and manpower resources at their disposal.[19] Recurrent complaints in Zambia about mismanagement and inefficiency in INDECO-run enterprises[20] must consequently be seen as one part of this overallpicture of structural dependence. Having risen rapidly up to 1974, total manufacturing production has stagnated since then.[21]

Agriculture is highlighted in all major speeches, but in fact continued to be neglected. Given the financial requirements of the mining and manufacturing industries and Zambia's limited resources this could hardly have been otherwise. Production for the market remained in the hands of private, essentially commercial and emergent, farmers. With inflation, however, their conditions of production deteriorated, all the more so as government kept producer prices fairly low. Only after serious shortfalls of the national staple maize occurred, due to reduced acreages cultivated and poor rainfall, and large quantities had to be imported were producer prices increased from K 9 per bag in the crop season 1978/79 up to K 16 in 1981/82. After 1980/81 had at last produced a good harvest again, the two following years saw renewed shortfalls due to poor rains.

Recognizing that the continuing drift of the rural population to the towns required an increase of agricultural productivity in order to statisfy the nation's needs, government in 1980 came up with a gigantic plan of establishing 18 20,000 ha state farms, two in each province.[22] It is obvious that enterprises of this size will require production of a huge industrial and technological dimension. Quite in line with Zambia's overall policies of state capitalism, it can confidently be predicted that they will produce results similar to other state-run enterprises of this kind. The country's structural dependence would be strengthened. Two years after this plan was launched its future was already uncertain. Finance and manpower both had to come from international sources, and donors appeared reluctant to engage in such oft-tried and oft-failed ventures. If this proved to be so, Zambia only stood to gain. Not least of all, foreign-financed state farms producing mainly for the local market would be an additional heavy burden on its worsening external debt situation.

For those concerned with their personal enrichment, foreign and local, dubious credit brokers and local partners out to make their cut, any deal involving high turnovers promises good business.[23] A feature of Zambia's political economy, which has attracted more than enough attention in the national press but little government action, is the widespread practice of the national elite, political leaders as well as government and parastatal bureaucrats, to use their positions of influence to enrich themselves or to establish themselves in business. Cases of corruption like "Kanyamagate" (misuse of relief funds, 1978) and "Winegate" (illegal import of wine from South Africa, Christmas 1980) can hardly be regarded as exceptional. These practices are enhanced in times of economic hardship characterized by tight state regulations, especially for foreign exchange allocations, and low political commitment. Zambia's conditions of exchange control and high inflation also increased dissatisfaction among the new business class who saw their profit-making endangered. For them more room for private capitalist enterprise had long been a necessary remedy for Zambia's economic problems in face of state capitalist inefficiency. In October 1980 Zambia experienced an abortive coup attempt, the alleged leader of which was one of the country's foremost businessmen and a former high-ranking parastatal bureaucrat.[24]

Dissatisfaction among workers about their worsening living conditions became increasingly apparent as Zambia's economic crisis deepened. Even though government continued to control prices of essential commodities, the cost-of-living increased at rates above 10% year after year from 1975 onwards, while workers' wages lagged far behind. Chronic shortages of basic goods completed the picture. The gains of the postindependence boom years were, therefore gradually eroded during the '70s. UNIP's relations with the workers and the trade union leaders were never really harmonious. To press for delayed wage increments workers in numerous state enterprises went on wild-cat strikes between 1979 and 1981, which at times led to violent clashes with the authorities. When in 1981 these strikes centred on the copper mines, endangering copper production and exports, President Kaunda intervened and ordered the detention of the Chairman of the ZCTU and two other trade union leaders whom he held responsible for what he saw as the workers' lack of discipline. Explaining his move, he underlined the need for foreign exchange from copper sales in order to restore economic stability and also referred to the IMF loan Zambia had recently secured.[25] When the trade union leaders were released a few months later, order had been restored, but tension between UNIP and the unions remained. Kaunda has good reason to worry about foreign exchange from copper sales. Given the inherited and since independence basically-unaltered structure of production, and given the material, e.g., consumption, interests of its ruling class, the national elite, the country's political economy is externally oriented. As so many other Third World countries Zambia turned to the IMF for aid to counter its balance of payments problems when copper revenue went down. A first loan of K 350 m. was negotiated between 1978-80. As the ailment persisted a new IMF loan of K 800 m. to be disbursed over three years between 1981-84 was agreed upon. But IMF loans have strings attached.[26] Notwithstanding its rigorous action against the trade unions Zambia failed to meet the agreed conditions, so that the IMF withheld further payments in 1982. At the same time it tightened the screws and raised new demands knowing that Zambia would have to come back for new negotiations. By 1982 its external debt was estimated to have reached $ 3 bn., and its debt service ration 45%. In January 1983 a new agreement with the IMF was signed involving a 20% devaluation of the Kwacha. After 20% in 1976 and 10% 1978 (a condition of the first IMF loan) this was the third devaluation since 1975. Furthermore, price controls on various basic goods were lifted to allow staterun enterprises to charge "economic" prices. Together with devaluation, prices were, therefore, under double pressure and immediately started increasing again, while wage increases were to be limited to a minimum. These measures invoked strong criticism from the trade union leaders who saw the workers carrying the brunt of the weight of this IMF-Zambian austerity programme. To appease them Kaunda appointed the Chairman and the Secretary-General of ZCTU on to the Board of ZIMCO, the apex of Zambia's state capitalist system. With the loan agreement signed, Zambia announced it was partially stopping external debt repayments while seeking a rescheduling from its creditors.[27] This was an all time crisis-point in Zambia's postindependence development; and given its continuing, if not enhanced, structural dependence on world market forces it will not necessarily be a turning-point.

The institutionalization of state capitalism in Zambia between 1968-74 could not prevent the problems the country has experienced since 1975 because the basic economic structures were left untouched. Zambia's political economy as it has developed is still characterized by an extremely uneven distribution of income.[28] The combination of a dominant state capitalist sector with ample room for private enterprise in diverse economic sectors serves the national elite. "The maintenance of a national private sector allows state capitalists who accumulate at the expense (and/or, I would add, with the help; P.M.) of imperial capital to branch out at a later period in private ventures."[29] In his speech announcing the Matero Reforms in 1969 President Kaunda had included a section on the "prevention of incipient capitalism" showing that he was aware of the problem. He said: "I do not want to see a small group of Zambians owning large cars, plush houses, wearing flashy clothes; whose conspicuous consumption is a continuous taunt to the rest of the nation."[30] State capitalism in Zambia has not prevented this happening.

Notes

1. D. Mezger argues this is precisely the effect price fluctuations on the LME are supposed to have in UCs. D. Mezger, *Copper in the World Economy*, London/New York, 1980.
2. A positive figure on item 11 indicates a decrease of reserves; a negative one, an increase.
3. In 1970 they had amounted to just K 3 m. See Bank of Zambia, *Annual reports 1975*, 1980.
4. M.R. Bhagavan, *Zambia's Impact of Industrial Strategy on Regional Imbalance, Social Inequality*. Scandinavian Institute of African Studies, Research Report No. 44. Uppsala 1978, p. 48.
5. See R. Hall, *The High Price of Principles: Kaunda and the White South*, Harmondsworth 1963.
6. A. Seidman, "The Distorted Growth of Import Substitution: The Zambian Case", in: *JMAS*, 12, 4 (1974).
7. Govt. of Zambia, *Report of the Commission of Inquiry into the Mining Industry*, Lusaka 1966.
8. C.S. Lombard and A.H.C. Tweedie, *Agriculture in Zambia since Independence*, Lusaka 1974.
9. S.A. Quick, *Humanism or Technocracy? Zambia's Farming Cooperatives 1965-1972*, Lusaka 1978.

10. Rep. of Zambia, *Zambia's Economic Revolution. Address by President Kaunda at Mulungushi,* April 1968, p. iii.
11. Ibid, p. 27-35.
12. Rep. of Zambia, *Towards Complete Independence.* Address by President Kaunda at Matero Hall, Lusaka, August 1969.
13. For a detailed analysis of the 1969/70 take-over agreements, see M. Bostock & C. Harvey (eds.), *Economic Independence and Zambian Copper,* New York 1972.
14. G. Lanning with M. Mueller, *Africa Undermined,* Harmondsworth 1979, p. 219 ff.
15. For a closer look at the political developments and the factional struggles in this period, see J. Pettmann, *Zambia – Security and Conflict,* London 1974; W. Tordoff (ed.), *Politics in Zambia,* Manchester 1974.
16. K.D. Kaunda, *Humanism in Zambia and a Guide to its Implementation, Part II,* Lusaka 1974, p. 111.
17. M. Bailey, *Freedom Railway,* London 1976; K.S. Mutukwa, *Politics of the Tanzania-Zambia Rail project,* Washington 1977.
18. R.H. Green, "Things fall apart: The World Economy in the 1980's," in: *Third World Quarterly,* 5, I (Jan. 1983).
19. F. Stewart, *Technology and Underdevelopment,* London 1978. See, in particular, ch. 3 on "inappropriate technology".
20. K.D. Kaunda, *Blueprint for Economic Development.* Address by the President at Mulungushi Hall, Lusaka, October 1979, pp. 47-8.
21. Rep. of Zambia, *Economic Report 1981,* Lusaka 1982, p. 162.
22. Rep. of Zambia, Project "Operation Food Production" 1980-1990, Lusaka, May 1980.
23. *Times of Zambia,* 1982.
24. In Jan. 1983 he was found guilty by the Lusaka High Court and, together with 6 others, sentenced to death.
25. Kaunda's speech is reproduced in full in *Zambia Daily Mail,* 28.7.1981.
26. C. Payer, *The Debt Trap: The IMF and the Third World,* New York/London 1974.
27. *Times,* 8.1.1983; *Observer,* 9.1.1983.
28. ILO, *Narrowing the Gaps. Planning for Basic Needs and Procuctive Employment in Zambia,* Addis Ababa 1977, p. 292.
29. J. Petras, *Critical Perspectives on Imperialism and Social Class in the Third World,* New York/London 1977, p. 92 (Chapter on "State Capitalism and the Third World").
30. *Towards Complete Independence,* p. 60.

Chapter 2
Were the Copper Nationalisations Worth-while?
by Marcia Burdette

In the late 1960s and early 1970s, the Government of the Republic of Zambia made a tremendous fiscal and political investment and became the majority shareholder in its mineral industry, the largest in majority-ruled Africa. This billion dollar industry had dominated the political, social and economic life of the region since the 1930s—its pre-eminence had not significantly declined with formal independence in 1964. It truly was the engine of the whole political economy of Zambia. The state participated in the mines through the purchase of a 51 % share in the two existing mining groups, RST and ZAMANGLO, in 1969 (Phase I). In 1970 the GRZ and the foreign mining companies created two new joint venture companies, NCCM and RCM under the management of the former owners but with the state as majority shareholder.[1]

Three years later the Government abrogated the contracts it had signed in 1970 with the two foreign mining conglomerates (AMAX inc., and the Anglo American Corporation of South Africa, Ltd.). From that date onwards,[2] NCCM and RCM were to be ,,self-managed" and a new parastatal organization, the Metal Marketing Corporation of Zambian Ltd., (MEMACO), was to market abroad the copper, cobalt, lead and zinc from Zambia's mines (Phase II).

Using any yardstick—finance, manpower, attention and efforts of state representatives—these actions by the Government cost the nation a great deal. The President, Dr. K.D. Kaunda, stated that the nationalisations were necessary to give the nation some control over its main economic sector and its own future.[3] Now, more than a decade after the first phase of the copper nationalisations in 1969, scholars are attempting to assess these actions-were they worth-while? Or perhaps more pointedly, what was gained from the participation of the state in the mining industry? And what was the cost? Further, what does the future hold for this giant venture?

As one might expect from questions that are both technically complex and politically sensitive, there is great disagreement on the issues and criteria. Lately some authors have approached the general question of costs and benefits of state participation in the Zambian mineral industry. Few have been more direct than Michael Woakes and Ronald Libby in a recent article in *The African Studies Review.*[4] In this piece, the authors argue that, in contrast to the great expectations of the late 1960s and early 1970s, little was gained for the country from nationalising the mines, and the cost to Zambia's future development was high.[5] They conclude that the bottom line on Zambia's participation in mining has been a financial drain on the state rather than the looked for exponential revenues in taxes and dividends.

Another analyst, Prof. Muna Ndulo,[6] approaches the issues with an eye to the legal methods used by the state to assert control over the industry.[7] To him the economic nationalist impulse to control the mining industry was more significant than economic calculations. But, he goes on,

> participation in the existing mines has proved to have overall benefits in the area of profits in that it has effectively increased government revenues from mining activities.[8]

To support his opinion on revenue rewards to the state, however, Prof. Ndulo chose the only year (1974) between 1973 and 1979 that the mines produced a dividend at all![9] In most of these same years, moreover, the mines themselves and the Government of the Republic of Zambia (GRZ) experienced a heavy drain to repay loans and redeem the bonds from the Phases I and II of the nationalisations. Thus, although Dr. Ndulo seems to conclude that the nationalisations were both necessary politically and economically and properly conducted legally, his point on the financial rewards needs some modification.

A third author, Dr. George Simwinga,[10] has examined the nationalisations and later the control of the state over parastatals, one of which was NCCM.[11] In an article[12] Simwinga argues that economic ownership does not translate directly into actual control. So Phase II of takeover of the mines was a natural outcome of economic nationalism in Zambia. Perhaps in his later work, he will reflect on the results of the nationalisation of this industry over time.

Dr. Chisepo Mphaisha has also expressed an opinion on the nationalisations in his thesis.[13] Because of the oligopolistic character of the copper marketplace, Dr. Mphaisha argues, a producer state or a cartel which does not have effective monopoly over a product is in no position to try to set the terms of its trade internationally. Not only is this true for Zambia as an individual producer but this also holds for the formal organization CIPEC[14] to which it belongs. In recognition of this situation, Dr. Mphaisha suggests that Zambia should try to modify her mining legislation to reduce the state's share from 51 % to 50 %; drop the requirement of 51 % on future mining development; and offer a series of incentives to foreign capital such as tax reductions, surtax concessions, special write-offs, etc.[15] One does not have to stretch this argument too far to assume that this author sees many losses from the nationalisation, particularly disincentives to foreign companies to invest in Zambia's mineral industry.

As this brief review suggests, the return to the Zambian state from participation in the mineral industry is both highly contentious and potentially a very political matter. But it is part of a necessary debate since future policy on mining may stem from these assumptions and assessments of past, present and future relations between the state and the mining industry. Yet to this author, the question of loss and gain has not been adequately posed. On the point of failed objectives, we ask, What in fact was intended? Much confusion exists over the concept of nationalisation itself. In essence, nationalisation simply means that a state takes over physical or financial assets found within its geographical boundaries from private enterprises, either domestically or foreign-owned. It is basically transfer of assets with authority vested in a parastatal or a ministry or in some cases reverting to private, though local, hands. The concept is often confused with other actions by a state, such as nonpayment of compensation for the takeover (expropriation or confiscation), the turning over of a percentage of the shares to locals (localization) or even the reorganisation of management so that workers assume all or partial control over the enterprise. Yet these specific actions are not requisite parts of a nationalisation. Rather they are possible further strategies of the leadership of the nationalising state. Thus the actual intentions and outcomes of any nationalisation should be subject to close analysis. What were (and are) the objective interests of those in control of the Zambian state in this matter?

To the issue of gain, surely we must measure gain in terms of the wider social and economic benefit over the whole period of the nationalised industry rather than simply dividends and taxes. Further, who gained what from these state actions? Losses should be tabulated by any student with awareness of problems in these mines as well as of the vagaries of the international copper market.[16] Also one needs to look at opportunities foregone by this use of capital, manpower, and resources in the mining industry. Finally, the future of the industry should relate both to its own technical and orebody potential and the place it is likely to hold in the production needs of the industrialized world.

In this chapter, we argue that to assess the intentions and outcome of the nationalisations of the mining industry in Zambia, we must first explore the nature of the dominant class in Zambian society. The policies of the Government of the Republic of Zambia (GRZ) towards the mines reflected a conscious or unconscious strategy for this locally dominant class to assert itself in the major productive sector of the economy. Because of the fragmented nature of this dominant group, various factions have contested the direction and detail of policy. Further, we suggest that this internal strife contributed to the serious economic crisis of the late 1970s although it is certainly not the only feature in this crisis. When the fractiousness in the dominant class was combined with a declining industry and a recession in the Western industrialised economies, the policies followed by the state led to a growing impoverishment of the masses of the local population. And it seems to be leading to a deepening indebtedness of the state to international capital.

In order to make this argument, we will reflect on three lines of analyses. First, we offer a brief political and economic history of the mining industry, with emphasis on the period prior to Phase II of the nationalisations. Second, the major developments in the industry since the mid-1970s will be set out in narrative form, emphasising production, transportation, technology and financial questions. Lastly, we will pose the questions of the value of the nationalisation in light of the nature of the group of control of the state and its objective interests and those of other classes in society. And from this analysis, we will speculate on some of the possible implications of these policies for all classes of Zambian society and conclude with a set of possible alternatives for the political class relating to the mining industry.

The Political Class in Zambia, and Political and Economic History Relating to the Mining Industry.

A local dominant class has been forming in Zambia since the assertion of nationalist control over the political apparatus in 1964. This class appears to be consolidating its position vis-a-vis other classes in society and towards external capital through its control of the state and the national economy. We use the term "political class" here to refer to this locally dominant class.[17] As with any class, it exists in relation to other classes in society, and in the Zambian case, the major ones are the workers and peasants. This local political class derives its existence from its power over the means of producing, of appropriating, and of distributing wealth in the society. But within Zambian society, because of the character of the colonial and federal political economies,[18] this political class has not been able to derive its dominance from the traditional or "classical" relations to the means of production, i.e. ownership of property, control over production and employment of labour. Rather, its dominance was established indirectly through the mediation of the state which it controls. Thus the degree of its pre-eminence derives from the extent of control over the state, and further, the control that the state has over sectors of production. One tool to gain access to these sectors has been state participation or partial nationalisations of various businesses. Because of the significance of the mining industry to the society as a whole, access to this particular sector has been a crucial part of the strategy of this formative political class. Specifically, this dominance is still being achieved and this political class is still being shaped. There is a growing debate within the literature concerning the nature and strategies of this locally dominant class.[19]

The embryonic political class in Zambia grew around the pole of the leadership of the nationalist movement which conducted much of the independence struggle. After ascending to political power in 1964, the nationalist leadership of the United National Independence Party (UNIP) quickly revealed a sensitivity to its dependent position vis-a-vis the mining industry. A symbiosis existed between the state and the external ruling class, composed of the mining companies and their allies. The foreign corporations needed the apparatuses of the new state to maintain order and services; the state needed revenues from the mines and the employment for a sizable portion of the organized labour force.[20] Initial policies of this embryonic group were to enlarge revenues, control party and state bureaucracies, and assert sovereignty over regions or provinces.[21]

It was not until 1968 that the nationalist core of the political class began to develop a strategy based on the direct participation of the state in the sector of the economy previously owned or controlled by resident or foreign expatriate capital. This core, led by President Kaunda, began a series of economic reforms known as the Mulungushi Reforms.[22] In April of that year, the President initiated a partial "nationalisation" of certain commercial and industrial enterprises, predominately owned by resident expatriates. Twenty-five firms operating in Zambia eventually offered the GRZ a 51 % share in their businesses, making the Government overnight the majority shareholder.[23] This pattern was employed by the state for later takeovers.[24]

The Mulungushi Reforms opened to local entrepreneurs and bureaucrats many productive sectors of the domestic economy. Without sufficient capital or credit facilities, Zambian businessmen would not have been able to force out the already-entrenched Asian and European businessmen.[25] It is unlikely that these businessmen would have spontaneously offered the GRZ a majority interest in their firms either. After the first Mulungushi announcement in 1968, a parastatal organisation, the Industrial Development Corporation of Zambia Ltd. (INDECO), was placed in charge of these partly-nationalised companies, and this organisation held the Government's shares in the subsidiary companies.[26] Although local managers and entrepreneurs were hired or received contracts to manage these partially-nationalised firms, by and large the Mulungushi reforms began the state capitalist phase for Zambia.[27] And the embryonic local class began to expand its membership and to gain supporters from other classes or portions of classes in society.

After five years of independence, this locally dominant class still did not control the mining companies although the state had gained considerable revenue from taxation privileges.[28] The Zambian copper industry remained at the bottom of an inverted production pyramid with the consumers of the industrialised world at the top and two international resource companies as intermediaries between the resource base in Zambia and the market. Even the terms by which the price of copper was sold was set outside the control of Zambians and was based on the price on the London Metals Exchange (LME). Despite various pronouncements of redirecting economic development into different sectors, copper was still "king" in 1969.[29]

This formative political class was in a delicate position in relation to these mining companies. After the Unilateral Declaration of Independence by Rhodesia (UDI) in 1965, the cooperation of the foreign mining interests had minimised the deep dislocation that this event had on the Zambian economy.[30] Yet the Zambians knew (or suspected) that they were slowly being drained of their investible surpluses by those same representatives of Western capital. As an example, in the years of good copper prices, profits were high in the mining groups. Yet the managers persisted in borrowing heavily on the local markets, undercapitalizing and increasing expenditures in invisibles (up from K 32.9 million in 1965 to K 64.7 million in 1967).[31] The very prominence of the mines in the Zambian political economy made it a target for a class that seemed to be evolving a strategy of expanding its economic power through control of enterprises mediated through state ownership. This strategy fits within an overall plan to develop the productive sectors of the economy via a vigorous import substitution policy for industrialization.[32] This plan demanded a heavy foreign exchange contribution and the major source of that precious tender was the mines. By 1969 the revenues from the mining sector provided almost 90 % of the foreign exchange earnings of the state. For an economy as import-dependent as Zambia, this was a vital feature. Another constraint on the political class was their awareness that Zambia simply did not have adequate manpower to operate the mines on its own.[33] As a legacy of colonialism and federal education and employment policies, not only did the independent government lack the technical staff, they did not have sufficient management personnel either. There was also a set of legal restrictions written into the Zambian Constitution concerning the behaviour of the state towards the owners of private property and mineral rights.[34]

The actions of the GRZ in 1969 to surmount these barriers are described elsewhere.[35] In summary here, it should be noted that in August of 1969 the GRZ requested that the two mining companies "offer" 51 % of their shares in the Zambian mines to the Government. After intense but relatively amiable negotiations led by the Chief GRZ negotiator, Andrew Sardanis, a new arrangement was worked out in December, 1969. The metropolitan companies and the representatives of the Zambian state entered into a partnership in the running of the two new mining corporations, NCCM and RCM.[36] Titular ownership of a majority share resided with the state. But effective management control (including the appointment of the operating executive, the Managing Directors of NCCM and RCM, the provision of technical and administrative personnel and the provision of all sorts of important services) rested in foreign hands. The international companies in turn received fees for their services and were to be repaid for their loss of 51 % of the shares through a complex scheme of bonds to be redeemed over time. Thus the penetration of the state into this sector of the economy was not accompanied by unequivocal dominance by state capital. Not surprisingly, then, this agreement was terminated by the GRZ in 1973.

At the beginning of Phase II of the nationalisations, the Government demanded an end to the junior partner status of the state. The contracts with the foreign companies were cancelled, outstanding debts (the bonds) were to be repaid almost immediately, and the GRZ made ready to alter the foreign exchange and taxation regulations written into the prior agreements. Problems soon developed over whether a "penalty fee" was due to the former owners of the contracts, the international companies AMAX and AAC-SA via their subsidiaries in Zambia. After tortuous and extended negotiations, a settlement was finally reached in 1975.[37] The GRZ agreed to pay the AAC-SA subsidiary K 33 million and to pay AMAX's wholly-owned subsidiary, RST International, the sum of K 22 million. In order to finance the initial redemption of the bonds, the GRZ borrowed $ 150 million Eurodollars. Now it owed an additional K 55 million in penalty fees to foreign-based concerns.

While all this was going on at head offices in Lusaka, the mining companies themselves continued much as before. Excepting the appointment of Zambian Managing Directors by the Government side, the mines went on with business as usual.[39] The foreign corporations seconded technical and administrative personnel to the Head Offices; many of the expatriate managers and technical staff on the Copperbelt itself extended their contracts under Zambian terms of service. Because of the continued reliance on many of the same people or the same companies, claims of total "self management" in the mines since 1973 need to be looked at a bit skeptically by students of these matters. Nonetheless, the obnoxious quality in the prior management contracts had been removed and the Zambian representatives had far greater access to decision-making than before Phase II. Through the next five years, the Zambian formative political class via the state slowly extended its control over the mining sector. Ironically, this assertion of greater Zambian influence in the mining industry coincided with its decline. The next section reviews developments in this industry after 1975 to explain this decline.

Developments in the Mining Industry

The years since 1975 have proved a disappointment to the political class. Since the conclusion of the negotiations with AMAX in early-1975, the Zambian political economy has been caught in a rollercoaster of events. The major purpose of this section is to explore these mining developments under the topics of price, production, transportation, financial and technical issues. Then the political actions impinging on the mining industry will be reviewed.

Discussions of mining in Zambia often reflect only upon the divisions of the major copper mines in NCCM and RCM. But there is also a lead and zinc mine at Broken Hill (NCCM); centralized services divisions for both NCCM and RCM; the Copper Industry Service Bureau (CISB); MINDECO Small Mines Ltd. which is responsible for minerals used in domestic and industrial use; the Maamba Collieries Ltd. (coal); MEMACO (marketing); and two feeder industries for the mines, the Ndola Lime Co. Ltd. and Mining Timbers Ltd.[39] There are also a few joint ventures with other foreign companies such as Mokambo Development Co. and MINDECO-Noranda Ltd.[40] and some precious gemstone recovery. Yet because the copper mines are the largest and traditionally the major source of profit and employment, the discussion below will tend to focus on copper and to a lesser degree on cobalt.[41]

Of the two mining companies, NCCM is the larger in overall sales and employment. Their production tends to average around 350,000 tonnes of copper per year, to RCM's 260,000 tonnes. Internal organisation also differs, as a reflection of their prior histories. But both companies have a majority of their shares owned by the GRZ and thus are equally subject to GRZ directives. In contrast with the early years of state ownership, their refined metals are now jointly marketed by the parastatal MEMACO. The effects of the international marketplace have thus tended to affect them similarly.

Price and Geopolitics:

Zambia has always suffered some disadvantages from its position as a land-locked state. Its location meant that in the last half of the 1970s, the major geopolitical events of the era—the Angolan Civil War, the Zimbabwean War and the Namibian struggle—all affected the Zambian state.[42] These regional upheavals have tended directly or indirectly to affect the mines. As disruptive as these geopolitical factors have been, the cyclical expansion and recessions in the advanced industrial states have been worse to Zambia's economy. These swings in economic health within the metropoles has reduced effective demand for copper and other metals driving down the price and encouraging the build-up of stockpiles which act to depress the price further. Thus in the 1970s the price undulated with the valleys of low prices of longer duration than the peaks. (See Table 1.) Lead and zinc had a slightly steadier pattern but since the tonnage and the value of these metals are smaller than copper, the relevance of these metals to the overall Zambian political economy is less telling than the prices of cobalt and copper.[43]

The bright spot in the late 1970s was the emergence of cobalt as a major "money spinner". Cobalt occurs in several of the Zambian mines and is produced as a by-product of copper production. It occurs in Chingola, Rokana and Konkola mines of NCCM, and Chibuluma and Baluba mines of RCM. With the price at around $ 5.00 per lb., its production as a by-product was only marginally profitable. But in 1978 and 1979 the producer prices escalated rapidly.[44] Fortunately at this time major new tonnage of cobalt came from RCM's roast-leach-electrowin plant[45] at Chambishi Mine. The industry as a whole gained K 35 million from sales of 1,823 tonnes of cobalt in 1978 and K1 129 million for sales of 2,987 tonnes in 1979,[46] compared with K 16 million for 1,704 tonnes in 1977. At one time the price for cobalt was so "positive" that 2,934 tonnes were airfreighted to overseas markets.[47] Unfortunately, the high prices did not continue into the 1980s although the price is still far higher than early 1977. Currently there is a significant surplus of cobalt in the world with 16,000 tonnes of cobalt metal overhanging the market. Zaire is holding about 14,000 tonnes while Zambia stockpiles about 2000 tonnes.[48]

Despite additional revenues from cobalt sales, widely fluctuating prices for copper and a generally low price hurt the Zambian economy deeply in the decade of 1969-79. The GRZ had scheduled for much of its revenue to come from mining. Three streams of revenue for the GRZ from the mines are: a tax on the mineral extracted (73 % now 75 %); an income tax on the companies plus a small withholding tax, and dividends from the majority shares in NCCM and RCM. The degree of Zambian governmental dependence on mineral revenues is revealed for the years 1970-79. (See Table 2.) Even in the years that copper contributed nothing to state revenues (1977-79), mining still represented between 94 % and 96 % of exports and most of the foreign exchange earnings of the whole economy.[49] When copper makes little or no profit, far less foreign exchange is available to the state. The mines are then strapped for monies for imports and for servicing of foreign debts. To bridge the gap, the Bank of Zambia steps in, and the companies and the state often resort to further foreign borrowing.

The price at which Zambian copper is sold is beyond domestic control. Despite the existence of a producer alliance (CIPEC), the prices for copper are still set according to the American producer price ($ 1b) or based around the LME price (£/tonne).[50] Consumption of copper, cobalt, lead and zinc, furthermore, are tied to the growth and contraction of the industrialised economies of the West and Japan. A ripple of decline of demand in Europe, Japan or the United States sends a tidal wave to those peripheral states (like Zambia) dependent upon these export markets for survival.

Costs:

On the domestic scene, the Zambian mining industry (particularly copper) seems trapped in a vice between static or declining production and rising costs of production and sales. In 1968, prior to the nationalisation, Zambia was a medium-cost producer of primary copper relative to the other major copper exporters.[51] Because of the reliability and high quality of the copper, there was a ready market. But by 1976, according to the Commodity Research Unit of New York, Zambia was one of the highest cost producers of copper in the world at 48.54 c/lb—a dubious honour shared with Zaire. Her costs are particularly at variance from the new exporters, Papua New Guinea and Australia producing at 27 c/lb.[52]

Table 1 LME Monthly Average Price for Copper Wirebars, 1970-1980

(per tonne)						
Year	1970	1971	1972	1973	1974	1975
Settlement and Cash Sellers Price	589	444	428	727	878	557
Year	1976	1977	1978	1979	1980	
Settlement and Cash Sellers Price	781	751	710	936	941	

Source: *Zambia Mining Yearbook;* 1979 and 1980 figures from RCM and NCCM personnel.

The RCM mines experienced the most rapid escalation of costs in the period. Costs (f.o.r. refinery) in 1976 were K 806 /tonne; by 1979/80 they had reached K1, 213/tonne. (See Tables 3 and 4.) Some of the increase can be accounted for by inflation and some by lower production which tends to increase the unit costs of production.[53] Whatever the reasons, the company

Table 2 Contribution of copper Industry to Domestic Product, Revenue, and Exports, 1970-1980

Year	Gross Domestic Product (K million)	Contribution Gross Domestic Product (K million)	%	Government Revenue (K million)	Contribution to Government Revenue (K million)	%	Copper and Cobalt Value of Exports (K million)	Contribution to exports %
1970	1,278	455	36	435	251	58	688	97
1971	1,189	268	23	316	114	36	480	95
1972	1,348	317	24	302	56	19	500	93
1973	1,591	506	32	385	108	29	703	95
1974	1,893	607	32	647	341	53	846	94
1975	1,583	204	13	448	59	13	479	93
1976	1,941	330	17	443	12	3	705	94
1977*	2,024	223	11	449	1.0	–	661	94
1978*	2,259	271	12	550	–	–	633	94
1979*	2,566	450	18	685	–	–	1,034	96
1980*	3,038	520	17	719	41	6	960	80

Source: *Zambia Mining Yearbook*, 1970-1979; 1979 and 1980 figures from interviews with NCCM and RCM personnel, 1981.

* provisional figures

+ Although the title is for copper, these figures include cobalt contributions as well.

Table 3 Costs of Copper in RCM Mines, 1976-1981[a]

Costs of Copper in RCM Mines, 1976-1981[a]
(f.o.r. refinery) (K/tonne)

Year	1976/77	1977/78	1978/79[c]	1979/80[c]	1980/81[d]
Mining	485	457	477	609	760
Concentrating	81	90	100	131	153
Smelting and Leach Plant	118	111	122	148	183
Refining	31	30	28	30	40
Mine General Expenses	77	89	105	204	157
Replacements[b]	41	32			
Depreciation[b]			76	91	87
Cost f.o.r. refinery	806	809	908	1213	1380

Source: RCM *Annual Reports,* 1976-1980. 1980 data is provisional.
[a]The years in this table are not strictly comparable because of changes in accounting procedures. Also, some years had lower production, therefore creating artificially high costs of production for that year.
[b]RCM adopted depreciation accounting in 1979 with effect from 1 July, 1979.
Results in 1979 annual accounts are restated to reflect this change.
[c]In 1979 RCM changed its financial calendar to align with the ZIMCO companies.
So these figures are for a 9 month period only from July 1 to March 31st.
[d]New financial year, April 1 through March 31st.

must generate income from somewhere for repayment of the loans and necessary capital expenditures as well as to cover production costs out of the profits. When costs go up, profits tend to go down if there is not a coincident increase in price. Thus there was a serious profits squeeze on RCM in this period, only relieved by the additional cash flow from cobalt sales in 1979 and 1980.

Estimates have been made[54] that around 70 % of the operating costs of the Zambian copper mines are "fixed". Thus management's ability to reduce costs measurably is constricted. Not surprisingly, one insistent directive from the shareholders to the two mining companies has been to slow the rate of increase in costs and the outflow of cash. Many of the changes recently instituted (and to be discussed further under "rationalization" plans) apply to this point. But a more traditional method of dealing with fluctuations in price is to expand volume and to reduce costs by cutbacks and layoffs and by pressing for greater efficiency. Here again the Zambian mining industry has run into problems.

Table 4 Costs of Copper Production in NCCM Ltd., 1975-1980[a]

Year Process	1975/76	1976/77	1977/78	1978/79	1979/80	1980/81[c]
Mining	340	333	409	398	482	562
Concentrating	82	69	104	95	122	158
Leaching, smelting and refining	155	165	172	219	254	312
Administration and technical services and mine general expenses	133	153	220	201	206	281
Major Abnormal Expenses		32	45			
Depreciation[b]				71	79	86
Cost f.o.r. refinery	710	752	950	984	1143	1399

Source: NCCM *Annual Reports,* 1975-1980. Figures for 1980/81 are provisional.
[a]Not all years are strictly comparable in this table since the method of accounting changed over the years. Figures are for the financial year of NCCM, which is April 1 to March 31st.
[b]NCCM adopted depreciation accounting in 1979.
[c]Provisional figures only for 1980/81.

Table 5 GRZ Accounts – Revenue and Expenditure, 1970-1979.

Year Category	1970	1975	1979
Expenditures Recurrent	274,989	580,991	676,033
Capital Fund	*239,332*	*245,560*	*149,839*
Total	514,321	826,551	825,872
Revenue Current	432,432	448,338	595,197
Capital Receipts	*239,284*	*169,792*	*206,323*
Total	671,726	618,130	801,520

Source: *Monthly Digest of Statistics,* "Government Accounts", Tables 32-35, pp. 29-31, Vol. XVI, Nos. 4 to 9 April/September 1980. (Lusaka, Zambia: Central Statistical Office).

Production:

Zambia's Second National Development Plan (SNDP), covering the years 1972-76, predicted that tonnage of copper from the Zambian mines would reach 900,000 tonnes per annum by 1976.[55] At present (1981) production is still less than 700,000 tonnes. Sections of the metallurgical plant are used at considerably less than capacity. This is not because of their inefficiency, according to technical personnel,[56] but rather because there is not sufficient ore coming into the concentrators, smelters and refineries. The shortfall in mining thus needs to be addressed.

One of the most productive mines on the Copperbelt, Mufulira, experienced a tragic cave-in in September of 1970, costing 89 lives and great losses of production and potential ore. The removal of this mine, which had been producing almost 190,000 tonnes per year, brought down overall tonnage figures dramatically and cut deeply into RCM's overall output. Ten years later tonnage figures from Mufulira have not achieved their pre-1970 levels, nor are they likely to hit this peak again. Rehabilitation and modification of mining methods at Mufulira have required the engineers to go deeper for ore with less overall production and more problems.[57] Other RCM mines have also experienced declining amounts of ore mined.[58]

Production at the NCCM mines also decreased. The total ore hoisted from Chingola, Konkola, Rokana and Bwana Mkubwa which was 17,363,000 tonnes in 1977, was down to 16,387,000 tonnes in 1978 and 16,208,000 in 1979.[59] Although production did not drop off sharply with this mining company, there was a downward trend nonetheless. Equally troubling is the slow decline in the grade of ore milled in both NCCM and RCM mines. It is in the nature of mining that ore grades are rarely consistent year after year. But as mines get deeper, it often becomes more difficult and more costly to extract the ore. In addition the orebody may narrow and twist. Thus the overall grade of ore declines and, unless there is an unexpected strike of a rich new orebody, overall copper production is likely to go down as well.[60] In 1979, a decade after the Phase I of nationalization, the volume of production of coper from both companies was 655,600 tonnes per annum, well below the old target of 900,000 tonnes.

The full effect of declining production from the major copper mines has been masked by some technical breakthroughs in the past few years. For example, the Chingola tailings leach plant is producing copper from the concentrator tailing which were considered to be untreatable in the past. Now Chingola tailings leach plant adds 75,000 tonnes of copper to overal NCCM production without additional mining costs.[61] Kalengwa Mine from RCM was "mined out" in 1978 but the residual stockpiles of low grade ore are currently being milled and added to overall production figures.[62] In terms of the ore actually mined, then, the decline is even steeper than estimates based on the tonnage sold.

One factor helping to account for lower production is the low copper prices and the commitments that Zambia, as a charter member of CIPEC, made on cutbacks in 1976-1978.[63] Still, most serious estimates of the static nature of copper production ascribe the root causes to problems with efficiency, skills, and declining orebodies.[64] More shafts have been sunk to keep production to its current levels but indications are that more new orebodies of sufficient grade or size to make for economic mining are not likely.[65]

Transportation:

The vice has visibly tightened since 1975. Increased costs of production and static volume of minerals extracted have been matched with a heavy financial and capital expenditure programme. This combination can be lethal to any industry. On top of this, the transportation bottlenecks of the late-1970s have deeply affected the Zambian mines. The major purchasers of Zambian metals are Japan, France, West Germany, Italy, India, the United States and the Peoples' Republic of China.[66] In order to sell to these customers, Zambia has to get the metals to the ports and loaded on to ships bound for these ports-of-call. Her colonial history as part of the southern African economic complex comes back to haunt her now. Traditional export/import routes have been first through the Rhodesian Rail system to South African and Mozambiquan ports and secondly, via the Benguela Railway to the Angolan port of Lobito, traversing part of Zaire). Wars of liberation and local rebellions have played havoc with these routes. Often the mining companies have had to resort to road haulage, a far less desirable means of transporting the metal to ports.

In the 1970s the GRZ engaged in a major construction scheme with the Republic of Tanzania and the Peoples' Republic of China to build a new railway line from Kapiri Mposhi in Zambia through the north-eastern part of Zambia and south-western part of Tanzania to the port of Dar es Salaam (DSM). TAZARA, as the new railway was named, seemed to many observers to be the answer to Zambia's export/import problems. It came at the most opportune time as well. By 1975/6 a real bottleneck had developed. The Benguela Railway was closed after August 1975;[67] the Rhodesian border had been sealed between 1973-8. Extant rail and road systems were simply unable to carry the bulk and weight of the copper shipments going out and the imports coming into Zambia. TAZARA saved the day in 1976/77 allowing the companies to clear their backlog of copper stocks. This route appeared to be a permanent solution even though there continued to be constrictions at the port of DSM.

Yet by 1979 the picture again had dimmed. The route to Beira was discontinued at the onset of the rains in December 1978 and the port was damaged in Rhodesian attacks. NCCM had to declare a "force majeure" on 15 % of its sales that year.[69] Shipments of metals through the Mozambican port of Nacala ceased in March 1979. Washaways, sabotage and strikes on the TAZARA in 1979-80 combined with labour disputes and disruptions on the main Zambian "line of rail" meant that the shipments of 645,208 tonnes of metal in 1980 were 56,736 tonnes lower that the preceding year.[70] One expensive outcome was that Zambia has sometimes been placed in the position of being an unwilling holder of copper stocks. Her backlogs were due in most part to the unreliability of the transport routes. NCCM stocks of copper increased from 27,000 tonnes in 1977 to 72,550 tonnes in October 1978.[71] RCM's stocks were worth K 25.7 million by 1978.[72] Mining, processing, transportation and invisible costs had to be covered but with less immediate return of income. This put the mines in a poor "cash flow" situation.

The "southern route" via Rhodesia and South Africa became more and more appealing to Zambian politicians and civil servants as well as the mine managers and marketing men, particularly after the metamorphosis of Rhodesia to Zimbabwe. In order to lessen the bottlenecks, the mining companies ship some metals out through the port of East London in South Africa. Although a greater distance than the Beira, DSM or Nacala routes,[73] this export route availability helped reduce backlogs of Zambian metals to 16,895 tonnes in 1979/80.[74] For RCM the "southern route" accounted for 55 % of total copper shipments in the first 9 months of 1980.[75] What effect such reliance on South Africa will have upon Zambian politics is uncertain.[76] But Zambia is again in the position of having a major export route traversing a potentially hostile regime. The long term consequences of this transportation imbroglio are difficult to predict. The Zambian mining companies intend to use the ports of Nacala and Beira again in the near future for the southern route is a costly one. Recent aid from China and some improvements in management of TAZARA have meant that the DSM route handled about 80 % of RCM production by mid-1981.[77] Therefore, in the equation of factors acting upon the Zambian mineral industry, transportation does not necessarily have to play a constant role in constraining Zambia's exports and imports. But the problems have not yet been settled by any means.

Whatever the current and future political implications, the disruption of transportation routes has cost Zambia dearly. The average costs to transport a tonne of copper (K f.o.r. mine station to c.i.f. UK and world ports) increased from K 64.183 per tonne (1969) to K 108.719 per tonne (1979).[78]

When these transportation costs are added to the overall costs of sales (including airfreight, insurance, sales commissions, etc.), the breakeven point[79] is quite high, relative to the average price for copper on the LME. For example, in the RCM mines in 1980/81 the overall breakeven point was K 1646 per tonne and the average price for copper based on the LME quotation was K 1608 per tonne.[80] The squeeze that this places on profits is hard, and relief is not in sight.

Because of this squeeze and some other factors, there has been some pressure to close the less productive mines rather than continue their producing copper at a loss. But this option is not as simple as it might seem. Closure of the less profitable mines will not cut costs dramatically since the overhead costs remain much the same and decreased overall production increases the unit costs of production. Also "mothballing" mines is an expensive and delicate process and the unemployment consequences are politically and economically untenable.[81] Another point rarely mentioned but equally significant is that Zambia must continue to export metals in order to obtain the foreign exchange necessary to service debts and purchase consumer and capital goods necessary for domestic production in and outside of the mines. Since import dependence has been a matter of policy, the effects of the mines' reduction of foreign exchange earnings is as much a consequence of political strategy as inescapable technical factors.

Finance:

The long squeeze on profits occurred along with a tendency for overall state recurrent expenditures to rise. As a crude measurement, the recurrent expenditures for the central government in 1970 were K 274,989,000 with payments on the capital fund account standing at K 239,332,000. These amounts totalled K 514,321,00. (See Table 5.) By 1979 recurrent expenditures had ballooned to K 676,033,000 though capital fund payments had shrunk to K 149,838,000. The total sum therefore was K 825,872,000. To cover the shortfall of revenues, both in the state and in the mines, mining officials along with GRZ and Bank of Zambia representatives went to the international marketplace in search of capital. Foreign capital came in four major forms: IMF loans, export credits and guarantees, bilateral governmental grants and commercial loans.

Although the IMF has not granted loans directly to the mines, the financial situation of the country has become intertwined with the Fund and thus it is a major backdrop for any discussion of finance and the mines. Since 1976, the IMF has become steadily more involved in the Zambian political

economy. In 1976 Zambia obtained SDR 38.3 million from the IMF's outstanding fund facility. By the end of that year, the Fund's holdings of Kwacha
(excluding oil and compensatory facilities) amounted to 136.2 % of quota.[82]
Two years later, a stabilization grant was extended to Zambia in the form of
two-year stand-by agreements with conditions attached.[83] Zambia was to
devalue the Kwacha (done in 1976 and again 1978), external debts were to
be paid off first out of these funds (also done) and the GRZ would promise
to look for aid from friendly governments, other international organisations
and private banks.[84] Sheridan Johns has referred to the set of policies as
"economic retrenchment."[85]

By the end of 1978, drawings from the Fund totalled K 270.6 million
(SDR 264.2 million) which represented 187.5 % of quota.[86] Finally, in 1981
another enormous loan-K 800 million (circa $ 1 billion) — was negotiated
between the IMF and the GRZ. At the time of writing, the conditions attached to this loan are not publicly available. But it is assumed that a large
percentage of the loan will go to pay the estimated K 500 million of debts
assigned to Zambia overseas.[87] One motivation to draw another large foreign
loan is that in 1978 and again in 1981, several major trading partners were
refusing to extend more goods on credit because of the scale of the nonsettled
outstanding debts. Such a termination of credit for import-dependent Zambia
could be a disaster both to the industry and to the development projects of
the state. The effect of these IMF loans, then, appears to be that despite its
massive scale, most of the money will never enter the country at all or aid it
in future development. Instead, it will circulate to the major creditors to
make Zambia's credit situation a bit easier and improve her balance of payments problem in the short term.

The impact of national finance upon the mines is complex. The mines
have occupied a privileged place in the political economy—seen in their ability
to obtain import licences and to externalise cash for payments abroad. But
they too were deeply affected by the wider downturn in finances for the
state in the last half of the decade. In order to continue operating and to
complete capital projects begun in the late 1960s and early 1970s, the mines
had to go to various sources for finance. The major sources of finance other
than the Bank of Zambia itself were export credits, supply credits, grants
from foreign governments and loans from private banking consortia on commercial terms.

A preferred source of finance was (and is) from loans extended through
the export support agencies of various industrial states, specifically the
EXIM Bank of the United States, the ECGD of the United Kingdom and
COFACE of France.[88] To use these facilities however, one is tied to procurement from these nations, not always the cheapest or most appropriate source
of supplies. Supply credits were not resorted to often by the mining com-

panies, according to one representative, because they are considered expensive.[89] On the other hand, some supply production schemes were entered into because of customers' demand for cobalt.[90] A few grants from foreign governments were forthcoming in the late 1970s such as the U.K. loan of 20 million to NCCM and RCM, tied to the delivery of copper to British customers. But just as the overall aid from the industrial states declined in the decade, so too direct governmental grants to Zambia dwindled.

Because of the tight squeeze on the companies, NCCM and RCM made extensive use of loan facilities abroad. With a heavy expenditure budget in the mid-1970s, NCCM went into the international loan market earlier than RCM. But both companies, through the Bank of Zambia, have negotiated some commercial loans abroad. The international institutions such as the IFC of the World Bank are often good sources of finance. But sometimes their conditions were unsatisfactory to the GRZ or the companies.[91] And whenever one takes that route, a certain slowness because of the bureaucracy involved has to be taken into account.

On the public record, RCM financial managers appeared to favour loans from the European banks such as the Indo-Suez Bank of France or the European Investment Bank. NCCM obtained large loans from a series of private banking consortia including the Citibank International Bank Consortium, the Mitsubishi and Mitsui group and Standard Chartered Ltd.[92] These commercial banks tended to be rather expensive since the gearing of the companies was not favourable.[93] But in order to bridge the gap between some international organisational funding and immediate project needs, the companies have sometimes resorted to expensive money such as the Barclays Bank International Credit Facility which extends loans based on copper "on the high seas" (i.e. past the bottleneck).[94] When comparing various sources of finance, however, the remark of one NCCM official is telling. "All sources of funding have a cost and you just have to get the best deal you can. But don't expect any favours from anyone."

With such unfavourable conditions on the money markets, it is not surprising that the mines turned to their shareholders to raise more equity. The minority shareholders (the foreign companies and some individual shareholders) were manifestly uninterested in investing further in an industry in which they had already been nationalised. So the GRZ, via the Bank of Zambia, became a major source of supply of finance for the mines in this period and will be for the foreseeable future. Altogether borrowing was heavy and the interest rates, particularly on short term borrowings, were stiff.

The Bank of Zambia extended its loans on the best terms available and in 1979 participated in a recapitalization scheme to be discussed further below. But the Bank usually acts as the intermediary rather than the actual source of finance for the mines. So the companies have heavy liabilities to external creditors as well as domestic sources of finance. Sometimes the interest rates have been so steep that the Government was forced to bail them out rather then to obtain the dividends expected from the mines. At other times the Bank has borrowed from the company accounts. By 1980 the total indebtedness of NCCM Ltd. was K 229 million, and for RCM it was K 218 million.[95]

Such heavy indebtedness was seen as a major problem to the Government and industry alike. The mining companies tried to reduce their costs. One major area for reduction was the capital expenditure budgets of the mines. In 1976 NCCM's total capital expenditure bill was close to K 40 million with K 19.6 million for major projects.[96] But over the lean years of 1977-80, this was pared down to the minimum necessary to finish vital projects. For example in 1977 a total of K 16.1 million was spent at the NCCM mines, compared with K 33 million in loan repayments and overdrafts.[97] How finance and technology interact upon one another is discussed in the next section.

Technology:

With new low cost producers coming "on stream" in Papua New Guinea and Australia, the large traditional exporters of copper are faced with a set of difficult choices. Either they shut down operations on their less profitable mines or they expand overall production and engage the newest technology to reduce costs and produce a competitive product. When an industry finds it necessary to cut back on new capital expenditures and thus new projects,[98] capital is saved in the short run. But it can prove very costly to one's strategy in the long run. Financial constraints affect the technological advances in the mines in a variety of ways.

With the loss of skilled personnel (mentioned in almost every official report on the Copperbelt since the early 1970s), the mines find it necessary to pay outside consultants for technical advice.[99] They also must offer high salaries to attract and retain the expatriate labour that they find necessary to run the mines. The most severe shortage appears to be at the mid-level of management, men with five to eight years of experience in mining and in particular those with backgrounds on the Copperbelt.[100] These people are crucial to the maintenance of production from the mines as the older mines go deeper and encounter more problems. But these people are scarce and expensive. Their salaries and emoluments add both to the costs of production and to the drain on foreign exchange since most of them externalise a portion of their salaries.[101] At this very basic level, technology and available finance work hand in hand. Another important area of technology is located in the metallurgical plant (concentrating, smelting, leaching and refining) where some breakthroughs have been made since the early 1970s on the processing of secondary materials and also improved extraction of copper itself. Cobalt has been mentioned but now gold, silver and selenium are also produced domestically.[102] As for the improved extraction of copper, considerable progress has been made in the reworkings of the tailing dumps and slag heaps as well as materials handling within the plant.

New shafts had also been sunk in this period.[103] But the overall effect of this additional engineering has been to maintain production at current levels for feeding into the existing concentrators. Some new concentrator equipment has been added to replace older machinery and also new acid plants provide for the new acid needs in the leaching processes. But the production of copper has not risen and the effect of the technology and expansion seems to have been to hold even production levels, to process more thoroughly the "waste" materials surrounding copper and cobalt mining, and to adjust to some changes in the inputs of mining that occurred because of geopolitics.

An example of the latter is problems at Broken Hill Mine (NCCM). Broken Hill Division produces zinc and lead and requires a particular grade of metallurgical coke for the Imperial Smelting Furnace (ISF). The major source of supply of that particular quality of coke had been the Wankie Colliery in Rhodesia. When the border was closed, this appropriate fuel was no longer available to Broken Hill and the technical personnel had to adjust to this alteration. The decision was taken to import coke from Germany which resulted in delays and caused considerable production losses and well as costly adjustments.[104] As one might imagine, technical difficulties abounded. So the overwhelming percentage of time of the skilled technical personnel at Broken Hill has been directed to solving problems that have to do with the Waelz Kilns and the ISF. In the meantime, production declined and profits for NCCM from this mine dwindled.[105]

Other examples of expensive and technically demanding projects are the anode slimes plant at Ndola Copper Refinery (now known as the Precious Metals Plant); the tailings leach plant at Chingola; and the new cobalt (RLE) leach plant at Chambishi Mine (RCM). A new RLE plant for cobalt is under construction at the Rokana Division of NCCM to extract cobalt from the cobaltiferous ore from the Nchanga Open Pit at Chingola, a sizable project. This proposal seemed so promising that the U.K. has lent 14 million in a supply contract for the cobalt from the mine which is still on the drawing boards![106] Such technical efforts have helped to maintain the level of production for NCCM and RCM, and to provide some new projects on the Copperbelt. But because of the expense of such projects, their economic viability in the long run is still in doubt.

A final major adjustment is required of all the copper exporters in the world because of the change in the nature of fabrication in the metropoles. In the past few years there has been a remarkably fast transfer from the old "hot rolling mills" for copper production to plants that produce continuously cast rods CCR plants require cathodes as feedstock rather than the wirebars. In 1970 the reported installed capacity for CCR was about 809,000 tonnes per year. By 1979 that had ballooned to 4,773,000 tonnes per year with over onequarter of the plants located in Western Europe.[107] Thus Zambia was faced with the choice of a switch in production from wirebar to cathode or a fight for the narrowing wirebar market. Once again the decision is not as simple as it may first appear.

In the mid-1970s the Zambian mines produced copper in several different forms but wirebars were preferred over cathodes 2:1.[108] With the demand from CCR plants for prime cathode rather than wirebars as feedstock, RCM switched over its production to cathode by 1979. Their calculation appeared to be that the loss of income from the cathodes (which are slightly less processed than the wirebar) would be compensated for by the reduced costs of production.[109] In addition, they hoped to gain a premium on their cathodes because they are high quality. NCCM, on the other hand, continues to produce several refined cast shapes as well as refinery cathodes, some leach cathodes, and blister and anode copper.[110] The motivations for this choice are complex.[111] The management of NCCM had some problems with product quality of the cathodes from the leaching process. The additional step of casting into wirebars permits them to reduce final impurities by blending with electrorefined cathodes and thus to obtain a good price on the market for the premium wirebar. And with the wirebar market less competitive because of the switch that most producers have made back to cathodes, NCCM hopes still to capture a good price for its wirebars.[112]

But the longer range implications of the move to cathodes is important too and there are at least two major arguments here. One point of view has it that by switching back to cathodes, Zambia's mining industry is stepping back upstream rather than in the downstream direction (towards more processing) that most industries choose to move in. Thus Zambia sells a "less processed" rather than a "more processed" final product. It might seem logical, given that no industry willingly relinquishes downstream potential, that the mines set up their own CCR plant and export semifabricated copper itself, thus retaining more value within the domestic scene. But there are serious barriers to such downstream integration. Although the CCR technology is not exceedingly sophisticated, it is in an expensive plant to set up. Authorities suggest that any additional profitability from setting up such a plant is not adequate to offset the capital expenditure. So the immediate and mediumterm gains from heavy capital expenditure are not so attractive.

Another argument holds that the switch to cathode is simply an alternative product form and one with the advantage of better quality and lower cost. Those using this line of analysis attribute distinct benefits to the move from wirebar to cathode. Some go further to suggest that the most positive movement for the Zambian mines would be to further fabrication within Zambia such as that now being done by ZAMEFA, a parastatal company which makes copper cables. If Zambia wants to break into the export market for cable, however, there are some trading barriers with which to contend. Semifabricated and fabricated materials face higher export tariffs against their import into the primary markets for Zambian copper-i.e. the EEC, Japan and the United States.[113] Marketing personnel are also concerned with the final product delivery. Given the long lines of shipment between the mines and the primary customers, there is some question whether either a CCR or a fabricated product would reach its destination in a form acceptable to a discerning buyer. The relatively fragile nature of these goods versus the hardy character of the wirebar also seems to mitigate against the establishment of further processing plants in Zambia.[114]

In order not to be left behind in this new CCR technology, the Zambian mining companies took another route. Together they formed a jointly-owned company, Mulungushi Investments Ltd. Through Mulungushi Investments Ltd., they acquired a 50% interest in a French CCR company (Société de Coulée Continue de Cuivre) along with the French company, Thomson Brandt.[115]

This seems a realistic strategy for the short run. But it effectively discourages the creation of further processing within Zambia other than the small amount of cables produced by ZAMEFA.[116] It also commits the industry, for the forseeable future, to the export of a refined but not fabricated product. It then behooves the mines to see that their equity in a French CCR plant produces profit, a strategy more tied to metropole than to Zambia.

Technical/marketing problems for cobalt have also emerged at the start of the 1980s. Zambia produces steadily increasing tonnages of cobalt metal but the giant in the field is Zaire. In 1978[117] the invasion of Shaba Province of Zaire along with a general world shortage of cobalt drove up the price. When demand was this strong, they could sell all the cobalt they could get to market. However, with the deepening of the recession in the West and the consequent lessening of demand for cobalt, the market for Zambian cobalt has gone "soft". The locally produced product also has a slight disadvantage in that it is slightly less pure than the Zairois product. To compete, the industry has directed much technological effort to further processing of cobalt and a vacuum refinery plant is being installed by RCM to contend with deleterious impurities. The target is the super-alloy market for jet plane engines, but in the meantime the stockpiles of current quality cobalt are growing.[118]

A discussion of these technical and financial features would be incomplete without recognition of the role of the Government. Because NCCM and RCM are partly state-owned (61 %), economic and technical decisions are intertwined with political ones. So the next section reviews major political choices made by the state which impinged upon the mining industry.

Political Developments Since 1975

Overt political involvement by the GRZ in the mines was far less apparent in the second half of the decade than in the first. Through its majority shareholding, its appointment of the Managing Directors and the "A" Directors and its quarantee of the Bank of Zambia loans, the Government's potential role on behalf of the political class was large. Yet, by and large, the industry was left alone to operate on a profit-making basis within the guidelines broadly set by the GRZ. Despite this overall policy of noninterference, some events and decisions did affect the mines and they will be discussed below.

The most potentially significant event was the Government's increase in its equity holdings in NCCM and RCM. With the uproar in 1969 and again in 1973/5, one could have expected considerable attention to accompany this decision by the GRZ. But in fact there was little visible concern expressed by the minority shareholders[119] it seemed as though they were not interested in extending their interest or investing more capital. Thus what occurred was an elaborate trade-off of the debts owned by NCCM and RCM to the Bank of Zambia for equity obtained by the GRZ and held in ZIMCO. The Government's share increased from 51 % to approximately 61 % in both NCCM and RCM. A portion of the debts were thus "capitalised" with the remaining portion of the loans converted into medium term loans repayable over six years, starting in 1980.[120] This trade received the approval of the minority shareholders whose equity was therefore reduced. Now RST, International, a wholly-owned subsidiary of AMAX, Inc., has 16.42 % of RCM; Security Nominees, an Anglo American company, holds 9.84 % of RCM; with the general public holding the remaining 13.12 % of RCM. ZCI Holdings Ltd., another Anglo company, now controls the remaining 39.9 % of NCCM.[121] Thus the effect of this move by Government was simply to finance the ailing mineral industry indirectly. Since the minority shareholders stood to gain from this new capital as well, no opposition was expected or appeared on the subject.

More fundamental to the workings of the mines has been the Government's policies and pressures on "rationalization." Basically what this had meant is the mines had been encouraged to blend together their operations whenever possible and to reduce any duplication and inefficiencies that have crept into the operations. With income from the mines nil, the majority shareholder was pressing NCCM and RCM to make whatever savings they could, including a pooling of resources, stores, purchasing, etc. These efforts culminated in 1980 with the President's announcement of a merger of the two mining companies into one giant conglomerate, Zambia Consolidated Copper Mines Ltd. (ZCCM).[122]

The Merger:

In the 1970s a series of "rationalization" schemes had been suggested to the mines by GRZ officials, but they had been rejected on grounds not altogether clear to this author. The persistence of two mining groups following Phase II of the nationalisations was largely an anachronism but one that carried some personal significance for management and operational levels and had some fiscal relevance to the groups of minority shareholders. With the decline of income from the mines and the need to raise more capital for investment and maintenance, NCCM and RCM management could no longer resist governmental pressures to merge their operations as rapidly as possible. The target date was 1981 or early-1982 at the latest. A countervailing force to a rapid merger had been the recognition that this merger has to be conducted with careful attention to legal obligations to the minority shareholders. But a scramble for position and power within the new ZCCM has no doubt also occupied much time and attention.

Governmental insistence on the merger is understandable. If properly conducted, there should be savings in salaries, emoluments, gratuities and overhead costs. Given the shortage of capital, there could be some more rational development of new projects on the Copperbelt. But there are also many fears, expressed by those involved in the mines, that the merger could create one enormous and unmanageable conglomerate. Top level management of the new ZCCM would have to be of the highest caliber in order to control such huge production. Previously, if one mining company guessed wrong on a particular strategy, it was not necessarily an industry-wide disaster, for the other company had been under no obligation to follow suit unless it seemed economically attractive. With a conglomerated company, particularly in the days of shortage of capital ahead, the tendency will be to direct all resources jointly towards a particular strategy. This has increased the chances of both industry-wide bonanzas and disasters.

Another concern of many within the existing companies is with organisational hierarchy. Instead of streamlining management, the top management may choose simply to merge the higher levels of both mining companies. A stratum of vice-presidents or assistant managing directors could be established between the divisions and the managing director. This could effectively increase the layers of bureaucracy between the operational level and the top management to such a degree that there is a lessening of communication rather than an increase in efficiency.

Whether these fears are justified or not, the decision has been taken by the GRZ to merge the companies. For the foreseeable future, the merger will require considerable exercise of corporate diplomacy and to be successful, will need a very strong-minded chief executive.

Works Councils:

Another governmentally-inspired development has been the creation of works councils on the mines. This is part of a national policy to establish these councils in an attempt to lessen industrial strife between management and labour. This programme was launched as an aspect of President Kaunda's philosophy of Humanism. For the mines, representatives of management were to sit together with representatives of labour (most likely individuals from the Mineworkers Union of Zambia — MUZ) and to „open lines of communication". Eventually these councils are to be permitted some participation in decision-making on the mines, but so far this has not occurred.[123]

Although much appears in the press concerning these works councils, for the mines at least, little relevance is attached to their existence by knowledgeable observers.[124] Far more significant is the growing autonomy and militancy of both the MUZ and the umbrella trade organisation, the Zambia Congress of Trade Unions (ZCTU) from the Government and the party (UNIP). The end of the 1970s and early 1980s have been characterized by frequent work slowdowns, stoppages, wild cat and organised strikes. The future seems to hold more such labour militancy.[125] This organised resistance may strike at the base of the already-weakened industry and might possibly inspire some repression from the state against the working people on the mines.

Government has also sponsored some new legislation affecting the mines. Some alterations have been made in the old Mines and Minerals Act of 1970 and the income tax provisions. The effective combined mineral and income tax rate for the mines increased from 73.05 % to 75.5 %. Also the Income Tax (Amendment) Act of 1976 exempted from tax provisions all dividends paid to Government.[126] But such legislation has really been only a minor adjustment to the system rather than any fundamental change.

MINDECO and MEMACO:

The political class also was deeply involved in the infighting over structural changes in the parastatal network in Zambia. In 1979 the Mining and Development Corporation Ltd. (MINDECO) had been charged with the overseeing of the mining companies and other mineral and metal production in the country. This parastatal was to cooperate with the Ministry of State Participation and the Ministry of Mines and to be subordinate to the supraparastatal, ZIMCO. At that time, President Kaunda served as Minister of State Participation and also held the portfolio for Mines. The Permanent Secretary, Andrew Sardanis, was appointed Managing Director (M.D.) of ZIMCO, the umbrella organisation. Initially he also served as Chairman of MINDECO.[127] Thus Government officials sat in positions of authority in the various parastatals which, directly or indirectly, affected the mines.

When Sardanis stepped down in January of 1971, the initial instrument for state participation (the ministry of the same name) was dismantled. In its place a new Ministry of Mines and Mining Development was established with Humphrey Mulemba as Minister. The President announced a major decentralisation of ZIMCO, the omnibus organisation, most of its activities now fall under the relevant ministries. Hence MINDECO was placed under the Ministry of Mines, and the Permanent Secretary of that ministry served as Executive Chairman of MINDECO.[128]

But what was the effect of these organisational shuffles? Many in the Government had recognised that under the 1969/70 agreements, the minority shareholders (the foreign companies) were still in effective control of the mines. There was some fear that the companies would not act in "national interest". So MINDECO continued with its overseeing of NCCM and RCM but without daily involvement in their operations.[129] Although MINDECO itself went through several top level changes, the staff remained more permanent and consisted largely of skilled expatriate personnel with backgrounds in various aspects of mining. The technical and management levels of NCCM and RCM appear to have found the involvement of MINDECO in its internal technical and financial decisions to be a considerable irritant. MINDECO staff, for their part, expressed scepticism about the bases for many decisions taken by NCCM and RCM management and pressed for a series of projects of their own.[130]

Thus an antagonistic relationship built up over the years between the mining companies and the parastatal. In 1974 with the cancellation of the management contracts, the Government removed NCCM and RCM from under MINDECO's jurisdiction and placed them under ZIMCO. MINDECO was subsequently demoted to overseeing the remaining operations—small mines, lime, timber, collieries, etc. In 1978 Dr. Kaunda announced that all subsidiaries of MINDECO would become direct operating subsidiaries[131] or ZIMCO thus depriving MINDECO of any functional purpose.

The politics that underlay these moves will be explored below. But the effect of these moves was that by 1974, the decisions of NCCM and RCM were only subject to scrutiny by the "A" Directors. ZIMCO and the Ministry of Mines. The "A" Directors tend not to have technical training but are businessmen and civil servants. Neither ZIMCO nor the Ministry of Mines have technical personnel with the expertise or time necessary to assess or counteract proposals by the mining industry adequately.[132] Thus it appears that the mines are indeed "on their own". With NCCM and RCM self-managing, it can be argued that they will work in accordance with the national economic interest without having to be so directed. But whether it is reasonable to expect any company organised primarily around the goals of growth and profits to work for the wider social benefit of the population as a whole is an open question.

In 1973 at the time of the announcement of Phase II of the mining take-overs, the President made public a decision to create a government-owned sales organisation, the Metal Marketing Corporation of Zambia Ltd. (MEMA-CO) This company created MEMACO Services Ltd., incorporated in the United Kingdom, to provide sales and marketing services for the parent company and for the mines in general.[133] Initially this parastatal operated through the agents previously used by AMAX and AAC to sell their Zambian-generated metals and minerals. When the price of copper was high, the job of marketing was relatively simple. However, with the slump in the price and increasing competition, the choices made by MEMACO Ltd. become more key to the profitability of the Zambian mining industry as a whole. Zambia is now slightly less dependent upon markets in Western Europe and North America, and MEMACO is said to be flexible in purchasing.[134] But aggressive marketing will be required in the future to find reliable customers for copper and to develop some special markets for the newly-processed materials, for example, the superalloy market for cobalt. So the relative importance of this parastatal to the industry as a whole has increased.

In conclusion, the reorganisation of the parastatal network at the end of the decade affected the mines indirectly.[135] ZIMCO assumed more direct power and MINDECO was removed. The current Director General of ZIMCO, James Mapoma, serves as Chairman of NCCM, Ltd., RCM, Ltd., and MEMACO, Ltd. He is the final authority on the industry's policies and future development and the major spokesperson for the mines. At this point, however, it is difficult to assess whether his personal or organisational role has penetrated into the mining industry any more than the prior parastatals. We conclude, therefore, that there is some residual autonomy that the mines have from the formal governmental structures although the overall goals are set by the state. So we return to one of our initial queries: What has been the cost of this intrusion of the state into this industry? In fact, Was this strategy worthwhile for the wider nation? To approach this question, we have argued that it is necessary to understand the process of class formation and class strategies under state capitalism. Now we point to the level of intraclass struggles that, over time, influenced state policy towards the foreign mining interests. This same strife, we believe, has posed a barrier to the formation of an appropriate stance for the national economy which is dependent upon a declining industry.

The Evolution of Factions in the Political Class

The evolution of a dominant local class has not been smooth in Zambia. Its consolidation has been affected by two major factors. First, the nature of the oligopolistic copper markets and international finance means that this domestic class must maintain a *symbiosis* with foreign capital. No matter how intense the confrontations with external interests, the economic survival of this governing class in Zambia is intimately linked to its export-dependent economy. The economy is linked to the needs and rules of the metropolitan countries and companies. So no matter how far the tensions go or how strong the rhetoric, unless this local dominant class alters the nature of the characteristic mode of production, this class must retain the ties with foreign capital and bow to its will in certain regards.

Second, the development of this political class has not occurred without a high level of intraclass friction. This often characterises a class holding an intermediate position between productive class and the owners of capital.[136] The struggle intensifies as the dominant class as a whole gains more access (through the state) over the surplus produced by the mines. In the struggle, we identify the tendency for two factions to develop in relation to the mining sector. We call them "technocrats" and "national politicians." Although part of the wider political class, these factions have differing strategies and approaches to state capitalism and thus have often been in conflict over policy vis-a-vis the mines.

Before we probe this point on factions, we must reflect back on the objective interests of the political class in nationalising the mining industry. What was expected from this assertion of state power in the productive system? The literature on the Government's desire to control the mines links these efforts to a larger national development strategy[137]—specifically, expansion and diversification of the mines; an increase in capital investment in that sector; and use of revenues from mining to develop productive and social infrastructure in previously unproductive areas of the country.[138]

Further, these companies with state equity might help encourage more tertiary business and stimulate agricultural production, thus answering many observers' developmental dreams.

But there is always a disparity (as well as an interaction) between subjective perceptions and intentions and the objective interests of the dominant class in any society. Although these goals may well have been stated and believed by many participants in the nationalisations, the state's actions drew the mines into a state capitalist sector and in an objective sense, gave the political class forming in Zambia access to the dominant engine of the political economy, hitherto controlled by external capital. As mentioned earlier, income generated from the Mulungushi Reforms of 1968 enabled factions of this class to acquire ownership for itself of some secondary means of production through the provision of high salaries and posts for its members in management positions and allowing allied classes more direct access through partnership in the companies. It also provided the state with some guarantees of expanded income[139] so that civil servants and politicians could continue with many of the postindependence social welfare programmes. Thus accumulation began in the commercial and service sectors following these initial reforms, but movement was indeed quite slow.[140]

This emergent class had objective interests in controlling the mining industry as well. Yet since the mines could not be parcelled out to individual owners or managers to create a more traditional bourgeois class, ownership has to reside within the state and power there as well. The conduct of state capitalism elicited the visible stirrings of intraclass frictions. The national politicians argued forcefully and eloquently for the state to extend its power over the mining industry. They were in power in the 1969 takeover and hoped that state participation would lead to additional revenues from this sector. Yet another tendency was building up at this same time around the pole of the nationalised industries. These we call the technocrats.

Usually educated in the West and often employed by the state or in private businesses with a more direct relationship with external capital, classical technocrats and independent entrepreneurs tended to identify as a group. Their skills, training and experience with capitalism tended to lead to an ideological predisposition towards "businesslike" solutions for social and economic problems of the country. They tended to accept the general precepts of Western capitalism and only allow for minimal deviation from these norms of behaviour. Thus these technocrats found themselves often in conflict with the national politicians who act more in accordance with their own political survival and do not appear so bound by the legalistic traditions of Western capitalism.

Although both factions belong to the wider political class, they had distinct political practices for dealing with the nationalised mineral sector. Their approaches stemmed from different perceptions of material interest as well as patterns of socialisation. The contradictions between their goals is suggested in the case study below. The combat contributed to (although certainly was not the only feature in) the failure of the GRZ side to avoid additional payments to foreign resource companies during the nationalisation negotiations.[141] This conflict may also result in inadequate planning for the difficult decade ahead.

To detail all the battles between factions over the mining industry would be beyond the scope of this study. But we will trace a set of encounters in 1973-75 which highlights how this intra-class combat affected the outcome of those negotiations.

Case Study: Phase II of the Nationalisations:

In the early 1970s several members of the technocratic faction served as managers within parastatals.[142] As the individuals with superior technical credentials and skills, they battled against national politicians, often their seniors. From these management posts they (the technocrats) displayed some amount of independence from the policies laid down by the national politicians while at the same time remaining within the wider bureaucracy of the state and party. One particular focal point of technocratic power was MINDECO. With a contingent of expatriate specialists in geology, engineering, finance and metallurgy on its staff, this parastatal was to be a major counterbalance to the power of the mines, still managed by the minority shareholderss, particularly the Ministry of Mines. Since head-on conflict over technical and management choices might have resulted in decisions favouring this group of technocrats, the strategy that appears to have been chosen by the national politicians was one of exclusion, and eventual removal.

In March of 1973 President Kaunda appointed a committee to look into the contracts of 1969/70 and to suggest means of cancelling the odious arrangements without violating international law or harming Zambia's financial reputation.[143] This committee took as within its mandate the reorganisation of MINDECO as well.[144] The Managing Director (M.D.) of MINDECO, one of the original facilitators back in 1970 and thus intimately affected by and knowledgable about these conflicts, was conspicously absent from this committee as were other key technocrats. Instead, the appointees tended to come from what we have identified as the national politician faction.

After a decision was reached to cancel the contracts by an immediate redemption of the outstanding bonds, certain members of this committee went overseas to raise the necessary capital on the Eurodollar market. This "search" subcommittee did not include members of the technocrat faction, again the people who would be most immediately affected by a change in the financial arrangement underpinning the partnerships with foreign capital. It appears this was part of the deliberate strategy to exclude technocrats and their possible allies until the last moment—the actual announcement of Phase II in August 1973.

Justification for this secrecy is offered by a former Minister of Finance who was part of the March Committee.

> It would have been improper to announce redemption because it would have upset the market straight away and the shareholders.[145]

Realistically, he was concerned that a premature announcement of the intential sources of finance. So the fewer officials that were involved, the better. But there is a long step between the reasonable desire to avoid a premature public announcement of the committee's intentions and the exclusion from the committee of various personnel such as the heads of INDECO and MINDECO who could have been strategic members of the committee.

A more convincing and all encompassing explanation for the secrecy relates to the factions question. The exclusion of certain obvious individuals from the March Committee was an expression of the political battles between these factions in this period. Initially a group from the national political faction had tackled the difficult task of extricating the nation from the binding portion of the earlier contractual arrangements with AMAX and the AAC-SA. In all likelihood, their hope was that they would emerge with greater legitimacy in the political class through a successful termination of the very unpopular 1969 agreements. They may also have desired to increase their faction's power through the castration of MINDECO and the placement of certain key parastatals more firmly under the formal bureaucracy.

This strategy, however, had some costs. It seems to have led these individuals to an interpretation of the initial contracts that later affected the progress of the negotiations and a penalty to the GRZ for the early termination of these contracts. The issue was whether the contracts automatically were cancelled once the bonds were redeemed. The GRZ argued "yes"; the foreign mining companies argued "no". Careful reading of the contracts indicates that the companies were on the stronger legal ground.[146] It is unlikely that the truth of the initial assumptions by the GRZ will even be known or acknowledged given the sensitive nature of the question. But when negotiations began in September of 1973, the multinationals' delegations had the distinct impression of confusion and disagreement on the GRZ side on this key point. They proceeded to take advantage of the disarray, hardening their resolve at the bargaining table. This seems to have resulted in their obtaining higher penalty payments form the GRZ for the abrogation of the contracts.

The battles between the factions did not end there. The political orientation of the March 1973 Committee was repeated in the composition of the first negotiating team appointed by the President in August of that year. Because of their tacit sponsorship of the redemption of the bonds and the termination (automatically) of the management contracts, a considerable amount of the national politicians' "capital" was bound up in the desire to emerge from the negotiations with *a politically acceptable settlement*. By this, we mean one which did not appear to give away too many concessions to the foreign companies and one which permitted the mines to continue operating for both sets of partners.

Interestingly, by the time of the first negotiating session in September of 1973, the M.D. of MINDECO, D. Mulaisho (a technocrat conspicuously absent from the March 1973 Committee), was included in the GRZ delegation.[147] Perhaps this addition was a belated recognition of the need for some continuity with the previous negotiating team from 1969/70. However, his addition following on the redemption of the bonds did not help ease the tensions between AMAX, AAC and the GRZ over the terms of the final settlement.

Meetings dragged on through December of 1973 without any substantive settlements. The national political team seemed unable to obtain any compromise from the foreign interests since they insisted on the point of no penalty fee. Then they began to be undercut by the vagaries of domestic politics. Next, a group of technocrats was placed on the team, after the election of December 5, 1973.[148] Of course, the ascent of these technocrats to power on the GRZ negotiating team would not have been possible without the support of the President and others within the top level of the state and party apparatuses. So this new delegation began with at least tacit political backing from the wider political class. Of necessity, however, this was an uneasy alliance since the national politicans predominated in the Party and the formal civil service top posts. Therefore they were often hostile to the style and goals of the technocrats. And individuals who identified with this nationalist faction held key positions within the contiguous parts of Government intimately connected with the negotiations.

Thus the progress of the next phase of negotiations continued to be marked by ongoing struggles between the different factions of the political class in Zambia.[149] In particular, a collision occurred between the former Minister of Mines and the new Minister of Mines—this extended from January to March of 1974 and personalised many of the internal contradictions within the political class at this phase. But such personal and political antagonisms should be understood as simply as another episode in the larger intraclass struggle of the period.

The new Zambian team that came into power in January 1974 was faced with many dilemmas. They had to try to appear to make progress in the negotiations because of pressures within the political class. But they faced strong resistance from the foreign companies' representatives who both stood on stronger legal grounds and sensed the confusion on the Zambian side. It became apparent that the minority interest would only be pacified by some concession on compensation for the cancellation of the contracts. Yet such a compromise was not politically possible for the GRZ team because of the opposition to it from the national politician faction within the political class, particularly vocal within the Cabinet Office and the Central Committee of UNIP.

Negotiations dragged on through another year of fruitless and often bitter talks. The sessions consumed a considerable amount of time of the delegates, which pleased neither side, but probably was most costly to the manpower-strapped GRZ. In December 1974, the American company finally gave in.[150] All that remained was for the GRZ to find a formula for subsidiary agreements after AMAX had agreed to accept a payment of K 22 million. Despite this sizable achievement for the technocrats on the GRZ team, events in domestic Zambian politics had their own momentum.

In January 1975 a series of difficult decisions had to be made and announced by the GRZ. The Budgetary Address revealed declining revenues for the state, especially marked in the mining sector. The government also had to decide whether to uphold its initial promises to reduce production of copper in accordance with the CIPEC proposals in an attempt to bolster the slumping price of copper.[151] As Chairman of the GRZ team, A. Kashita, who was also the Minister of Mines, awaited replies from the mines themselves concerning possible areas for shutdowns and layoff. Before the meeting with the Cabinet scheduled for the 30th of January 1975 to discuss these cutbacks, he was asked to leave his post, both on the team and in the Ministry.[152]

One reason given for Kashita's dismissal was that he had given Zambian approval to the CIPEC cutbacks without Cabinet approval.[153] He denies this allegation; others support it. But his removal was in effect the outcome of the festering conflict between the factions of the political class. In his own account, Kashita says,

> Since September of 1974 there has been an effort to get rid of most of the most capable people in the GRZ who were not real politicians... Chikwanda, Vernon Mwaanga and myself. We're all part of the educated and technical elite and had to be gotten rid of.[154]

Although this is a very personal statement, it is similar in tone and content to many other comments concerning conflict between technocrats and national politicians in this period. Kashita proved to be a good target because he is an outspoken person and a bit abrasive. He also had the misfortune to be the "messenger bearing the bad news". To many, he appeared to be following in the footsteps of Sardanis and attempting to become an "economic Czar". In retrospect, he was a prominent member of the faction that was undermined by another because of the downturn in the fortunes of mining and a series of unpopular policies he invoked.

The effect of this dismissal on the negotiations was that when the AMAX delegation arrived in Lusaka on January 24th, to sign the final papers which had been battled over for 17 months, they found no one willing to sign for the GRZ.[155] Another episode began in the talks. This time it centered around not whether to pay compensation, or how much to pay, or even over how long a period of time to pay it, but rather who in the Zambian political class would take responsibility for the final settlement?

In what appears to have been an effort to gain more time, negotiations reverted to the subsidiary agreements and continued through January.

> After Kashita was fired, the last stages were conducted by Chiwenda (the Permanent Secretary). He did a subsidiary agreement. . . Mawema and David Farmer drafted lots of final agreements. AMAX finally agreed that the Anglo Agreements should be seen as a precedent.[156]

As one AMAX negotiator remembered it, "I thought they (the negotiations) were going to go on forever."[157] A settlement was finally signed in February of 1975 although the new Articles of Association for RCM were not agreed to until December 1975.

In the final analysis, the eighteen months of delay in these negotiations had cost the GRZ and the MNCs the time and energies of skilled officials. Perhaps because of a misinterpretation of the 1969/70 agreements, the GRZ was forced to pay an additional penalty fee of K 55 million to the two foreign companies and shareholders.[158] With the actual settlement in the copper industry concluded, the copper price began a long slide into the slump that persisted into the early-1980s. Therefore the additional and short term income so eagerly looked forward to from the alteration of the foreign exchange rules, taxation provisions, and contract agreements has proved elusive for the political class in Zambia.

Post-1975 Developments:

Since the conclusion of these negotiations in 1975, the mining industry has fallen on hard times. Ironically, the assertion of greater Zambian control over the mining industry coincided with its decline. We strongly emphasise, however, that the nationalisations did *not* cause the decline. But the expected and immediate gains of revenues for the state were not forthcoming. In terms of the class composition of Zambian society, was the whole effort worth-while? Who gained and who lost from these nationalisations? And what does the future hold for this state-controlled mining industry?

Stated plainly, the prime gainers from the Zambian nationalisations of the mining industry were the international resources companies, AMAX, Inc. and the Anglo American Corporation of South Africa, Ltd. First, they obtained a reasonable settlement for their loss of initial assets in 1969/70.[159] Second, for three-and-a-half years, they were handsomely compensated for their services as managers of the companies. Had they been the sole owners, these costs would simply have been tabulated into the overall overhead and thus subtracted from sales revenue before net profits were calculated. Third, upon cancellation of these contracts in 1973, AMAX and AAC-SA received immediate monies for their outstanding bonds,[160] and an additional K 55 million in penalty fees from the GRZ. Granted, it took some time for these monies to be actually externalised to their creditors; nonetheless, by 1978, the final payments had been completed.[161] If and when the Zambian mines again make profits, these companies will receive dividends from their remaining minority interest in NCCM and RCM without further capital investment. Fourth, some unforeseen benefits to the foreign companies included that the cash flow from the Zambian nationalisations occurred when both MNCs were heavily committed to investments throughout the world.[162] Further, the heavy capital expenditure on maintenance and new projects on the Copperbelt has not been borne equally by the international companies but almost totally by the mines themselves and the Zambian state. Such consequences were not planned by AMAX or the AAC-SA but were fortunate (for them!) nonetheless.[163]

The prime losers, we would argue, have been the poor, and lower and middle income groups in Zambia. In an effort to promote Zambian exports and to limit imports at times of economic difficulty, officials have taken a series of steps that have eaten into the living standards of these people. For example, officials have devalued the Kwacha several times, sometimes at the behest of the IMF.[164] This has increased the cost competitiveness of the export sector but has also increased the costs of some vital imports such as petrol and food. The burden has been especially heavy on the urban and periurban lower and middle income groups.

Since the mining industry provided almost no revenue to the state from 1976-1979,[165] and at the same time the state incurred heavy liabilities to keep the mines operating, much of the national reserves and capital available domestically went to the mines. Recurrent expenditures of the state have continued to grow[166] so that the need to locate more revenues from other sectors of society has become more urgent. Consequently, income taxes on the middle income groups have increased rapidly, many social service schemes have been deferred or cutback, and inflation has continued to climb. Life for the average Zambian is more difficult than in the period prior to the take-overs.

Again we hasten to add, one cannot place the blame on the Zambian decision to nationalise the mines for the downturn in the international market for copper. Rather had the nationalisation step not been taken, the country still would be starved for capital since under the old tax and royalty formula[167] the state would have received low income from the mines as well. Still, in order to service the debts accrued in order to take over a majority share in the mines, the state incurred heavy debts and these must be repaid at current market rates of "rolled over" at even higher interest rates.

What of the effect on labour, particularly the mineworkers? One policy that appears to be an outcome of state participation has been the decision to keep open mines that probably would not be operating under current market conditions if there were purely commercial considerations in mind (e.g., Kalengwa Mine). Thus some benefits have accrued to these mineworkers and staff and, of course, the wider family and commercial structures around the Copperbelt and farther-flung mines. But, it should be noted, the partnership of the state with foreign enterprise has also permitted management to hold down wage demands with strong party and bureaucratic backing.[168] Although by far the best-paid wage sector, the mineworkers' actual standard of living has been reduced by inflation and the lessening of services hitherto available to them. A current outcome from the squeeze on these workers is the disruption in the organised sectors of the economy, particularly the mines. This is likely to increase in the future.[169]

Finally, to the political class itself, was the decision to nationalise the mines worth-while? The infusion of state participation into the mining industry has given the political class more access to the life blood of the country. The political benefits that stem from popular recognition of the increase of power of the state are hard to measure but surely they have contributed to the political power of the dominant class which not only controls the state but has a strong hand in the key sector as well. However, the economic consequences have been more mixed.

The conclusion of the negotiations over Phase II (in January 1975) coincided with a rapid downturn in the copper price. Since that time, a large flow of income from the mines to the state has not been forthcoming via dividends or taxes. The state has been squeezed for revenues. But the political class as a whole seems to be doing quite well with members obtaining handsome salaries and benefits as state managers in the government, parastatals or the mines proper. Many of the original technocrats have dropped out of formal government and some analysts argue, they are directing themselves along the lines of a more traditional bourgeoisie, trying to accumulate the means of production for themselves and their descendents.[170] Others have cemented ties with foreign capital, functioning as local managers for the MNCs or even partners in some local subsidiaries.

The overall health of the political economy is still linked to the mining sector. And the prognosis is not good. A foreign exchange crisis of the proportions of that which existed between 1976 and 1979 could create a serious problem for all the factions of the political class. Private entrepreneurs had problems in obtaining capital or import licences at that time. State managers and civil servants suffered from serious shortages of necessary materials such as spare parts; this was also a factor in the static nature of copper production in these years. Those most closely allied with foreign capital fared the best comparably since they could afford to wait out the crisis, safe in an awareness that the top levels of the MNCs are solvent. But the overall losses to the political class that followed shortly after the conclusion of Phase II were deep and hit at their base in the production of copper and the foreign exchange generated by it. Such a threat to the economic base of the political class can result in heightened tensions with other classes in society and in particular efforts to break any autonomous power of the working classes.

Simmering discontent within the political class, so apparent during the negotiation of Phase II, again manifests itself. Although the arena has changed, the existence of factions continues, and the battling amongst them as well. Those involved with state management press for continued copper production combined with strenuous efforts to reduce costs. But running the mines for any long period at a loss is a questionable strategy. Those in the national politician faction tend to recognise the bind but are politically committed to certain policies that increased costs to the mines rather than reduced them—for example, holding open high costs mines. In 1977-79 groups of technocrats and entrepreneurs allied to form a vocal chorus demanding such steps as the reopening of the route to the south despite the political and economic embargo on Rhodesia. More recently they have pressed for increasing trade links with the cheapest regional producer of manufactured goods, South Africa. This rubs against the policies invoked by the national political faction.[171] So far the factions that are most drawn to foreign capital or which have achieved the most individual ownership of the means of production find themselves out of political favour. The national politicians are in ascendence politically and in alliance with the formal civil service. But they will be hard pressed at a time when the economic survival of the nation is tied to the fortunes of a declining industry.

Possible Alternatives for the Future

Problems in the technical and financial arenas for copper and cobalt exporters in the 1980s are intimidating. The mining of these metals depletes the national resource base permanently. Indications are that the expected life of the major Copperbelt mines is around thirty more years.[172] Projections are for increasing problems in sustaining production at the current level for the near future. Therefore the policy options are somewhat constrained and tend to fall into three general categories. The first option would consist of continuing with the status quo, permitting a few minor alterations to deal with immediate crises. A second direction would be the actual denationalisation, totally or partially, of the mines. And a third set of policies would substantially alter the connections between the Zambian mining industry and the consumer nations. It would demand a redirection of the resource for domestic rather than international use. Each of these alternative strategies could demand extensive argument and analysis which is beyond the scope of this Chapter. But a brief survey of the options appears appropriate in a discussion of the future of the industry as a whole.

The most likely alternative would surely be the first. Because of a lack of consensus within government and possibly a lack of full understanding of the seriousness of the situation of the mining industry, it is possible to foresee a policy of maintaining production, closing only the most costly mines. National development finance could continue to be funnelled in this sector, with the political class hoping for rapid upturns in the demand for (and presumably then the price of) copper and cobalt. If, however, the price remains as low as it was from 1977-80 (averaging K 1437/tonne)[173] and there is no major decrease in the costs of production and sales, there is some question of the very ability to maintain production at all. In regard to the least profitable of the mines, there are some strong arguments for placing them on a "care and maintenance" basis, until an upswing in price.[174] Such a route is undoubtedly costly in social terms and so far has been avoided by the management of the mines under some pressures from the government.

The second direction would involve a total or partial denationalisation of the mines. These actions would be conducted to reattract foreign capital and therefore increase the technology available to the mines, decrease the unit costs, and perhaps even produce copper at a satisfactory profit. Some nations have chosen this route and have, in fact, experienced an influx in direct foreign investment in response to their denationalisation of ownerships. But most suggestions to denationalise the mines do not seem to take into consideration certain domestic and international realities. To reinvite foreign capital to exploit Zambia's minerals would require offering them something lucrative for their efforts, technology and capital, such as a tax holiday or full write-offs on all capital expenditures. Hence, no revenues would come from that area to the state although there might be some expansion of income from the industry as a whole. Second, whatever new technology the international concerns might bring, it will be costly and will not slow the rate of depletion of the Zambian mines, although it might increase marginally the rate of extraction of metals from the ores. It should be remembered that it is in the interest of the multinational resource companies to use the best possible methods and technology to extract the highest rate of materials at the lowest cost and often in the shortest period of time. Thus Zambia would return to its pre-1969 dependence with little benefit from its considerable efforts to control its own economic future. And the clocks cannot realistically be turned back.

The challenge that faces the political class for the 1980s and beyond is to construct a reasonable strategy based on a declining industry. The third alternative relies on that ability and will. The nationalisation decision placed the locally dominant class in a position where they can use their pivotal role in the industry to reorientate it for the national benefit in the long run. Examples of such reorientation would include a redirection of a growing portion of the metals for domestic and regional use. Currently the Zambian market is not capable of absorbing its own metal production. But many metal products are being imported—for example, zinc roofing sheets—which could be produced locally without a highly sophisticated industrial base. Also Central and Southern Africa is rich in extant and potential hydroelectric energy plants. The demand from this sector for copper cable should grow relatively rapidly, and Zambia could be a regional supplier. This argument, is based on an understanding that a continued dependence on foreign markets for sale of metals and import-dependent development plans will not help Zambia develop its own political economy. Such an alternative, however, would take time as the economy would slowly be redirected towards the local and regional markets, even if this means a decline in production in the short run and a permanent loss of her international market share.

To face the choices for the future will demand considerable unity and fortitude from the political class as a whole, and those are characteristics it lacks. The pulls on the different factions will no doubt result in different strategies being put forward and a difficulty for any one faction to remain in power long enough to make and carry through decisions. In all likelihood, the technocratic faction will demand mine closures and careful mining in recognition of Zambia's need to play the international market as carefully as possible. They will have considerable support from the technical and financial layers of the mines themselves. But the national political faction is under pressure to try to maintain revenues from the state—for this is the base of their political future as well as a key area of employment and social quiescence. Thus for them, the route of continued and even increased production is most enticing. Probably they will try to encourage the mines to do what now appears impossible—increase production and decrease costs.

So the real question then is whether the intermediate position that the political class has between labour and external capital will pull it apart. Will the battles between factions in Zambia make a coherent strategy for the mining industry improbable, if not impossible? The leeway in the system in the late 1960s provided by high copper prices and relatively high profits from the mines is not likely to be repeated in the early-1980s. Thus the challenges are even more overwhelming and more immediate.

Notes

1. Three general sources on the 1969 takeover are Charles Harvey and Mark Bostock, eds. *Economic Independence and Zambian Copper: A Case Study of Foreign Investment* (New York: Praeger Special Series, 1972); M.L.O. Faber and J.C. Potter, *Towards Economic Independence: Papers on the Nationalisation of the Copper Industry in Zambia* (Cambridge, England: at the University Press, 1971); and A. Martin, *Minding Their Own Business: Zambia's Struggle Against Western Control* (London: Hutchinson of London, 1972, Reprint by Penguin Books, 1975).
2. *Times of Zambia*, September 1, 1973.
3. See, *Towards Complete Independence, Address by His Excellency Dr. K.D. Kaunda to the National Council of UNIP at Matero, August 11, 1969* and other speeches by President Kaunda which express this hope.
4. Ronald T. Libby and Michael E. Woakes, "Nationalization and the Displacement of Development Policy in Zambia," *The African Studies Review* 23,1 (April 1980): 33-50.
5. *Ibid.*, pp. 43-44.
6. Dr. Ndulo is a former Professor and Dean of the School of Law at the University of Zambia.
7. "Domestic Participation in Mining in Zambia," *Development in Zambia*, ed. Ben Turok (London: ZED Press, 1979), pp. 49-70.
8. *Ibid.*, p. 55.
9. 1974 was the last year that the mines produced a dividend to the share holders until a small one in 1979.
10. George K. Simwinga, formerly senior lecturer in the Department of Political and Administrative Studies at the University of Zambia, is currently Director of Training at the African Centre for Monetary Studies in Dakar, Senegal.
11. See, G. K. Simwinga, "Corporate Autonomy and Government Control of State Enterprises", *Administration in Zambia*, ed. William Tordoff (Manchester: Manchester Univ. Press, 1980), pp. 130-138.
12. See G. Simwinga, "The Copper Mining Industry of Zambia: A Case Study of Nationalization and Control," *What Government Does,* ed., Mathrew Holden, Jr. (Beverly Hills, Calif.: Sage Publications, 1975), pp. 84-93.

13. Dr. Mphaisha teaches in the Political and Administrative Studies Department at the University of Zambia. His thesis is entitled "A Study of Zambia's Copper Policy: Nationalisation, Market Intervention, Deep Seabed Mineral Exploration" (unpublished, Ph.D. dissertation University of Pittsburgh, Public and International Affairs Department, 1979).

14. CIPEC stands for the Conseil Intergouvermental des Pays Exportateurs de Cuivre (the Intergovernmental Council for Copper Exporting Countries). It was founded in 1967.

15. Mphaisha, *op.cit.*, pp. 239-241.

16. An interesting effort in this direction was demonstrated in a Master's essay by Mathias Musonda Mpande, entitled, "Market Instability and International Commodity Arrangements" (unpublished M. Engineering thesis McGill University, Canada, 1977).

17. For a fuller discussion of the term and application to the Zambian situation see, by the author "The Political Class in Zambia: Technocrats versus Nationalists," paper presented to the African Studies Association, Los Angeles, October 31-November 3, 1979.

18. A good summary of these features is found in James Fry, "The Economy," Tordoff, *op.cit.*, pp. 43-67.

19. The nature of this locally dominant class has been dealt with by Richard Sklar in *Corporate Power in An African State: The Political Impact of Multinational Mining Companies in Zambia* (Berkley, Calif.: University of California Press, 1975); Ben Turok, "Zambia's System of State Capitalism," *Development and Change* 2 (1980): 455-478; and Carolyn Baylies, "The State and Class Formation in Zambia," (unpublished Ph.D. dissertation, University of Wisconsin, 1978).

20. In 1977, as well as being the largest single employer outside the public sector, the mining industry alone accounted for 35 % of the GDP, 45 % of governmental revenues and 95 % of total export earning, according to the Bank of Zambia, *Report and Statement of Accounts for the Year Ended December 31, 1977,* pp, 26-27.

21. An excellent review of these events is contained in Andrew Roberts, *A History of Zambia* (London: Heinemann, 1976) and some older material contained in R.I. Rotberg, *The Rise of Nationalism in Central Africa: The Making of Malawi and Zambia, 1973-1964* (Cambridge, Mass.: Harvard University Press, 1965); Gerald Caplan, "Barotseland: The Secessionist Challenge to Zambia", *Journal of Modern African Studies* 6,3 (October 1968); and D.C. Mulford, *Zambia: The Politics of Independence, 1957-1964* (London: Oxford University Press, 1964).

22. *Zambia: Towards Economic Independence,* Address by His Excellency, Dr. K.D. Kaunda to the National Council of UNIP at Mulungushi, 19 April 1968 (Lusaka, Zambia: Government Printer, 1968).

23. *Ibid.*

24. One sector where this pattern was not successful was in finance. In November 1970, the GRZ announced the nationalisation of all banks and insurance companies in the country. Three big international banks, however, avoided giving a majority share to the Government, although all insurance activities and a majority share of the smaller banks went to the state. See, *Take Up the Challenge,* speeches made by His Excellency the President to UNIP Council, Mulungushi Hall, 7-10 November 1970 (Lusaka: Government Printer, 1971) and the account offered by Sheridan Johns, "The Parastatal Sector," ed. Tordoff, *op. cit,* pp. 104-129.

25. An interesting evaluation of the potential for Zambian businessman is provided by

A.A. Beveridge, "Converts to Capitalism. The Emergence of African Entrepreneurs in Zambia" (unpublished Ph.D. dissertation, Yale University, 1973).
26. The general outlines of these parastatal changes is contained in Johns, *op.cit.*
27. A state capitalist model, according to James Petras, "attempts to devise a different pattern of industrialization which links the various phases of the industrial effort − from technological innovation through assembly − within the bounds of the nation state. The key strata initiating and seeming to direct the conversion from neo-colonialism (externally induced expansion) to state capitalism − via evolution, coup, popular uprising or some combination − are the state sector employees (civil or military)... thus it 'borrows' socialist forms (one party state, socialist rhetoric, etc.)· to accomplish capitalist ends − the realization of profit within a class society." "State Capitalism and the Third World," *Development and Change* 8 (1977): 1-17. For an application of this analysis to Zambia, see Turok, *op.cit.*
28. Government revenue was K 63.7 million in 1963-4 (figures transposed from the pound to the Zambian Kwacha) and it rose to K 432.4 million in 1970 with the value of mineral production at K 299 million in 1964 and K 759 million in 1969. *Monthly Digest of Statistics*, vol. 7, no. 3, 1971, Tables 15 and 29.
29. Charles Harvey, "Growth and the Structure of the Economy," in C. Harvey and M. Bostock, *op.cit., in* which Harvey argues that a vigorous policy of import substitution had been instituted after independence. But the level of imports continued to rise and so did the need for more export-derived foreign exchange.
30. Richard Sklar, "Zambia's Response to the Rhodesian Unilateral Declaration of Independence," *Politics in Zambia* ed. W. Tordoff (Manchester; U.K.: Manchester University Press, 1974, pp. 320-362.
31. Martin, *op.cit.*
32. See Harvey, *op.cit.*
33. By comparison, in 1969 less than 1 % of the employees of the Chilean companies were foreigners whereas in the Zambian mines in 1972/3 almost 58 % of the staff positions were filled by expatriates.
34. Chapters 3 and 7 of the Constitution of the First Republic of Zambia.
35. Martin, *op.cit.,* Bostock and Harvey, *op.cit.,* and Faber and Potter, *op.cit.*
36. NCCM was Nchanga Consolidated Copper Mines Ltd., owned 51 % by the GRZ and the remaining 49 % was controlled by Anglo Group companies. RCM was Roan Consolidated Mines, owned 51 % by the GRZ and the remaining 49 % shared by AMAX, Inc. RST, I.I., Anglo companies and various private shareholders. They have been merged into the new Zambia Consolidated Copper Mines, Ltd. (ZCCM).
37. See author's thesis, "The Dynamics of Nationalization on the Periphery of Capitalism: Negotiations Between AMAX Inc., the Anglo American Corporation of South Africa, Ltd., and the Government of the Republic of Zambia." (Unpublished Ph.D. dissertation Faculty of Political Science, Columbia University, October 1979).
38. From interviews with personnel in NCCM and RCM both in Head Offices and on the Copperbelt, 1975-1976.
39. *Zambia Mining Yearbook,* 1976-1980.
40. Mokambo Development Company Ltd., is a joint venture of MINDECO Ltd. and Geomin of Rumania. MINDECO-Noranda Ltd. was a joint venture with Noranda Mines Ltd. of Canada.
41. The emerald industry in particular has considerable potential to generate foreign exchange in Zambia but it has been the focal point of great internal struggle over smuggling, illegal digging and corruption in high places. See, *Republic of Zambia:*

Report of the Commission of Inquiry into the Emerald Industry (Lusaka, Zambia: Government Printer, August 1979), and *Times of Zambia* and *Zambia Daily Mail* articles in May of 1980. Uranium mining has also received considerable publicity of late, but there is a question whether deposits are available in quality and size to make mining it an economically viable venture.

42. Eight states – Tanzania, Mozambique, Malawi, Zimbabwe, Botswana, Namibia, Angola and Zaire – border on Zambia.
43. Although the prices were steadier, lead and zinc prices did not keep up with inflation in the period.
44. The production price began an upward movement from $ 5.40 per pound in early 1977 to a peak of $ 25.00 in February 1979. The free market price hit $ 40.00 in February 1979. S.C. Lowe, paper presented at Gorham International Inc. meeting, "Cobalt Crisis," April 30-May 1, 1979.
45. RCM, *Annual Report 1979* and interview with Consulting Metallurgist for RCM, Mr. Ian Knight, 8 July 1981.
46. RCM, *Annual Reports,* 1976-1980.
47. MEMACO, *Annual Report 1980,* p. 13.
48. From interviews with RCM personnel, June-August 1981.
49. *Zambia Mining Yearbook,* 1975-1979 and interviews with RCM and NCCM personnel.
50. See annual reports of the companies and prices listed in the financial press.
51. Ann Seidman "Introduction," *Natural Resources and National Welfare: The Case of Copper,* ed. Ann Seidman (New York: Praeger Special Series, Praeger Press): Table 1.1, p.5.
52. Commodity Research Unit of New York, 1976.
53. Information from financial officers at RCM, 1981.
54. According to NCCM and RCM personnel, these figures are of the right magnitude for all operating costs.
55. Republic of Zambia, *Second National Development Plan.* (Lusaka, Zambia: Ministry of Development Planning and National Guidance, 1971), particularly Chapter III, "Mining," pp. 85-92.
56. Interviews with metallurgists and mining engineers, 1981.
57. Interview with Mr. Hanson, Acting General Manager, Mufulira Mines, July 1981.
58. The tonnage of ore mined at Chibuluma, Chambeshi, Luanshya-Baluba, Luanshya and Kalengwa Mines in 1977 was 8,926,000 tonnes and by 1979 it had reached 7,677,000 tonnes. These aggregate figures can be misleading since tonnage will often reflect a particular stage in mining or any particular problems that come up underground as much as overall mining potential. But most personnel interviewed agreed that there was a downward trend at both mining companies. *Zambia Mining Yearbook, 1977-1980.*
59. *Zambia Mining Yearbook, 1977-1980.*
60. A general rule in mining is that new mine shafts are sunk to exploit the richer parts of the orebody first. Thus, later mining tends to hoist ore of lower grades than the initial ones.
61. The figure of 75,000 tonnes of copper was supplied by Mr. H. Matschke, Consulting Metallurgist, NCCM, 1981.
62. *Ibid.*
63. The cutbacks of production agreed to by the CIPEC members were of the order of 10 % in 1974, 10 % in 1975 and 15 % in 1978.
64. According to the Bank of Zambia, in 1979 there were "production problems af-

fecting growth in output including the deepening of mine operations and falling grade of mined ore. A loss of skills through the high rate of expatriate labour force turnover has also been a continuing problem. Despite the easing of the problem of foreign exchange availability during the course of 1979, the supplies situation for spares and other inputs still remained tight as a result of long lead times between the placing of order and their receipt." *Bank of Zambia Report, 1979*, p. 21.

65. Interviews with both NCCM and RCM personnel.
66. *Zambia Mining Yearbook, 1979*, Table 2, p. 23.
67. RCM, *Annual Report 1979*, p. 7; recent reports indicate that the Benguela Route may be reopened soon but the question of UNITA control in that region must be settled first.
68. From corporate reports and newspapers, the Zimbabwe-Zambia border was re-opened in 1978 but only to metal shipments.
69. NCCM, *Annual Report, 1978*.
70. MEMACO, *Annual Report, 1980*, pp. 12-13.
71. NCCM, *Annual Report, 1979*, p. 7.
72. RCM, *Annual Report, 1978*, p. 6.
73. Days in transit comparisons for these routes are as follows: average of 21 days for Beira; 15-20 days for DSM; 14 days to Lobito; and 25-30 days for East London. James Matale, Commercial Dept., NCCM, July 1981.
74. MEMACO, *Annual Report, 1980*, pp. 12-13.
75. RCM *Annual Report, 1980*, p. 8.
76. There is much speculation on South African influence upon the Zambian leadership but very little of it is documented or established beyond doubt. A recent controversial account of the Zambia/South African connection is included in Phyllis Johnston and David Martin's, *The Struggle for Zimbabwe*, (London: Faber and Faber, 1981.)
77. Interviews with RCM personnel.
78. Figures drawn from *Zambia Mining Yearbooks* and corporate reports.
79. That point where the company either makes a loss or makes a profit.
80. Interview with RCM financial personnel.
81. So far major layoffs have been avoided in Zambia by keeping open some less profitable mines. Paring down has been achieved largely by attrition. Cost reduction measures invoked by the government include for the mines to reduce their labour forces and the amount of work done through outside subcontractors, reduce the scale of operations at some high cost mining sites and to purchase spare parts and equipment from cheaper sources than hitherto. See, *Bank of Zambia Report, 1979*, p. 21.
82. *Bank of Zambia Report, 1976*, pp. 60-61.
83. The full implications of the GRZ reliance on the IMF facilities is beyond the acope of this study. But some provocative parallels can be found in the case studies included in Cherly Payer's *The Debt Trap: The IMF and the Third World* (New York: Monthly Review Press, 1975).
84. *Bank of Zambia Report, 1978*, pp. 64-65.
85. Johns, *op.cit.*, p. 123.
86. *Ibid.*, p. 67.
87. A recent statement of that belief was included in an article entitled "The IMF Comes to Our Aid," in the new newspaper called the *Financial Review of Zambia*, Vol. 1, no. 1, June 1981.
88. EXIM Bank is the Export/Import Bank of the United States, an agency of the

federal government; ECGD is the Export Credit Guarantee Department of the United Kingdom. In order to extend large foreign loans, both France and Britain require that their credit guarantee organisations clear them first before the commercial banks extend the loans.

89. Interview with RCM financial personnel.

90. *Ibid.*

91. Such a problem emerged in 1977 over the financing of Phase III of the Chingola Leach Plant when the company (NCCM) withdrew its mandate to a lead bank to obtain financing. This mandate was given to IFC which in turn offered conditions that were not satisfactory to the GRZ or NCCM. Therefore the whole matter was postponed until 1981 when the refinancing discussions got underway again with the World Bank.

92. The European Investment Bank gives preferential terms to members of the Lome Convention with the EEC and Zambia is a member. Similar terms are often available from other European banks such as the Indo Suez Bank of France.

93. Gearing is calculated by a ratio of the company's liabilities to its shareholder equity. It serves as a gross measurement of the financial extendedness of the company plus its own shareholders confidence.

94. Interviews with RCM personnel. These short term loans can be rolled over every 90 days, with a combined interest plus commissions rate of nearly 7 per quarter, thus almost 28 %.

95. NCCM, *Annual Report, 1980,* and RCM *Annual Report, 1980.*

96. NCCM, *Annual Report, 1976.*

97. NCCM, *Annual Report, 1977.*

98. A heavy portion of these costs are recurrent expenditures while the capital expenditure budget usually measures expansion and growth in an industry.

99. A certain amount of consultation is expected to be contracted abroad since it makes little economic sense to keep specialists in all fields on staff. The fees are usually quite high since they often are for a few very highly skilled experts in a particular area. According to an industry spokesman for RCM, however, an extensive use of outside consultants is not particularly wide-spread in the Zambian mines.

100. Interviews with mine managers, 1981.

101. The higher ranks usually tend to externalise more of their salary than the lower levels since they do not require all of it for immediate living expenses and local taxes.

102. At the Precious Metals Plant in Ndola.

103. See *Annual Reports* of both NCCM and RCM.

104. Interview with Mr. Matschke, Chief Consulting Metallurgist, NCCM, Ltd., July 24, 1981.

105. See NCCM, *Annual Report, 1975, 1980.*

106. NCCM, *Annual Report.*

107. MEMACO, *Annual Report, 1980.*

108. *Zambia Mining Yearbook, 1970-1980.* Over this period, the name of this document changed several times but it is generally listed under this title.

109. Interviews with RCM personnel, 1981.

110. NCCM, *Annual Report, 1980* and *Zambia Mining Yearbook.*

111. According to Mr. Matschke, NCCM sells "high grade cathodes; a certain amount of leach (electrowon) cathodes in an attempt to establish a market for them; wirebars (made from a blend of electrowon and electrorefined cathodes); billets (made

from the same mix) for ZAMEFA, a Zambian cable maker; and some anodes (blister) which are rejected by the toll refiner (RCM) to avoid resmelting costs." July 24, 1981.
112. *Ibid.*
113. The customs duties on copper goods vary greatly, depending upon the degree of processing of the good. A Table of figures for 1972 is reproduced below.

Custom Duties on Copper Goods – 1972
(in c per pound of copper)

Code	Copper Goods	EFC	USA	Canada	Japan
74.01	Blister	0	3.1	3.1	5.6
74.03	Wrought bars, rods, angles, shapes, sections angle	8.0	8.1	7.7	16.3
74.05	Wrought plates, sheets and strip	8.0	8.1	12.5	17.5
74.07	Tubes and pipes	8.0	3.8	5.3	18.8
74.08	Tube and Pipe Fitting	7.5	9.9	17.5	10.0
85.23	Wires, insulated electric cables	11.0	7.4	7.5	15.0

Source: Mpande thesis, *op.cit.* Appendix, p. 257 which he drew from OECD reports.

114. Additional concerns are that freight charges are higher for rod than wirebar and the rod would have to be packed and crated for long distance delivery.
115. MEMACO, *Annual Report, 1980,* p. 6.
116. ZAMEFA produces a small amount of cables domestically.
117. According to S.C. Lowe, *op.cit.,* p. 5.
118. Interview with Mr. Mapsen, General Manager, Chibuluma Division, RCM, July, 1981.
119. From interviews with mining personnel and head office representatives.
120. NCCM, *Annual Report, 1979,* p. 2 and RCM, *Annual Report, 1978,* p. 1.
121. *Ibid.*
122. See report in *Africa,* No. 119, July 1981, p. 140.
123. A brief description of the reasons behind the creation of these works councils and their effectiveness is available in Robin Fincham and Grace Zulu. "Labour and Participation in Zambia," ed. Turok, *op.cit.,* pp. 214-225.
124. See particularly the responses of the miners in R. Fincham and G. Zulu, *op.cit.*
125. According to a speech by Pres. Kaunda in 1979, there were 44 illegal strikes involving 10,846 workers; 1980 the number of strikes doubled involving 21,921 workers and in the first 6 months of 1981 there were 84 illegal strikes involving 46,399 workers. *Times of Zambia,* July 28, 1981, p. 1.
126. *Zambia Mining Yearbook, 1979,* p. 7.
127. From interviews A. Sardanis, August 22, 1975.
128. A fuller discussion of this decentralisation of ZIMCO is included in S. Johns, *op.cit.,* pp. 111-116.
129. According to Dr. Simwinga, in this period reports were prepared by experts in technical fields and sent on to the operating companies and then on to a technical liaison committee. This committee included a representative from NCCM and

RCM. After this technical liaison committee's deliberation, the project went on to the Board of Directors for discussion and approval. Simwinga, "The Copper Mining Industry of Zambia. . . " *op.cit.,* pp. 89-98.

130. Information from discussion with participants in 1975-1976.
131. Information from interviews, 1981.
132. Although there are technical personnel listed on staff at the Ministry of Mines, they are few in number and often without sufficient background or time to oversee properly the operations of the operating mining companies.
133. MEMACO, *Annual Reports.*
134. See *Monthly Digest of Statistics,* "Trade with Selected Countries," Table 26, Vol. xvi, no. 10-12, October/December 1980, p. 24, and *Zambia Mining Yearbook, 1979,* "Copper Sales to Customer Countries," Table 2.
135. Kenneth D. Kaunda, *Address at the Official Opening of the First Session of the Fourth National Assembly,* Lusaka, 18 December 1978 as reported in the *Times of Zambia,* 19 December, 1978.
At this time, MINDECO lost its subsidiaries to ZIMCO. On the new ZIMCO Board sat the Prime Minister, now responsible to approve all managing directors, general managers or chief executives of the subsidiary company.
136. For another study of a local class pulled in different directions; see, John Saul, "The State in Post Colonial Societies: Tanzania," *Socialist Register 1974* (London: Merlin Press, 1974): 349-72.
137. Bostock and Harvey point to this strategy and in the later works of Harvey, he explores the import-substitution nature of the whole development plan.
138. Libby and Woakes, *op.cit.,* p. 35.
139. In fact, much of this income has proved elusive, and several INDECO companies have been chronic money losers. The parastatal as a whole reported a loss in 1975-76. S. Johns, *op.cit.,* p. 122.
140. Some information on local accumulation is available in C. Baylies, *op.cit.,* and Morris Szeftel. "Political Conflict Spoils and Class Formation in Zambia, (Unpublished Ph.D. dissertation, University of Manchester, 1978).
141. Much of this argument is developed in the author's paper at Los Angeles, ASA, 1979, *op.cit.*
142. Individuals who served first as Executive Chairmen in this period later assumed the posts of Managing Directors.
143. According to Mr. John Mwanakatwe, former Minister of Finance, this committee included himself, Humphrey Mulemba; the Minister of Trade; Mainza Chona; the Governor of the Bank of Zambia, Bitwell Kuwani, Lishomwa Lishomwa, the President's Economic Advisor, and the Permanent Secretaries of the Ministries of Mines, of Finance, and of Legal Affairs.
144. Interview with H. Mulemba and J. Mwanakatwe, 1976.
145. Interview with J. Mwanakatwe, February 6, 1976.
146. Such is the opinion of a lawyer, Mr. John Niehuss, who served on the GRZ back-up team in 1969/70. An outline of his legal opinion is available in Appendixes of of Bostock and Harvey, *op.cit.*
147. From AMAX International corporate records of who attended each session of negotiations.
148. In that election 29 of the 72 sitting MPs, lost their seats, including three Cabinet Ministers and ten Ministers of State; see Tordoff "Introduction," *Politics, op.cit.,* p. 11.
149. The information in this section was derived from various sources. Individuals will be mentioned only in regard to isolated or different opinions from the rest.

150. Interviews with AMAX representative upon his return from Lusaka in late February 1975.
151. The proposed CIPEC cutback in production at this time was to be 10 % as put forward at the Ministers meeting in Lima in November of 1974.
152. "I was fired." Interview with A. Kashita, December 3, 1975.
153. Interviews with A. Kashita and other members of the GRZ.
154. Interview with A. Kashita, December 4, 1975.
155. Interview with Dexter Walcott, a former Vice President of AMAX Inc., January 31, 1975.
156. Interview with Alan Dodd, former Financial Controller of ZIMCO, INDECO, and MINDECO, October 1, 1976 who was also involved in the negotiations from time to time as an advisor.
157. Interview with Denis Acheson, former President of Amax International, London, September 29, 1976.
158. At this time K = $ 1.56. K 22 million went to AMAX Inc. and K 33 million went to Anglo American, totalling K 55 million or about $ 86 million.
159. For example, from the 1969 nationalisation, RST received about K 144.5 million which included both compensation for the loss of shares in the Zambian mines and also about K 60 million in funds that had been "blocked" since 1968 by the new externalisation of funds regulations introduced in the Mulungushi Reforms.
160. In August of 1973 there were $ 226.3 million in bond form outstanding.
161. Interview with AMAX personnel, 1978, New York.
162. For further information on this, see author's thesis, *op. cit.*
163. Representatives of both companies deny any gains from the nationalisations but when the figures are pointed out, they tend to concede that there were some residual gains.
164. The Kwacha was devalued by 20 % in July 1976 and another 10 % in March of 1978.
165. See Table on p. 33.
166. *Monthly Digest of Statistics* and *Bank of Zambia* reports confirm this statement.
167. The pre-1960 taxation of operating mining companies included a royalty tax to be paid on production and without regard to costs. This tended to act as a disincentive to the mining groups to open mines with lower grade ore or higher costs. For a fuller picture of the problems with the prior taxing system, see Charles Harvey, "Tax Reform in the Mining Industry," in Bostock and Harvey, eds., *op.cit.*, pp. 131-144.
168. For further analysis of the effect that a joint venture with local state foreign capital upon local Zambian wage rates, see author, "Beyond Nationalization. The Partnership Between the Political Class in Zambia and the Foreign Mining Companies, 1960-1973," paper presented to the African Studies Association meeting, Philadelphia, Pa., October 15-18, 1980.
169. For the first six months of 1981 the incidence of strikes or labour disruptions has grown dramatically, according to the Zambia Federation of Employers as reported in the *Times of Zambia*, July, 1981.
170. Again see the work of Baylies and Szeftel, *op.cit.*
171. The outlines of the dissent are discernible in the pages of the *Times of Zambia* coverage of the National Assembly debates and question periods and in the *Hansard*.
172. A rapid drop-off in production is predicted for the early part of the next century but some mines will have a longer life, possibly another 40 years.
173. LME figures.
184. These arguments are currently heard from the technical and managerial levels of the operating companies.

Chapter 3
A. Participation or Powerlessness:
The Place of Peasants in Zambia's Rural Development
by M.C. Bwalya

The basic rationale for peasant participation in development is to motivate self-reliance so as to ensure a wider and more equitable distribution and utilization of scarce local resources. In the past seventeen years since political independence, Zambia has employed a variety of strategies intended to enhance peasant participation in development. The success or failure of the participatory strategies has obviously varied from strategy to strategy and situationally though they have not led to a fundamental transformation of peasant socioeconomic positions. I wish to express the view that peasant powerlessness rather than participation has underlain these strategies. What follows is an attempt to exemplify this view and to offer suggestions for the eighties and beyond.

Peasant Participatory Strategies in Zambia

The tem "peasant" as used here, is a shorthand to describe the majority of rural producers who usually sell part of their produce in order to sustain their subsistence. In strict Marxist terminology, they would be referred to as "petty" commodity producers: those rural producers who rely largely on household labour for the production of partly consumption and partly exchange values. In short, peasants will be seen, in as broad a way as possible, as small-scale rural commodity producers.

Zambia's attempts at increasing peasant participation have been of two basic types. There has been, firstly, the effort at improving peasant participation in production and in the distribution of the benefits of the product. Here can be grouped the various programmes, such as co-operatives, agricultural settlement schemes, rural reconstruction, etc., which are aimed at mobilizing and organising rural people to engage in self-sustaining production, employment and income generating activities. Then, there has been the effort to improve peasant participation in power. The series of actions regarding the devolution of government such as District Councils, Ward Development and Village Productivity Committees, are aimed at bringing decision making power to the locality, among peasants. A discussion of participation cannot be complete unless it touches both forms which Zambia has employed.

I. Programmes for Participation in Production

From the point of view of the peasant, the various programmes aimed at increasing his capacity for productive engagement have failed to reach him. To him, they are a deliberate camouflage to obscure his exploitation and consequent exclusion from sharing fairly in the available resources and benefits of the country. A few examples will suffice.

i. *The Cooperative Instrument*

As is well-known, the co-operative strategy has not met with much success as an instrument for peasant participation in production. From the youthful enthusiasm and attendant expansion following their Presidential launching in 1965, cooperatives began to decline from a peak of 1,121 in 1969 to just under 700 in 1979 (Bwalya, 1980).

Although the decline has been attributed to a broad range of problems, chief among them was the incessant feuds among cooperative members for control and dominance. Cooperatives became the battle grounds for fighting between the better-off farmers for preeminence and selfish access to resources at the cooperatives' disposal. The fighting did not only crush the peasants underfoot, but it led to the dislocation and destruction of cooperatives themselves.

Moreover, in the few cases where cooperatives have been relatively successful, their structures and operations did not adequately fit in with the philosophy of peasant participation on which they were intended to be based. The most successful of those cooperatives (e.g., AFIF, ECU, NCU, SPCU, etc.), have become dominated by their administrative staff and the few local economic and political notables. These tendencies certainly are not commensurate with the objective of peasant participation in development, since peasants are excluded from sharing not only in decision making, but also in the benefits of such cooperatives.

ii. *Settlement Schemes*

The idea of family farm groups which would be encouraged and assisted in agricultural production with a view to increasing their incomes greatly influenced the introduction of settlement schemes. Blocks of demarcated and prepared land were settled by selected people for purposes of agricultural production. With government assistance in form of loans, technical and extension advice, marketing facilities and initial clearing of the plots for settlement, each of the settlers was expected to engage in the production of specified cash crops. From these, they were expected to generate an income to enable them to pay off their loans as well as meet other subsistence needs.

But, like the cooperative movement, settlement schemes met with even greater difficulties in enhancing peasant participation. Firstly, the numbers of settlement schemes introduced throughout Zambia were very few, far-spaced and unevenly distributed as the following examples show.

1. While Serenje District, with a population of 53,000 in 1969 had three settlement schemes, Mpika District with a population of 59,000 in the same year had only one scheme. At most, each of these schemes only supported a few people, thereby defeating the original intention of widespread peasant participation in development.

2. Settlers were not only expected to have some education and the basic skills needed for carrying out agricultural production, they were also expected to produce crops prescribed by the scheme management. The first factor entailed a biased preference for the already better-off rural households to the exclusion of the needy peasant poor who are the majority. The second factor discouraged potential settlers from joining, as they would not grow crops of their own choice. This was not only to limit the settler's own production planning but it justified a feeling that settlers were mere government production workers — not their own masters on their plots.

The consequence of these factors was to dampen the peasants' enthusiasm to join and also to limit the motivation and commitment of existing settlers to incomes and the capacity for self-perpetuation.

iii. *Other Programmes for Production*

Other peasant participatory programmes such as the Rural Reconstruction Centres, Intensive Development Zones, and more recently, the Multi-purpose Cooperatives and the Lima programmes have been introduced. But they have all met difficulties in initiating genuine peasant participation in the form of creating rural employment opportunities and increasing the quantity and coverage of peasants' incomes. Thus, the standard of life in rural areas has remained generally low while the poorest of the peasant population have an increasingly diminishing change of participating effectively in the formulation, implementation, and in the benefits of rural development policies in Zambia.

The Machinery for Implementation

In order to service the various peasant production programmes, a series of parastatal organisations were introduced to supplement the efforts of the conventional government departments. These parastatal organisations were created, expanded or reconstituted from colonial or early independence formats between 1970 and 1979 with the aim of catering for the development of rural people, among whom the peasants are the majority. Organisations such as the Rural Development Corporation (RDC), National Agricultural Marketing Board (NAMBOARD) Tobacco Board of Zambia (TBZ), Cold Storage Board (CSB), Dairy Produce Board (DPB) and the Agricultural Finance Company (AFC), were reconstituted to render credit, marketing and production extension services to rural/peasant producers. The capital investments in these parastatals totalled up to K 33,754,000 in 1972; K 17,616,000 in 1973; and K 10,887,000 in 1974; and even for lesser amounts in the years up to 1979. This would seem to indicate an increasingly deminishing activity after 1972 (*Mid-term Review*, SNDP, 1974, p. 46; RDC, *Annual Reports*, 1975-1979). The rural parastatals have exhibited similar vacillations to the rest of the Zambian economy and in this sense they serve to illustrate the declining role of the state in rural and peasant development. A few examples will suffice.

i. *Credit provision*

The AFC, a subsidiary of the RDC, was reconstituted from a credit body with roots in the colonial government. As the Land and Agricultural Bank, the body did not provide credit facilities to village or peasant producers or Africans in general. Only in the late 1950s was a small number of Africans organised into Peasant Farming Schemes (Hellen, 1968; Dresang, 1975; *RDC Annual Report*, 1975).

At independence, the new government expanded the Bank under the name of Credit Organization of Zambia (COZ) with a view to extend services to village/peasant producers under liberalized security and qualifications requirements for granting loans. It was argued that only then would the dominantly poor rural Africans be accommodated and given a change to participate in production, self-sustained employment and income generation. Indeed, by 1968, K 19.7 million worth of loans had been handed over to farmers.

But the bulk of the loans had supported larger commercial farmers near the railway rather than small peasant producers. This was partly because in the early days of independence, the government had a private enterprise orientation and partly due to a state structure which favoured better-off producers. Thus, only K 2.0 million per year was issued to small scale or peasant and cooperative producers numbering some 309,000 (Lombard and Tweedie, 1973, p. 79; Bwalya, 1980, *passim*). It is clear that in *per capita* terms, the peasants receive a tiny fraction of the cake. Although large sums were given in loans, *albeit* in a biased way, poor accounting procedures, inadequate skilled manpower, low repayment levels of less than 30 % annually finally forced COZ to close with an accumulated loss of K 20 million in 1969.

The closure of COZ and the introduction of AFC in 1970 was a tactical disaster as far as village and peasant producers were concerned. As it turned out, AFC adopted more stringent credit policies and aimed at making substantial profits from its activities. AFC's emphasis on certain levels of security and the requirement that former COZ debtors pay off their previous debts before being granted loans have scared away and excluded the majority of peasants with potential and desire for farming. In particular, this has led to lack of interest, a kind of powerlessness, toward reviving defunct cooperative farms, since even if only a few of the former members wished to work on the cooperative farm, they would be required to repay the total debt owed by previous members.

Other credit organisations include (a) the Cattle Financing Company, formerly the Grazier Beef Scheme. Virtually all borrowers from this agency are commercial farmers of which few could be found in the remote areas where peasants are in the majority. Again, it could be said that peasants are not given adequate funding and other supportive services. (b) The Commercial Banks, for example, especially after the 1970 Mulungushi Reforms, have been a source of credit to farmers. In 1975 for instance, over K 10 million worth of agricultural loans came from Commercial Banks. But the strictly commercial conditions upon which Commercial Banks have continued to base the granting of loans mean that only Commercial and Medium level (line-of-rail) farmers are able to gain from this source. Only TBZ has attempted to assist peasants by organising them into family production units and providing them with credit, training and technical and marketing services. However, it requires to expand its activities in order to cover more peasants throughout the country.

ii. *Marketing Facilities*

An important example of a marketing and supply − servicing parastatal which predated independence is NAMBOARD. This was the biggest agricultural marketing organisation in the country before the spread of Cooperative Marketing Unions in many provinces. As well as having a monopoly over marketing grain in which it assumed the importing monopoly, NAMBOARD had the responsibility for marketing and supply of production inputs (e.g., fertilizers, seeds, insecticides, etc.) and maize, sorghum, sunflower, groundnuts, beans, cotton, fruit and vegetables. It was instituted to serve the very small village or peasant producers who were unable to arrange for their own marketing and supply facilities.

But in fulfilling its function of residual buyer, and being in perpetual financial defecits, NAMBOARD has kept the prices and incomes of peasants equally perpetually low. Moreover, judging from the many complaints about the peasant's produce being left to rot at marketing depots, it may be clear that as an organisation, NAMBOARD is a source of frustration and a sense of abandonment for many a peasant interested in participating in agricultural production.

Furthermore, NAMBOARD staff tend to prefer to deal with and assist producers near the main roads and District centres. Surveys in Serenje and Mpika districts (Bwalya, 1975 and 1980, respectively) confirmed this tendency even though the situation in Mpika is less clearcut. In Mpika, most peasant respondents thought that the Northern Cooperative Union (NCU), in place of NAMBOARD, was the only government agency which reached them even though it was blamed for low prices and delays in paying for the produce.

Other service and marketing parastatals and government programmes include the CSB and DPB. The CSB buys and sells graded cattle in competition with private enterprises. Like NAMBOARD, CSB is the residual buyer of animals, but it often down-grades them to far below their market values which has led to charges of exploitation of village or peasant animal producers. The DPB on the other hand, buys milk from farmers and usually processes it into manufactured products before selling it to consumers. But few peasants are affected by DPB (especially in provinces with low animal populations), as not many of them engage in milk production on a large scale.

The Pilot Agricultural Mechanization Scheme (PAMS) was aimed at helping small-scalepeasant producers to cultivate their land and increase hectareage, but it has since died a natural death. At the end of July, 1968, 183 tractors had been distributed throughout rural Zambia through PAMS. However, high running costs and lack of spare parts and mechanical services made it an expensive service to peasant producers. This rendered it a failure.

Its withdrawal has an adverse effect on peasant producers who rightly thought of the action as a sign of the government's increasing lack of interest in them and their interests to improve production. Today, the only tractor loans available are to individuals on a long-term loan basis. This clearly benefits the already better-off or politically influential individuals while putting the poor peasant majority at an even greater disadvantage.

In general, the proliferation of parastatals has had the consequence of building up an unprecedentedly large bureaucratic bourgeoisie, dependent on state coffers for its existence and reproduction. As one report discovered, (Mwanakatwe Salaries Commission, 1975), the public service alone increased in size from 21,863 in 1963 to 58,013 in 1974. Superscale positions rose from 184 in 1962 to 1,298 in 1975, and personnel emoluments rose from K 33,563, 424 in 1964/5 to over K 109,952, 959 in only 10 years. Similar figures are not available for parastatal growth, but indications are that their growth was even greater and more dramatic.

Such an expansion of the bureaucratic machinery and structure can only reroute potentially productive funds into unproductive, mostly luxury consumption activities by the state employees. Moreover, in spite of the friction that may inevitably exist between the parastatal executives, top politicians and civil servants, there is a considerable similarity of orientation on many issues of policy. For example, the top levels of the parastatal management and the political and civil service bourgeoisie have close dealings with foreign capital (Eriksen, 1978, p. 20). Moreover, parastatal personnel have tended to be highly mobile and have often acquired business interests during their tenure of parastatal office. Similarly, among the upper levels of civil servants and politicians has emerged a class of property-owners, dependent upon the state and the party for: access to loan facilities; gaining management experience; high salaries; contracts with diverse sources of capital; and access to knowledge (Eriksen, 1978, Bwalya, 1980).

This means that a "dominant coalition" exists at the national level involving the various elite groups who use primarily the state and party machinery to gain preferential access to available resources, for their collective identification, and for the maintenance of their privileged positions. The National Council of UNIP, the National Assembly, various ministerial and parastatal bodies and committees and the elaborate multinational corporations and foreign companies which have proliferated since independence, can be seen as the institutional bases — institutional bases through which the various national elite groups identify themselves and gain consensus for the national policies concerned with the sharing of national resources amongst themselves and their immediate clientele to a greater exclusion of peasants.

II. Programmes for Participation in Decision-making

Zambia's postindependence efforts at effecting participation in decision-making have been lumped under the generic term of decentralisation. As it should be understood, decentralisation encapsulates two related concepts of deconcentration and devolution. The former refers to the delegation of administrative functions to the lower levels of the government administrative hierarchy. The latter, on the other hand, refers to the placement of decision-making power and responsibility in elected people at the locality. The major concern in this section of chapter 3 is this latter aspect of decentralisation, although it is imperative that the practice of deconcentration be touched upon briefly.

i. *Administrative Decentralization*

Following a period of indecision after Zambia's independence up to 1968, the government embarked on a programme of decentralisation which was launched with the 1969 Administrative Reforms. Under these reforms, local-level government was strengthened by giving the District Secretary more powers while at the same time introducing Governors and Cabinet Ministers at District and Provincial levels, respectively, who were politicians. The expectation was that these would expedite decisionmaking and consequent project implementation. Furthermore, it was anticipated that such reorganisation would enable greater involvement of the local people (hence participatory democracy) and better and relevant decisions, since these would be made with direct understanding of the situational problems.

But only junior and inexperienced Cabinet Ministers and later Members of the Central Committee of the party (MCCs) had generally been posted to provincial levels. Therefore, major policy decisions and project priorities were still made at the national level with only little or no local-level contributions or consultation. The allocation of the number of schools, hospitals, industrial plants, etc. to each province or district is decided at the national level and announced to the people strategically just prior to elections and often abandoned altogether after the elections. This seems to have been the case with the Mercedes Benz Truck Assembly plant for Kasama.

It may therefore be argued that the deconcentrative efforts of decentralisation were merely aimed at "administrative penetration" (van Velzen, 1973). By this type of penetration, the national bourgeoisie (or elite) strive to involve themselves at the local community level to ensure more or less coercive law and order, provide limited social services such as schools, health centres and agricultural extension services, as a means of identifying a few strategic locals to whom some resources spilling over from the centre can be allocated. These would be the local people to whom the duty of maintaining local order and a semblance of popular participation is delegated. Administrative decentralisation or simply deconcentration as it has been applied in Zambia therefore does not fundamentally encourage peasant participation in government. The following discussion of efforts at devolution in Zambia will tend to show that rather than popular peasant participation in decision-making, the efforts are a smokescreen for the identification and consolidation of a few eminent local men to maintain order while sharing among themselves the bulk of the available resources and wealth of the area to the exclusion of peasants.

ii. *Popular decentralisation*

Early in 1965, Local and Rural Councils were established by the postindependence government to coordinate and undertake local activities. Shortly afterwards in 1966, Provincial and District Development Committees (PDC and DDC respectively) were established to coordinate the implementation of the First National Development Plan programmes. Then, under the Village Registration and Development (1971) Act, Ward Development and Village Productivity Committees (WDC and VPC respectively) were created to enable local-level (grass-root) participation in policy making and the coordination of local hierarchies.

In the interests of coordination, of bringing decision making to the locality, of improving the quality and relevance of decisions to the locality, and of increasing motivation and commitment to the projects, such a series of committees was inevitable. But rather than the proclaimed intention, the development committees were deployed to bring the hitherto unorganised groups of the local elite (or bourgeoisie) together, rather than the peasant poor. This promoted their sense of identity and helped these elites to isolate themselves from the grass-root peasants.[1] Thus, the objective of popular participation in decision-making was overshadowed by the aim of coordination among and consolidation of the elite groups. A brief discussion of the various local committees will illustrate the point.

Village Productivity Committees (VPC)

Most studies have reported that VPCs are largely nonexistent in many districts in Zambia (de Jong, 1977: Ollawa, 1979; Bwalya, 1979, 1980). The Village Headmen have tended to use their traditional authority rather than the powers conferred by the 1971 Village Registration and Development Act to get things done. This situation further substantiates the mutuality of the different local notables.

But even if, and when, the VPCs were operating properly, they already had a bias in favour of the already-established elites. The limiting size of the VPC executive (approximately 8 members out of an estimated average of 500 people in a village) means that only the politically, economically and socially powerful could get in. For example, one Ndileni Simon VPC in remote Chief Chiundaponde's area in Mpika District[2] had the following members: Village Headman, (son of area chief); Dickson Changwe (big local farmer and businessman owning a lorry) and four other members, including a teacher, who were all visibly better-off (more affluent) than other villagers (Bwalya, 1980, p. 281). Another VPC, called Ching'andu, had a relatively rich local businessman and farmer as chairman, an educated man as secretary/ treasurer, and six others who were either of royal blood or were formerly in government or other employment. Similar reports have been made by Ollawa, 1979 Maramwidze, 1980 and Chikulo (forthcoming Ph.D. Thesis) in Central and Southern Provinces respectively. They indicate that peasants do not in fact get the chance to participate in decision-making on policies and projects affecting their locality.

Moreover, the method of election of VPC Executive members by show of hands is not exactly domocratic. As one unsuspecting informant stated in Mpika, election to VPC office "depended on who was relatively more educated or economically well-off enough to fit in with the WDC or top leadership when they visited the area or when he went to meetings with them."[3] In this context, the peasants could be said, somewhat involuntarily, to isolate themselves from taking leadership positions. In effect, they can be said to have allowed to take place a process of their own exclusion from power, information and resources which in turn has limited their ability to increase production while increasing their inequality. This process maximizes peasant powerlessness rather than participation.

Ward Development Committees (WDCs)

According to the Village Registration and Development (1971) Act, the WDC is the executive arm of a Ward Council. The Ward Council and WDC are chaired by a Ward Councillor, who in principle is the only popularly-elected leader at the subdistrict level. In practice, he is usually nominated from amongst constituency party leaders for candidature by the Regional or higher party levels. Thus, not every active member of UNIP is free to stand for elections. As for the ordinary peasant, "he rather tends to look upon these committees as created for him, over him and without him" (Kapteyn and Emery, 1972, p. 18). But it is at the ward level that the play of power and the exclusion of peasants begins to be active.

In one example, the District Governor sponsored a big local businessman for election as Ward Councillor. The Councillor, as is very common throughout the country, once elected, was given a free hand in appointing other members of the Executive. In the example in question, he went ahead to appoint two village headmen, an Agricultural Assistant, three businessmen, the headteacher of the local primary school and a Credit Union Treasurer, as the other WDC members. All these people were visibly relatively more affluent than the majority of the local people and had vested interests in WDC's activities. The example suggests that the WDC could be used as a personal business meeting or for plotting the strategy for sharing out potential resources to the WDC officials' own benefits (Bwalya, 1980).

Indeed, as it turned out, one of the main priorities to emerge from the new committee was to build a shelter along the road for travellers to rest. Such a priority may seem to derive from an innocent increst to serve the travelling public. However, the Councillor's bar and shop were directly facing the selected location of the proposed shelter. The travellers would be substantial and captive customers of the businesses. Another priority project was the expansion and upgrading of the local school; a rather obvious influence of the headteacher on the WDC. Even if the expansion of the school was of interest to the local community, it would mean upgrading the status of the headteacher.

An important reason why WDC is the meeting ground for the local elite is that it scrutinizes applications for short-term and seasonal loans, for trading licences, and other activities before appropriate authorities take action (de Jong, 1977). Our interest here is that exclusive membership of WDCs by the local bourgeois groups benefits them, while increasingly disadvantaging the peasants and other local poor to relative poverty, inequality and powerlessness.

The District Council (DC)

Before its establishment early in 1981, activities of the DC were undertaken by the Rural Councils and DDCs. These two bodies have been absorbed by the DC but, like its predecessors, it is the major body for maintaining linkages between the administrative, party and traditional elite at the expense of the peasants.

First, political leaders and traditional chiefs are either appointed or *ex-officio* members of the DC. Therefore, contacts are forged between Councillors, traditional chiefs and district level administrative and technical staff through the DC. Such contacts can and do conscientise the various elite groups to their similar identity, which often forms the basifs for local "class" distinctions. Secondly, the DC is the body within which decisions are made over district development activities of any importance. It is in the DC that WDCs' priorities are fought out between different Ward Councillors and other local notables and the stronger voices backed by strong power bases come out as winners.

Thus, for example, Chief Chikwanda in Mpika District, with generally more educated and economically better-off councillors, was able to skew DC resource allocation to his advantage. For instance, 21 out of the 66 wells and boreholes (31 %) approved for the 1976-78 period went to Chikwanda's area, which had no more population than other chiefs' areas in the district. Three out of five bus-shelters constructed in 1976 under Rural Council auspices were located in Chikwanda's area. Similarly, out of 63 schools, 13 were located in this chief's area. This was more than each of the eight other chief's areas in the district, even though the differences in population between the areas were not high.

The skewed allocations in favour of Chikwanda's area were clearly due to the concentration of economically well-off households in Chikwanda's area. They were able to argue more convincingly and to use their positions to coerce both the administrative and technical staffs and the other council members to accept their demands. By lending support on technical grounds to the projects they have sympathy with, the staff exercised effective control over the allocation of available resources. The result is allocation of excess resources and benefits to the already affluent, to the exclusion of the not so affluent. peasants from such benefits, the logical consequence of which is peasant inequality and powerlessness.

Moreover, peasants have also complained about the large number of local-level participatory committees. At the village level, there were Village Political Committees (VPC), Village Productivity Committees (again VPCs), Parent Teachers Associations (PTC), UNIP Branches and the traditional village structures, many of whose functions coincided. With no clear allocation of specific responsibilities to the different committees (although at times one or other function might be emphasized), it often happened that all were disregarded. The promulgation of committees took too much of the peasants' time as well as causing confusion of roles. By and large, therefore, the VPCs are not development linkages and stimulators of local mass participation in developmental activity, for which they were created.

In partial conclusion, it can be said that the essence of the slogans and realities of "decentralisation of government" and "participatory democracy", so predominant in the later part of the "First" and early part of the "Second" Republics, can be seen more as a strategy for effective control by the national elite (or bourgeoisie) of the premises of legitimate action of the peasants than as a genuine call for their free and independent mobilization. This renders the peasants powerless in their strive for socioeconomic and political participation.

Broad-based Peasant Participation

The solution for beyond the '80s is broad-based peasant participation in planning and development. The Western "political" connotations notwithstanding, participation as it should be conceived beyond the '80s may be political, social and/or economic, but necessarily has to hinge upon three fundamentals: information, power and benefit, and resource sharing.

i. *Information Sharing*

Genuine and effective participation depends on adequate supply and dissemination of information to all participants. As the Zambian case above has shown, no amount of structural change can allow effective participation as long as the people concerned (in this case, peasants) do not possess the basic information. Information is both a prerequisite and a basic tool for rational analysis, formulation, implementation and evaluation of any policy or programme of action. Thus, effective involvement of more peasants in decision-making depends on their understanding of the issues at play and the socioeconomic implications of the available choices. This cannot be easy but for a vigorous programme of educating peasants so as to afford them the necessary knowledge on matters over which their participation is required.

ii. *Power Sharing*

It would be futile, as we have seen in the case of Zambia, to talk of participation when the acclaimed participants have no power to adopt, reject, or even modify as they wish, projects for their own advancement. For peasant participation to be genuine and complete, peasants in the '80s will have to be given power over, and control of, the intruments of decision-making. This is inevitable because structural reorganisation alone without decentralisation of decision-making power (or devolution) can only inhibit effective peasant participation precisely because power to decide remains in central (at most administrative) organs of government.

iii. *Benefit/Resource Sharing*

Widespread distribution of available resources and the benefits that accrue from them are a major determinant of effective participation. Participation cannot be said to be complete, even if, as in present day Zambia, a semblance of institutions purporting to provide it exists, as long as only a minority of the people have access to the goods and services of a society. In this respect, participation can be maximized by expanding economic investments and activities in the rural sector, which in turn expresses itself in employment creation, income redistribution and the introduction of rural programmes supportive of peasants.

Within this rationale for participation in the 1980s, local or peasant producers will have (a) increased quality and relevance of decisions, since decisions will be made with the specific needs of the locality or peasants in mind; (b) increased chances of success and effective peasant mobilisation as they will be committed to their own decisions as beneficial to themselves; (c) a tendency to motivate a sense of self-reliance and a wider and more efficient utilisation of local or peasant resources.

Notes

1. See B.B. Schaffer, "Political Integration", IDS Discussion Paper No. 53, 1974. He discusses integration and voluntary isolation of the Itinerant Irish from the better-off people by various mechanisms.
2. Mpika District is on the Southern boundary of the Northern Province with the Central Province of Zambia.
3. This was the Chief's retainer while in the company of the author during research fieldwork, 1978. See Bwalya, 1980, p. 281.

Abbreviations

AFIF African Farming Improvement Fund
ECU Eastern Province Cooperative Union
NCU Northern Province Cooperative Union
SPCU Southern Province Cooperative Union

References

Bwalya, M.C. 1979. "Problems of Village Regrouping: The Case of Serenje District of Zambia", D. Honeybone and A. Marter, eds. *Poverty and Wealth in Rural Zambia.* Communications No. 15, Lusaka: Institute for African Studies.
— 1980. "Rural Development and Agricultural Transformation in Northern Zambia". Ph.D. Thesis, Norwich: University of East Anglia.
de Jong, L. 1977. "Organization for Participation in Rural Development" ARD Report. Amsterdam, Lusaka.
Dresang, D. 1975. *The Zambia Civil Service.* Nairobi: East African Publishing House.
Eriksen, K. 1978. "Zambia: Class Formation and Detente", *Review of African Political Economy, No. 9.*
Hellen, J. 1968. *Rural Economic Development in Zambia,* 1980-1964. Weltforum Verlag.
Kapteyn, R.C.E. and Emery, C. 1972. "District Administration in Zambia" Lusaka: ARD.
Lombard, S. and Tweedie 1973. *Agriculture in Zambia since Independence,* Lusaka: NECZAM.
Maramwidze, N.A. 1981 "RDSB-IRDP Socio-Economic Survey of Rural Households in Serenje District". Lusaka: RDSB. (Mimeo)
Mid-term Review, Second National Development Plan, 1974. Lusaka: Ministry of Development Planning and Finance.
Mwanakatwe, J. Report of the Commission of Inquiry into the Salaries, Salary Structures and Conditions of the Public Services and Parastatal Sector" Lusaka: Government Printer.
Ollawa, P.E. 1979. *Participatory Democracy in Zambia,* Devon: Arthur Stockwell.
Rural Development Corporation, *Annual Reports,* 1975-79.
Schaffer, B. 1974. ed. *Administrative Training and Development: A Comparative Study of East Africa, Zambia, Pakistan and India,* N. York: Praeger.
Van Velzen, T. 1973. "Staff, Kulaks and Peasants" L. Cliffe and J. Saul, *Socialism in Tanzania,* vol. 2, Nairobi: East African Publishing House.

B. The State and the Peasant Farming Sector: Small Scale Agricultural Production in Economic Development
by David Evans

It is generally conceded that the development of Zambia's rural sector has been the most neglected and the least succesful area of overall economic strategy. There is a wide and persistent disparity in incomes and standards of living between rural and urban areas, and national food scarcity is frequently under severe pressure, with the result that scarce foreign exchange needed for productive investment has to be diverted to the importation of food. The decline of copper prices in recent years, rapidly increasing import prices, and the severe disruption of communications and trade caused by the Rhodesion conflict have all contributed to Zambia's present economic difficulties, but failures in the rural sector are long-standing and are the result over a long period of the lack of a consistent and determined policy for the revitalisation of the rural areas, and of the small-farm sector in particular.

Unbalanced Development The neglect of the peripheral areas of predominently subsistence agriculture in Zambia has long historical roots. At Independence in 1964 Zambia inherited a highly dualistic economy. Along the central line of rail running from the then Rhodesian border to the Copperbelt were all the visible signs of "development"; towns, mines, factories and large-scale settler farms. Away from the line of rail the situation was in sharp contrast: a large hinterland of poor smallholder agriculture, remote from markets and starved of services and infrastructural investment.

Mining and commercial interests, which dominated colonial policy, looked upon the surrounding rural areas merely as reserves of cheap labour, not only within Zambia itself but also for the mines and farms of Rhodesia and South Africa as well. Any development of "native" agriculture would have been against mining interests, for it would have made it more difficult to extract sufficient low-wage labour. Moreover, the imposition of rural taxes, which had generally to be paid in cash, increasingly forced out the able-bodied males of the peasant hinterland to seek wage-employment, and further increased the disruption of traditional agricultural systems. Thus started the rapid rural out-migration which has continued to the present time, and which is a powerful force retarding the development of the smallholder agriculture of the periphery.

Large-scale "settler" farming, established mostly on the better class lands along the line of rail, displaced the indigenous peasant cultivators to remoter "reserve" areas. Large commercial farms, given preferential treament in pricing and other administrative measures on top of their natural locational advantages, constituted a buffer between the growing demand for food and the remoter small-scale producers. Peasant agriculture was thus less able to respond to growing market opoortunities and a very large proportion of marketed agricultural output came from a small number of highly-capitalised commercial farms. Only belatedly, towards the close of the colonial era, was any attempt made to promote a broader-based development of agriculture that would include the smaller producer. A report of an official commission in 1938 admitted that "although the Department of Agriculture has done valuable work in relation to such crops as coffee and tobacco it cannot be said that it has made any substantial contribution to the present solution of the problem of native agriculture".[1]

Post-Independence Rural Development The long-standing forces which had led to the stagnation of the rural periphery could not be quickly reversed. Despite the wide variety of interventionist measures that have been taken since independence, and despite the repeated pledges from the country's political leadership that the development of agriculture was a priority aim, rural sector development has been slow and faltering. The rural exodus has continued at a rapid rate, for there was in the first decade of independence a substantial growth of urban employment (as also in wage levels) in public administration, construction and the new import-substitution industries. Political interests were mainly geared to urban modernisation and development, and pricing policy and price controls were for a long time much more weighted in favour of low food prices for the benefit of the urban consumer and the employer of labour, than towards raising agricultural producer prices. Over a long period agricultural prices have been held well below import-parity, but even so, costly food subsidy measures have had to be introduced.[2]

There has been a very substantial expansion of the national communications network of major routes, but the minor feeder roads to serve the dispersed rural communities have received very much less attention and their poor state has inhibited small-farm marketed production. Major difficulties too have been experienced in the timely supply of imputs through the established state marketing institutions, and credit and other services to small-scale producers have reached only a minority. In spite of many initiatives, credit and marketing services to the peasant farmers are still a problem, and the institutions concerned are severely handicapped by liquidity problems. One of the great misfortunes of the present situation as it affects the small farm sector is that at the very time the full realisation of the need for expansion of the lagging agricultural sector has finally been brought home, the resources and means for achieving this should be so constrained by financial stringency.

There are three major issues relating to farm policy during the 1980s which will be raised here, namely, price policy, uncertaincies over agricultural credit and marketing arrangements and, finally, the precise role that is envisaged for the peasant sector in national food expansion programmes.

Statutory Pricing Policy Past agricultural expansion strategies have been frustrated by very low producer prices. Since about 1979, state-controlled agricultural producer prices for the main marketed products, and maize in particular, have been very substantially raised, but there still is a need for a regular and systematic price review procedure that would take account of cost inflation, interrelationships between the prices of different commodities, cost of food imports, the returns to small-scale producers, and distributive justice as between rural and urban populations. Frequently in the past, individual price changes have been announced on an *ad hoc* basis, and too late before the next planting season to allow for adequate advance planning. Price policy, too, should cover a wider range of products so as to take particular account of the peasant agricultural sector. Low prices and a weak marketing organisation for commodities like cassava, beans, sorghum, fish, charcoal, and honey — products characteristic of small producers — are a powerful disincentive to expansion of production for the market, and to the consequent improvement of the incomes and productivity of small rural producers.

Marketing and Credit In 1980, the Government announced that the marketing operations that had previously been the responsibility of the National Agricultural Marketing Board in each Province would be taken over in 1981/82 by Provincial Cooperative Unions. Some prolongation of the takeover was allowed for in Provinces where no Cooperative Unions had previously functioned, such as North-Western, Western, and Central Provinces, but even so, the rapidity of the transfer of marketing functions poses considerable dangers to the emergence of an effective cooperative marketing structure. Building up a strong base of primary societies, and creating from scratch the complex financial and administrative structures needed for an efficient provincial marketing system will take several years to effect, and there are fears that there could be a temporary disruption of services, to the smaller producers in particular, in areas where the cooperative movement is now only in embryo.

Under the revised system the cooperatives will continue to be financially dependent on Government. Finance will have to be provided for takeover of

Namboard operations and for working capital, and the Ministry of Finance will have to make annual provisions for restitution of handling charges and the differential between producer prices and prices to the millers and other producers. The new cooperative system will be characterized by increased vulnerability to liquidity shortages, and guaranteed bank overdrafts for the short-term crop financing and the processing of seasonal crop loans will need to be extended from the present three months or so to an average of about nine months, with consequent higher interest liabilities. Previous experience of delayed and inadequate provision of finance from the Ministry of Finance for agricultural marketing functions raises doubts about an improved performance under the new system. Prompt payment to farmers is vitally important, and under the new system the necessary short-term financing of the Cooperative Unions will only be liquidated when payment is effected for produce sold to millers and to Namboard, and when commision, subsidy and restitution payments are received from Government. Unless the cooperative system can be funded sufficiently to overcome liquidity problems, serious disruptive effects on agricultural development may occur, and the new system may hold few advantages over the former Namboard operations, with all its past deficiences.

Uncertainty also exists about the extent to which credit facilities to smallholders will be operated through the cooperative system, and the precise provisions that will be made in this context by the Agricultural Development Bank that had been expected to start operations during 1981. Credit facilities for short-term crop financing are at present inadequate and are generally available to only the larger producers. In remote districts like Kabompo and Zambesi, for example, only 279 loans were given by the Agricultural Finance Company to farmers in the 1980/81 season, and their average value was no less than K 709, far in excess of the requirements of a typical small producer of their districts.[3]

The Role of Smallholder Agriculture Production units in Zambian agriculture cover a wide range of forms; from state and parastatal farms and ranches, large-scale commercial farms run by private companies and individuals, medium-sized family farms, government-sponsored group farming projects such as settlement schemes and Rural Reconstruction Centres, right down to the smallest, mainly subsistence, smallholding. The urgency of the need to expand agricultural production has often given rise to somewhat hurried state interventionist projects of a large-scale nature, presumably in the hope that large increments of output might quickly be obtained. This technocratic bias in agricultural policy is exemplified by the ten-year "Operation Food Production" which sets out, for example, to establish in each Province two very large state farms of an average size of 20,000 hectares, "highly equipped technically in terms of organisation, planning, farming methods and machinary".[4]

However necessary these large-scale projects by the state may be for exploiting production opportunities in particular areas of the country, or for specific crops such as wheat and sugar, there is no doubt that many previous ventures into State farms and government-sponsored enterprises, like the Rural Reconstruction Centres, have proved costly in both capital and operating costs. It may be that their disappointing performance is due more to hasty planning, inadequate preinvestment research, and poor management rather than to intrinsic faults, but the major policy issue arises whether small but broad-based increases in production from the generality of small-scale producers would not in total add up to a more effective and more economical means of achieving the nation's food production objectives than a few major projects spread over the country. Whatever their effects in terms of increments of production, large-scale projects contribute less to the Humanist objectives of a more equitable distribution of income and the creation of rural employment opportunities than would a policy in which small farm expansion was the paramount and dominating policy aim. President Kaunda gave eloquent expression to this problem of policy emphasis in a speech to the National Council of UNIP in 1968 when he stated, "If we equate development and progress only with the number of tractors used, with the number of big projects, with a small number of well-looking areas, and with the town only, then we will soon face very big problems. Development that is restricted to only a small part of the ecomic sector, to only a few regions, to only large-scale production, and to only highly capital-intensive techniques, is, in my view, no development at all".[5] The policy problem is not a question of following the one or the other direction; both may be necessary, but the present danger, and a serious one, is that the concentration of resources, as well as of planning and administrative effort, will be diverted away from the vigorous promotion on a broad front of the small-scale peasant sector. Recurrent funds now available for government services in rural areas, such as for agricultural extension, road maintenance, schools and health clinics, are so depleted that the major share goes on salaries, without the means for the effective performance of the assignsed tasks.

Zambia's past development strategies have had an urban bias, with import-substitution industrialisation and urban modernisation playing an important role. But the "easy stage" of industrialisation (cement, textiles, brewing, food processing, oil refining, the assembly of components etc.) has been completed with only small increases in urban employment relative to such a fast growing population. The severe check to economic growth during the latter part of the 1970s arising from the balance of payments crisis has highlighted the need for faster growth of the rural sector. It is to this sector that government must increasingly look for the answers to the problems of growing unemployment and unequal distribution of income, as well as the country's future security in food supplies.

Notes

1. *Report of the (Pim) Commission to Enquire into the Financial and Economic Position of Northern Rhodesia,* Government Printer, Lusaka 1938, p. 136.
2. Doris Jansen Doge, *Zambian Agricultural Pricing and Marketing Policy,* World Bank, Washington 1979.
3. *Minutes of the North-Western Province Crop Forecasting Committee,* April 1981, Department of Agriculture, Solwezi.
4. Republic of Zambia, *Operation Food Production 1980-1990,* State House, Lusaka, May 1980.
5. Kaunda, *Presidential Address to the National Council of the United National Independence Party,* Mulungushi, April 1968.

C. The Rural Malaise in Zambia:
Reflections on the René Dumont Report and the State Farms Project
by Klaas Woldring

This chapter, which complements the previous ones, is based on a conference paper which I presented to the annual conference of the African Studies Association of Australasia and the Pacific, held in Sydney in August 1981. The theme of that conference was *Food, Famine and Population*. As a political economist just returning from a contract in Zambia it seemed appropriate to attempt an assessment of one of Zambia's major problem areas: rural underdevelopment. However, I do not claim any expertise as an agronomist or an agricultural economist and, therefore, this is not a chapter by a typical expert.

Certainly, I have become very interested in these problems and the research visit to Zambia by Professor René Dumont in September-October 1979 greatly stimulated this interest. More recently the K 400 million Operation Food Production — a ten-year plan — of which the State Farm Project is the major composite part, has provided the antithesis of the Dumont proposals and the philosophy behind them. It is within this framework of opposites that my paper was developed. In between the poles lies a gamut of policies and attempted policies which caught the fancy of the government at one time or other. Remarkably, in the final analysis, I have come to the conclusion that the poor record of rural development in Zambia is first of all a political problem and, secondly, a management problem. There is no lack of national resources, awareness of problems or even know-how. But the political will to implement definite policies effectively, and the managerial and financial discipline to see through policies and projects appears to be sadly lacking in Zambia. The explanations are partly to be sought in external, neocolonial relationships and perhaps partly in cultural factors but whatever the reasons the Zambians will have to find the political will to overcome such handicaps and to produce a leadership which is both more determined and able to deliver the goods than the present bureaucratic bourgeoisie which is uninspiring and unproductive.

Experts have come and gone and many projects by a great variety of Western and socialist countries have been and are being undertaken. Whilst such aid can be productive of frequently localised development and growth it has also brought confusion, discontinuity and new forms of dependence.

The ideas of Dumont, which correspond to a large degree with those expressed in the I.L.O. Study on Zambia, *Narrowing the Gaps* (1977/80), present a challenge which — whilst rejected by most African elites of both capitalist and socialist orientation — has still not been met. The Dumont ideas, to my knowledge, have not been tried seriously anywhere and they have therefore not been proved wrong. What we do know is that all manner of other rural policies have been tried in Africa and there is very little to show for them. Nearly everywhere in independent Africa there are massive rural problems and food shortages. Undoubtedly, an enormous diversity of agrarian systems exist in Africa and the causes of failure, domestic and external, are many and complex. It may be wise nevertheless — especially after a period of persistent and widespread failure — to see what the alternative suggestions, stressing self-sufficiency and the traditional base, have to offer.

Part A — Background: The Rural Sector — Policies, Structure and Performance

In 1977, the I.L.O. Report on Zambia, *Narrowing the Gap* — a study completed in September, 1975 — could still state reasonably optimistically that whilst things were pretty grim for most of the rural population there were definitely some plusses to be noted:

> Many impressive developments have taken place in Zambia's economy since Independence. The country's economic and social infra-structure has been transformed almost beyond recognition. Industry has expanded rapidly. Even agricultural production in selected fields has grown considerably. The large but fluctuating flow of income and foreign exchange from the mining sector has sustained Zambia's position as one of the richest countries of sub-Saharan Africa. It has provided directly or indirectly the source of investments of over K 3,500 million from 1965 to 1974.

Even so, the Report continues:

> In spite of these enormous expenditures, the majority of Zambians have so far gained little from them and most of the rural population have not benefitted very much. And the fact remains that a large number of Zambia's population, urban as well as rural, still lack the basic necessities of life.[1]

The Basic Needs approach advocated by the 1975 mission — and quite in line with President Kaunda's Mulungushi Declaration of 1968 — was reappraised by a further ILO group in September, 1980. In the Preliminary Draft we read:

Zambia's goals for meeting the basic needs of all the population by 1980 remains far from achieved. . . malnutrition, particularly among children, has almost certainly increased. . . . Two major constraints on Zambia's development explain the setbacks. Deterioration in the international economic environment, world recession and the Zimbabwe War made extreme difficulties of Zambia. But also, and perhaps of comparable importance, domestic distortions of priorities within Zambia have meant that goals and plans for broad-based development and rural advance have not been carried into action. Rather the reverse. Long-standing tendencies have asserted themselves and the urban sector and large-scale modern industry have pre-empted the lion's share of resources pledged in plans for rural survival, employment creation and basic needs services for all.[2]

A few statistics illustrate the plight of the Zambian economy at once:

Changes 1975-1979 (real terms)[3]		
GDP per head	declined 46 %	(from 1974-79)
Private consumption per head	declined 32 %	
Government recurrent expenditure total	declined 20 %	(30 % from 1975-78)
Government capital expenditure	declined 65 %	

As the mission points out, such declines are *extremely large* by international standards and among the largest in developing countries in recent years.

The colonial heritage, as far as agriculture is concerned, is that this sector was always secondary to mining. Furthermore, highly preferential treatment was given to the settler farmers in virtually every respect. About half of the 1200 expatriate farmers left at Independence and the privileged status of the others was withdrawn. Robert Klepper has demonstrated, however, that in spite of this change and several attempts at rural development (some ill-conceived and usually poorly-executed) the inferior status of agriculture was still very much a reality in 1978.

The basic structure of the economy remains heavily biased toward the production and export of minerals as it was in the colonial period. The nation imports large quantities of foodstuffs and relies heavily on a relatively small number of commercial and emergent farmers for its domestic agricultural output.[4]

The rate of urbanisation in Zambia since independence has been extremely fast. The proportion of urban to total population (5.6 million total in 1980 Census) has continuously increased from 20.5 % in 1963 to 29.4 % in 1969 and to 43 % in 1980![5] In absolute terms, the urban population, according to the preliminary results of that Census, recorded a growth rate of 6.7 % per year (1969-1980) whereas the rural population increased annually by only

1.1 %. The average annual growth from 1969-1980 was 3.1 % as compared to 2.5 % in the 1963-1969 period (the previous population census years). This represents a doubling time of 23 years. Clearly, this pattern indicates that urban dependence on the rural sector has grown considerably and that rural development and food production for self-sufficiency is in fact Zambia's primary concern.

Right through the period that I worked in Zambia I witnessed a definite and growing awareness of the need for urgent and massive improvements in this sector amongst the elites and in the population generally. Professor Dumont was again invited by the President although the recommendations following his earlier visit, in 1967, had not been made public (a sign of desperation?). This time, too, the Report had a first printing of only 500 copies and very few of these copies went outside the Cabinet's strong room, where they still are. (One somehow reached the University's Library.)

President Kaunda's concern is reflected in his address to the first Party extraordinary Council Meeting a Mulungushi Hall on 21st April, 1981. He said:

> It must be the Party's primary objective to ensure the successful implementation of the Operation Food Production programme. A Training System for various grades of agriculturalists will be an ancillary programme to the Operation Food Production which must continue to be the nation's preoccupation.[6]

Kaunda furthermore stressed the projected role of the new district councils (a controversial measure which aims to bring about effective deconcentration of decision-making) in assisting the central government in this new drive.

What policies have been tried in the postindependence period and why have most of these gone wrong? With the exception of some success stories like sugar production and poultry farming — industries established and managed by multi-nationals — and sunflower, overall production of most other crops and products is insufficient to meet national demand, let along cater for export. These include wheat, cotton, oilseeds, tea, coffee, rice, salt, milk, milk products and tobacco. Maize production has been just sufficient in most years but in 1979 and 1980 low productivity, bad harvests and storage facilities problems brought Zambia to the brink of famine. Large quantities of maize had to be imported from Kenya, the U.S., Zimbabwe and even South Africa at prices well above that paid to local farmers and, of course, in precious foreign exchange. Poor economic conditions have forced Zambia to increase imports from South Africa again especially over the last two years. In fact, imports from South Africa were the second largest group in 1980.

Even in the more prosperous period agriculture's contribution to G.D.P. declined from 13.7 % in 1965 to 9.4 % in 1974 with two-thirds of the agricultural share originating in the traditional sector (this means that two-thirds of Zambia's population working in traditional rural occupations earned only 6 % of Zambia's national income). Furthermore, in the same period agriculture's contribution to exports declined from 2.3 % in 1964 to 1.4 % in 1974, while the value of food imports increased from K 18 million to K 45 million.[7]

Thus by 1975 Zambia had to import 99 % of its wheat, 95 % of its rice, over 80 % of its dairy products and vegetable oils, two-thirds of its cotton and around half of its potato and beef requirements.
(Beef imports were stopped in 1975.)

Many observers have commented on the persistent gap between words and deeds. Although the intensity and frequency of the government's statements/ promises to introduce drastic reforms have increased over the past two years they are by no means new. The 1975 I.L.O. Report reads:

In contrast with the Government's declarations about the urgency of the need to transform the rural sector, and the priority to be given to rural development in national planning, one is struck by a neglect of agriculture, by the low priority given to rural activities in the allocation of economic resources and skilled manpower, and, overall, by the absence of a clear and coherent framework for rural development, within which decisions are taken.

There is a long trail of R.I.P.s or near-R.I.P.s. Best known among them are the State Production Units (since 1964), Cooperatives (since January, 1965) and the Rural Reconstruction Centres (launched in 1974). The cooperatives were quite enthusiastically received by the people and by June 1970 there were 1,280 of them of which 805 were registered as agricultural producer cooperatives. There were however many infrastructural handicaps associated with *these* cooperatives (any 10 people could form one). The rapid numerical expansion took place without the necessary preparation in terms of organisation and education. Stephen Quick[8] has argued that the government provided far *too much* money in loans and subsidies to cooperatives. They were incapable of utilising the capital, tended to treat the money as income rather than investment funds and were unable to repay. There were high transport costs and there was an excessive plurality of functions like marketing, credit, building and producer cooperatives. With management skills and know-how thinly-spread, problems were guaranteed to emerge. The lesson was learnt nevertheless. Cooperatives should be within the existing village systems; they should be multi-purpose and should be run by trained personnel.

In practice, from 1970 onwards the government began to concentrate on individual peasant households in an essentially capitalist fashion.

Another attempt was the Rural Reconstruction Centre Programme. The objective here was to recruit and train school leavers in all skills of rural development. This was primarily an effort to keep the youth in the rural areas and provide them with employment. After training they would be employed in rural occupations where possible within the cooperative framework. In 1975 this appeared to have the making of a major programme which was to involve 250 centres evenly spread throughout the country, and close to 250,000 people. This programme also got off the ground with substantial financial support as well as equipment. The R.R.C.s flopped in spite of this. Dumont rejected the R.R.C.s as well as the recommendations in the Third National Development Plan to revive them, give them still more means and to increase the number of participants per centre from 100 to 800. His view:

> But the young people don't want to live in the R.R.C.'s, they are running away, one after the other. Once more the T.N.D.P. seems to be composed of wishful thinking. The planners have probably never been in one R.R.C.; how could one make a good plan without any knowledge of the rural situation; without studying on the spot the villages and villagers' problems?[9]

Infrastructural provisions such as rural clinics, schools, transport and roads have deteriorated severely since 1975. In particular:

> the effectiveness of *government field staff* in virtually all the operating Ministries has been sharply reduced in the last few years through transport difficulties and lack of petrol. A case study of Serenje and Samfya Districts prepared for us by the National Institute of Public Administration provides numerous examples. Our own analysis of the budget allocations for petrol and vehicle maintenance of the Ministry of Agriculture shows a reduction by 1980 to one-fifth the level of 1972, in spite of an increase of both vehicles and staff. We have found officers confined to base for months on end through lack of transport.[10]

Public transport remains appallingly inadequate, in spite of a growing number of buses and only modest increases in fares in the 1970s. Although the number of rural buses has increased by 11% between March 1979 and 1980 the number of buses out of operation in 1980 was still 42% of total rural stock. Under such circumstances not too much can be expected from ambitious, top-down Government programmes.

Charles Elliott in a working paper for World Employment Programme Research[11] divides Zambian society into four economic groups.

Group	Numbers	% of Pop.	Av. Income/hd. K	% of Total Income
Poor farmers and subsistence producers	850,000	70	40	25
"Informal" employees and urban unemployed	300,000	25	120	27
Prosperous farmers	20,000	1	424	6
"Formal" employees	50,000	4	287 (estimate)	42[12]

He contends that pressures on rural households (Group 1) are threefold: (a) increased pressure on local land (there is an abundance of land but not local land with access to facilities and labour supply); (b) increased household demand for cash (due to capitalist penetration, urban inflation and lowering of real income); (c) pressure from a wide range of social penetrations into traditional village life.[13]

He divides the first group in Stratum 1 and 2 poverty level. Stratum 2 represent the "poverty of isolation of the subsistence producer". Elliott argues that this spectrum (of ideal types) begins with "the farmer who has the resources, motivation, and, to a degree at least, managerial skills to grow a range of modern crops but who finds that his attempts to do so are continually frustrated by poor prices, inadequate delivery systems, corrupt distribution of credit, ineffective marketing and distortions in the rural labour market".[14]

His main and most significant comment on the other group (Stratum 2, which he considers the largest number of the rural poor) is revealing:

> The current debates on the form of rural development policy (e.g. Intensive Development Zones, R.R.C.'s or multipurpose co-operatives) *have absolutely no importance whatsoever* as vehicles by which rural poverty in Zambia is to be eliminated.[15] (His emphasis.)

I would like to conclude this section by drawing attention to another kind of dichotomy to which Elliott refers earlier in his, to my mind, excellent and certainly most informative study. I quote at some length:

> The unusual feature of Zambia – indeed the feature which makes it a mandatory area of study – is the unresolved tension at the heart of official decision-making between two normative approaches to rural development strategy. To represent it as a tension between two clearly defined and mutually exclusive polar opposites is, of course, to simplify: if the reality were as stark as that, the tension might possibly have been resolved in the fifteen years since independence. In fact, in the capacious minds of Zambian leaders, and particularly of her President, ideas that are inconsistent when academically dissected can co-exist either because both are needed to maintain the confidence and support of different groups upon which the government is variously dependent, or simply because in the heat of decision-making under pressure they are never presented or internalised as coherent, though mutually exclusive, bodies of thought.
>
> The first, and easier to identify and describe, is a technocratic view of rural development that is concerned with the need to maximise agricultural output, to ensure the efficient use of scarce resources, and particularly public resources. Such a view puts rural development in a macro-economic context and is therefore concerned to ensure that agriculture fulfils given structural roles within an overall strategy of economic development. Dominated by variants of neo-classical economics, this approach is supported not only by aid donors and multilateral agencies but also, though sometimes ambivalently, by a number of senior Zambian politicians and civil servants, usually western trained.

The second approach is much more concerned with the ideological issues that surround the political economy of agriculture. This is not to imply that those who adopt this approach have a settled solution to those issues. That they certainly do not have; indeed one of the fundamental difficulties of Zambian rural development has been not the conflict between the ideologies and the technocrats but the confusion within the ideological group and therefore their inability to reach any consistent accommodation with the technocratic group. The ideological group is centred on the President himself whose attempt to provide a Zambian political ideology in the shape of Zambian humanism has been more successful at raising issues than at solving them. Thus, in the name of Humanism, various forms of co-operative have been favoured, allegedly on the grounds that this re-creates a traditional form of Zambian village culture, but both the ambiguities of different forms of co-operatives and their relationship with traditional village forms of co-operation have never been adequately explored and expounded. Almost simultaneously the ideal of the individual peasant family farm has been reasserted with no apparent awareness of the potential conflict between co-operative forms of organisation and the ideals of individual enterprise. Although state farms and state production units have received relatively less public support from the ideological group, they have not been actively opposed with the result that three quite different forms of agrarian organisation have been in both the public and bureaucratic consciousness simultaneously. Given the constraints on the capacity of the Bureaucracy (and supremely in the area of rural development) it is no wonder that resources have been switched from one to the other in a bewildering and confusing series of policy shifts, which have left not only officials at provincial and district level lost and demoralised, but also farmers themselves increasingly sceptical of the sincerity of governments' intentions towards them.[16]

Part B – The Dumont Philosophy

With this background sketch behind us – inadequate as it must be – we may now look at the philosophy which underpins and some selected items of the Dumont Report. Dumont has some 20 books to his credit of which *The Hungry Future* (1966), *False Start in Africa* (1966), and *Utopia or Else?* (1973) are some which have appeared in English. He is an anti-Soviet socialist of long standing and has written at length about the population explosion, the expected shortages of food, natural resources and fuel. It struck me how close Dumont's ideas often are to postindustrial, alternative thinking. Yet, he has been saying these things well before others, perhaps better-known.

As I witnessed at two seminars in October 1979 at the University of Zambia, somewhat to my surprise initially, he is distrusted by many Marxist-Leninists. They severely attacked him for "wanting to put the clock back", a "traitor to the cause", one who advanced a neocolonial solution to Zambia's rural problems which would in fact ensure continued underdevelopment. It was obvious that Dumont is frequently misunderstood by the hardline Left of the Third World. There is of course a real difference to which I shall refer later. Dumont also ran into criticism from the Technocrat Right. A supposedly "progressive" white commercial farmer, Guy Scott – a former admirer of Dumont – now regards his ideas as unpractical.

Finally, the Dumont Report came as a shock to the Zambian bureaucratic bourgeoisie based mainly in Lusaka. He didn't have a good word for them, not surprisingly.

> Unlike many other developing countries, Zambia in 1964 received a lot of copper money which made her believe that this state of things would last forever. And she built a town civilisation, on the line of Western developed countries; more low-density areas, over-expensive buildings (International Airport, Mulungushi Hall, Cairo Road skyscrapers, University campus, University Teaching Hospital, etc.). The town planning was designed for a private car civilisation with very long distances between different areas, and perpetuating a kind of apartheid between low-density high density areas and squatter compounds; between posh villas and slums. The rich people don't like to see poverty at their door."[17]

The high investments that were made were mostly unproductive investments with recurrent expenditure very costly to maintain. Referring to the 12-fold increase in the price of oil between 1970 and 1979 (Zambia imports 5 million barrels a year) Dumont urges alternative forms of energy. He estimates that by the year 1990 all the revenues from Zambia's copper may not be enough just to pay for oil! The Western Model is in a "condition of hidden bankruptcy, hidden by constant inflation, which allows the rich countries to increase the price of equipment and industrial goods and to perpetuate the plunder of the Third World."[18]

White farmers and agronomists have "modernised" Zambian agriculture, relying mainly on external inputs: tractors, heavy machinery, pesticides, and chemical fertilizer; at the expense of local resources of labour, animal energy and organic manure, which are now despised. The part replacement of traditional agriculture by the Western package after 1964 – for which the great majority of Zambian farmers were not ready anyway – created the condition for rural poverty and malnutrition. Concentration on the "Western enclave" is a gigantic error. Dumont is opposed to costly wheat schemes (in terms of irrigation and fertiliser), whilst rice and maize are typically tropical crops, and condemns the manufacture of polished rice whilst "only dehusking the paddy is much cheaper" and unpolished rice healthier. (As people coming from Australia, where a variety of brown bread is available nearly everywhere, it was surprising to only find white bread in Lusaka!) The malnutrition theme runs like a threat through his Report but, he writes:

> ... the main evolution in Zambia since Independence is the increasing gap between the urban privileged minority and villages, between rich town people and poor peasants. This widening gap is threatening the future of Zambia; in economic, sociological and political terms.[19]

He describes the townspeople as a "wasting civilisation", also "a nation within a nation". This wasting nation of public servants and white collar workers believes that all buildings, big hospitals, stadia, public halls, large airports and rich houses in splendid surroundings are a sign of development:

> ... those cars are wasting every day, in towns, the oil which is badly lacking in all rural areas, which are without enough buses and trucks. Air-conditioners, lifts, electric fans, excessive lights are wasting every day the electricity not available in rural areas.

The National Development Plans (especially II and III) advocated the need to reduce the urban-rural gap but, writes Dumont, just like in India, "without any result in practice".

Foreign advisors — for whom this generation of Zambians rightly or wrongly still seem to have some respect — draw up these plans in the main and then return to the safety (and comparatively high-level consumption) retreat in the Western World to monitor progress — as they see it. Dumont recommends to the Zambians. Have confidence in yourselves and in particular don't be afraid of your African values and traditions. Get the best out of them — they are the social fabrik of your society without which "progress" means nothing. Wasn't that what the Independence fight was all about? What has happened to that spirit?

The Report furthermore highlights the *serious* deficiencies in education and health in the rural areas (six provinces were visited). Dumont claims for instance that at least 30 % of rural children suffer from severe malnutrition (Kwashiorkor and Marasmus) with a weight below 70 % of normal.

He is convinced that the agricultural situation is worsening "day after day". That "everything is late: finance, supplies, marketing, payment for crops, repayment of loans, etc.". This is due, as I found out, to Zambia's very sluggish and inefficient bureaucracy. At virtually every level of the bureaucracy one has to wait a long time for action. This is not the place to illustrate with examples, but it is clear that the effect on rural development is devastating:

> Because of late loans and late supplies of inputs, some crops are planted late; everybody knows that early planting, in tropical climates, with a short rainy season and uncertain distribution of rains, is the first condition of success. With a lower yield resulting from late planting, because of delayed payment for their produce, many farmers are not in the position to repay their loans."[20]

In all fairness, just in recent months the government has at least made promises to speed up payments and deliveries. The appointment of Mr. Humphrey Mulemba as Secretary-General of U.N.I.P. (No. 2 position) and Prime Minister Mundia (No. 3 in the hierarchy) (both generally well-regarded) would seem to have had a positive effect on government performance. The bumper maize harvest this year may also provide the respite necessary to find a new direction.

Dumont does have praise for some of the existing state enterprises, e.g., the coffee plantation in Ngole, Northern Province, and the Kafubu Dairy Farm near Ndola (exceptions rather), but his real concern is for the 500,000 "forgotten farmers". This is virtually the same group Elliott has identified — the subsistence farmers — who seem to fall outside the scope of government policy, yet should be the main target of that policy.

The Dumont thesis really boils down to this: the thrust of rural development must be towards motivating and guiding the traditional farmers; to use their existence and values as a base, to improve that base by appropriate methods and technology and by involving them 100 % — using their own local language. The very occasional visits of (frequently incompetent) government extension officers will not inspire this (largest) group. Merely good intentions of better support systems are also inadequate. It must be accepted and be seen to be accepted as the nation's most serious task, and that, Dumont says, is precisely what is lacking. The target group, in practice (credit facilities, extension support), has been the emergent Zambian farmers — a very small group.

Dumont also keenly observed the atmosphere of urban insecurity which prevails in Lusaka and the Copperbelt towns. The main explanation for this is the strong rural-urban drift since independence, deteriorating rural-urban terms of trade and very high urban unemployment. The "Grow more Food" and "Go back to the Land" calls are senseless however, unless the conditions on the land are made much more attractive for people to go or return there. This involves a truly radical and wide-ranging shift in policy such as, for instance, paying (substantial) loadings to civil servants, teachers, doctors and nurses to work in the rural areas. Although this has been mooted on several occasions at salary inquiries in the 1970s, unbelievably the Lusaka-based commissioners have never seen sufficient merit in this argument (which presumably would reduce their own salary increases).[21]

Dumont is clearly opposed to large-scale, capital intensive rural development in Zambia and, I think, in the Third World generally. A "poor" Zambia, he suggests, needs labour intensive technology that does not eat away the foreign exchange needed for oil and costly spare parts. He rejects the recommendations in the Third National Development Plan (1979) as "more of the same that doesn't work". Priority must be given to "basic needs" for all Zambians rather than the luxury needs of the men and women who, really quite sadly, muddle along in the Kafkaesque bureaucracy, not to mention the largely unprofitable parastatals.

Dumont demonstrates that where conditions are right the repayment of loans — earlier a severe problem — can be achieved without much difficulty.

He refers here to the success story of the Family Farms project amongst the Tonga people in Southern Province.[22] We cannot delve too deeply in Dumont's more detailed suggestions here on account of space constraints, but a general picture has emerged of the thrust of his philosophy.

In an article in the *Times of Zambia* (8-11-1979) the earliermentioned Guy Scott, a postindependence white settler farmer, who has acquired a nation-wide reputation for successful commercial farming and experimentation with new crops and varieties, criticised Dumont.[23] His faith is in scientific, Western-style agriculture because "like the shoe factory replaced the cobbler" the scientific agriculturalist will replace the traditional peasant. This is both an ethnocentric and a conservative view of progress (evolution), which suggests that Western-style "progress" will continue to spread to other peoples and areas and develop in more or less the same fashion because "they'll see the advantages of it". This view clearly betrays a woeful lack of understanding of the basis of Western "progress" and the reasons why this "progress" is most unlikely to spread further to the Third World in the existing International Economic Order.

Critics from amongst the Zambian bureaucracy (informal communication) – the focus of attack by Dumont – although quite mute, are really primarily concerned with their privileged position. Their position is therefore hardly worth considering. Zambian academics trained in the U.S. and other Western countries in the sixties and early-1970s criticise Dumont from the perspective of outdated and indeed *false* modernisation theories. They conceive of progress as a Western process and hope for the stages of growth, as they have been taught. To them Dumont represents potentially at least one step back. They, too, want industrialisation, to "catch up" as it were and to deny this to Zambia is a new form of discrimination as well as colonialism.

These sentiments are understandable. Zambians have not lived through the extended industrial revolution and are therefore not products of a Western industrialised society. Thy should they be interested in putting that *behind* them?

A rather small group of vocal University Marxist-Leninists naturally see the traditional sector as preindustrial. Marx himself saw the peasantry as of no use to the revolution and as in a state of *imbecility* even. His development orientation – insofar as it existed – clearly has an urban bias. The fact is that Marx has little to offer to this situation. Externally, Lenin's thesis on imperialism applies, but solutions for that will have to be found in an external framework. Internally, improvements in Zambia are possible regardless of the external situation, at least this is what Dumont argues. To him there ist no point in imitating the Chinese or Russian models nor does Dumont romanticise the traditional village in any way as has been claimed by some critics. Actually, he has a keen and quite realistic perception of what can be achieved with improved, relatively inexpensive methods and technology using traditional structures and institutions as a base, as a point of departure – but no more and no less than that. Although bot Dumont Reports have been virtually suppressed, it is not inconceivable that his ideas will prove to be very influential, not only in Zambia but all over Africa, in times to come.

Part C – Operation Food Production and the State Farms Project

Comrades, I salute and address you in the name of the Revolution! During the period between the 12th to the 16th of May, 1980 the Central Committee of the United National Independence Party met in Lusaka to discuss an operational programme aimed at fighting against Poverty and all its offshoots of Hunger, Ignorance, Disease, Corruption, Crime and, above all, the Exploitation of Man by Man. Subsequently, this programme was tabled before Cabinet for implementation. I am happy to report to the nation that both the Central Committee and Cabinet in the revolutionary spirit of participatory democracy discussed with candour and approved the programme I am presenting to the Nation.[24]

Elsewhere the President outlined the basic objectives of this K 400 million scheme. Among them:

a) To feed ourselves because no-one will feed us if we don't.
b) To become a granary of Africa and the world.
c) To make agriculture the basis for industrialisation and industrialisation the basis for agriculture.
d) *A key objective of this programme which the nation must note is to begin doing something and to talk about that something while doing it.*

Operation Food Production will involve the following institutions:

1. Large-scale commercial State Farms.
2. Rural Reconstruction Co-operatives (re-invigorated).
3. The Zambia National Service (also re-invigorated and rationalised).
4. Producer Co-operatives.
5. Peasant and family farms co-operating through common funds, common dipping tanks, common marketing facilities and a common machine centre.
6. Private commercial farms some of which are already establishing common services and imparting scientific know-how to co-operatives and peasants.

1. *State Farms*

We intend, therefore, to establish in each Province two State farms to cover *an average* of 20,000 hectares each. (These sizes will certainly vary according to local conditions and logistical reasons.) Each of these farms will be highly equipped technically in terms of organisation, planning, farming methods and machinery. Some of these farms will be operational in the next season and all of them should be in production in the 1981/82 season. The plans for these schemes are already at an advanced stage and experts have also begun working "on the ground" in some of the areas.

2. *Rural Reconstruction Co-operative Centres*

The Party and its Government, taking into consideration past experiences in implementing this programme, will ensure that the scale of production of these Centres will increase to a minimum of 1,000 hectares if such Centres were properly located, i.e., near water and on rich soils.

3. *The Zambia National Service*

The Party and its Government further intends to programme National Service Production Units taking into account relevant strategies to make them economically viable by providing trained professionals to manage and guide large-scale commercial undertakings. The National Service Production Units will undoubtedly set the pace in reducing the ever-escalating cost of food in the nation through increased supply of a wide range of agricultural products. Experts have already begun working on this programme.

4. *Producer Co-operatives*

Zambia has had its share of successes and failures in this area. We have now finished serious studies on the causes that led to a slow development of our producer co-operatives making it possible therefore to find solutions and alternative strategies for their prosperity. Already the country boasts of a number of farm training institutes and a National Co-operative College, all earmarked for the planned development of these co-operatives.

5. *Peasant and Family Farms*

In keeping with our revolutionary objectives, the "Operation Food Production" will entail the regrouping of Zambia's scattered villages through a deliberate strategy to boost production while encouraging a spirit of pooling resources together for the common good of our peasant community. This will be done through providing common dipping tanks, marketing facilities, a common fund, a machine tool centre, schools, clinics and other amenities. The sizes of their plots with the aid of adequate equipment will be increased. It will then be possible to provide enough requisite knowledge of production and rational planning of peasant production while instilling a spirit of co-operation.

6. *Private Commercial Farms*

The State has little problems in this area except ensuring that during this period the real producer prices of agricultural crops will increase for the farmers, without spreading the burden to the consumer through high mealie-meal prices.[25]

It should be noted that the State Farm Project was not planned for in the Third National Development Plan. Apparently it came from within the National Development Planning Commission which is headed by Dr. Leonard Chivuno, who did his academic training in Moskow. The Minister for Agriculture, Mr. Chikwanda, opposed the idea and resigned subsequently. Opposition was voiced by the Zambia Farmers Union. Mr. David Mazimba, the Chairman, warned that the move would fail unless the authorities reorganised existing agricultural programmes:

The Union is still not convinced with the formation of State Farms at this stage. The government should solve the farming problems before they think of State Farms.[26]

The Chairman then went on to detail how existing programmes could be strengthened which amounted to a wide-ranging attack on political and administrative incompetence by the government. The recurring theme in this and similar attacks is that the President is a good man but that he is surrounded by quite a few dishonest and/or incompetent senior advisers.

The State Farm Project was received generally with a good deal of scepticism. The *Times of Zambia* came out against it and made s strong plea for multi-purpose cooperatives based on the village structure.[27] The President himself had been very impressed with the operation of such cooperatives during his month-long tour through Eastern Europe, the Middle East, Asia and the Far East in September, 1980.

What has been the progress to date with these State Farms (according to a recent government publication)?

1. All 18 State Farms have been identified, two in each province.
2. All 18 State Farms have been registered as Companies.
3. Preliminary investigations by both experts from countries willing to assist Zambia and local experts in the Ministry of Agriculture and Water Development have been made on the following:

(a) *The Lusaka South-West State Farm* – to be developed by the Peoples Republic of Bulgaria. A feasibility study leading to the planning and possible commencement, on a small-scale, of production during the next season will be started by experts from Bulgaria.

(b) *Solwezi State Farm* – a team of Japanese experts made preliminary investigations on this farm together with Zambian experts. A detailed study is now under preparation by the same team of experts which should lead to development of this farm on a joint-venture basis with the Japanese. It is intended to develop a large-scale irrigation system so as to raise more than two crops in a year.

(c) *Musaba State Farm – Luapula Province* – preliminary investigations were made by the Chinese Agriculture Specialist team together with Zambian Officials on this farm. From the preliminary information gathered the Peoples Republic of China has agreed to assist Zambia in developing this farm.

(d) *Masasibi State Farm – Southern Province* – a team of Russian experts made preliminary investigations on this farm and agreed to assist Zambia in developing this farm. A follow-up detailed study is to start in February. It is planned to start production on a small scale during the 1981/82 season. A large-scale irrigation system is also planned for this farm.

(e) A number of French companies have gathered preliminary data on one State Farm in Kaoma District, Western Province (Kalumwange State Farm) and also some preliminary information on Munkumpu State Farm on the Copperbelt and Mtirizi State Farm in Eastern Province.

(f) *Mswebe State Farm in Central Province* – Tate and Lyle of Britain have agreed to assist Zambia develop this farm on a joint-venture basis. A technical study on this farm was already carried out by Tate and Lyle. A project proposal has already been

worked out by Tate and Lyle and is now under consideration by the government.
(g) *Mpika West State Farm* – a team of Chinese experts made preliminary investigations on this farm.
(h)*National Irrigation Project* – a team of experts from Iraq made a preliminary study on the possibility of establishing a National Irrigation System.[28]

Conclusion

The State Farm Project potentially has the makings of a new disaster. Going by the record of policy implementation it is hard to see how an economy under severe stress could provide the thrust for such largescale enterprises.

Zambia is not without donors and apart from those mentioned several other Western and socialist countries have pledged cooperation with the project. Many donor countries are already involved in other rural development schemes, e.g. the West Germans in North-Western province, the Dutch in Western Province and the Fins in Luapula Province. The Swedes (S.I.D.A.) have been operating schemes in Eastern and Northern Provinces for years. Several of these projects run over a period of 15 years at least, are already based on the "basic needs" approach and try to reach the 500,000 forgotten farmers.

These projects operate within the overall framework of the Integrated Rural Development Programme (I.R.D.P.). They represent small steps in the right direction (as I see it) but greater and longterm success can only be expected if government policies move away from grandiose schemes, become consistent and reliable, and implementation is much improved. There are of course other policy aspects which have not been discussed in this chapter but which are very important, e.g., the vexed pricing policy (especially with reference to maize and fertiliser[29]) and the more technical questions of what hybrids should be used and by whom. These must remain beyond the scope of this chapter and are in any case outside the sphere of my competence.

Is there any hope in spite of the failures and the necessary scepticism? I think so. A new generation of Zambian scholars and managers, well aware of the shortcomings of the postindependence leadership, is knocking loudly on the door. The basic material resources are available. The K 480 m. loan granted by the International Monetary Fund in mid-1981 will at least provide a breathing space to rethink and restrock. Operation Food Production does have aspects which, with political will and determined management, could succeed. We cannot take past experience as a definite determinant of the future. There is no doubt that Zambia's agriculture is in deep trouble, but it is not without a hope of recovery.

Notes

1. I.L.O., *Narrowing the Gaps – Planning for Basic Needs and Productive Employment in Zambia,* JASPA, Addis Ababa, January 1977, p. 2.
2. I.L.O./JASPA, *Basic Needs Under Pressure,* Preliminary Draft, October, 1980, p. 1.
3. Ibid, p. 4.
4. Robert Klepper, "Zambian Agricultural Structure and Performance", in Ben Turok (ed) *Development in Zambia,* Zed Press, 1979.
5. Republic of Zambia, *1980 Census of Population and Housing,* Preliminary Report, January 1981.
6. *Times of Zambia,* 22nd April 1981.
7. *Narrowing the Gaps,* p. 76.
8. Stephen A. Quick, "Bureaucracy and Rural Socialism: The Zambian Experience", Stanford University, Ph.D. Dissertation 1975 – referred to by Klepper, op.cit.
9. Rene Dumont, *Towards "Another Development" in Rural Zambia,* Draft Report, November 1979, (assisted by Marie France Mottin).
10. *Basic Needs under Pressure,* p. 7.
11. Charles Elliott, "Equity and Growth – Unresolved Conflict in Zambian Rural Development Policy", I.L.O., January 1980 (working paper).
12. Ibid, p. 4A.
13. Ibid, pp. 13, 14, 15.
14. Ibid, p. 25.
15. Ibid, p. 20.
16. Ibid, pp. 8, 9, 10, 11.
17. Dumont Report, p. 4.
18. Ibid, p. 5.
19. Ibid, p. 7.
20. Ibid, p. 16.
21. Elliott states: "Typically the most experienced and able technical and professional staff are found in Lusaka."
    The O'Riordan and Mwanakatwe Salaries Commissions rejected the idea of loadings although advocated in the Simmance Report on Decentralisation.
    Last year's salaries inquiry (1980) led to substantial increases for public servants, but rural loadings were again knocked back.
22. Zambia Information Services, *About Zambia,* No. 10, *Family Farms,* June 1974.
23. *Times of Zambia,* 8th November 1979, "The Trouble with Rene".
24. Republic of Zambia, *Project: Operation Food Production, 1980-1990,* State House, 23rd May 1980, p. 1.
25. Ibid, pp. 6-8.
26. *Times of Zambia,* 18th August 1980.
27. *Sunday Times of Zambia,* 5th October 1980.
28. Zambian Information Services, *Progress Report on Operation Food Production,* undated – early-1981.
29. See Chungu Mwila, "The Determination and Past Trends of Maize and Fertiliser Prices", Occasional Paper, Rural Development Studies Bureau, University of Zambia, May 1980.
    Times Review of *Sunday Times of Zambia,* 30th September 1979: Arthur Simuchoba, "The Big Switch – Why Farmers no longer want to grow maize".

Chapter 4
Public Enterprise and Industrial Development:
The Industrial Development Corporation of Zambia (INDECO)
by Roger Tangri

Since the attainment of political independence in 1964, and particularly since the series of partial nationalisations between 1968 and 1970, Zambia's parastatal sector has grown to occupy the central position in the national economy. State-controlled enterprises today play a key role in most economic sectors including Zambia's mining and manufacturing industry, wholesale and retail trade, hotels, finance, energy, transport, agricultural services and marketing. Over half of the total gross domestic product per annum is estimated to originate in the parastatal sector and the parastatals together provide just over one-third of the formal wage employment. The activities of parastatals are therefore of prime significance in shaping the future economic structure of Zambia and in determining the nature of the development of the national economy.

The parastatal sector in Zambia is made up of enterprises in which the state holds at least majority ownership, or a controlling interest, and which are organised outside the main lines of the departmental and ministerial structure of government.[1] Zambia's parastatals are created either by special legislation and are referred to as statutory boards or corporations, or they are state-controlled limited companies incorporated under the provisions of the Companies Act. This chapter focuses on parastatals falling under the latter category. The state-controlled companies are generally grouped under one of the several wholly government-owned holding companies, and the latter in turn are wholly-owned subsidiaries of the Zambia Industrial and Mining Corporation, Ltd. (ZIMCO).[2]

INDECO and Manufacturing Industrial Development

One of ZIMCO's subgroup holding companies is the Industrial Development Corporation of Zambia, Ltd. (INDECO). This chapter focuses on INDECO which has, since independence, been the government's principal instrument for the implementation of its industrial policies. As one of the largest and oldest members of the ZIMCO group, INDECO reflects in good measure the parastatal sector in Zambia.

INDECO already existed before independence, when it was a small development finance company fulfilling the conventional functions of a development
bank, mainly the provision of finance and other assistance to private enterprise manufacturing industry. From 1965 INDECO became a major instrument of government industrial policy in Zambia. At first the government
pursued a general policy of INDECO participating in, or setting up where
necessary, industrial enterprises and of otherwise providing fiscal incentives
for prospective foreign and Zambian private enterprise.[3] The political and
economic confrontation with the white-ruled south, especially after Rhodesia's
Unilateral Declaration of Independence, gave a powerful stimulus to manufacturing in Zambia. Most of the industrial expansion was in the private
sector but INDECO expanded rapidly as well. By the end of 1967 it had
been transformed from being primarily a financing institution to one emphasising direct capital participation and management of its subsidiary companies. This transformation was reflected in the increase of INDECO total net
assets from a 1965 sum of K 4.9 million to a 1967 figure of K 35.5 million.

By the late 1960s, the government had become increasingly convinced
that most foreign-controlled and resident expatriate companies, which still
made up most of the private sector, were more preoccupied with fast and
high returns and with transferring large portions of their profits abroad than
they were with local reinvestment and Zambianisation of management and
production personnel. At the same time, President Kaunda was seeking to
combat large-scale private capitalism in order to achieve an economic and
social order based upon the quasi-socialist principles of Zambian Humanism.
In April 1968, Kaunda announced that the government was acquiring majority shareholding in a number of large-scale, predominantly resident expatriate
enterprises. It took over majority shares in a total of twenty four companies
— in the brewing, retail and wholesale, distribution, construction, road
transport, and timber industries — and vested the shares in INDECO.[4]

INDECO was suddenly entrusted with great responsibilities. The terms of
payment of the acquisitions were actually negotiated by INDECO which was
to hold and manage the assets together with those of the enterprises in which
it was already engaged. INDECO's total group net assets trebled from almost
K 36 million in 1969 to K 108 million in 1969. A large part of this massive
increase was the result of the acquisition of private enterprises, but a substantial portion represented investment in the development of new projects
since independence (K 46 million out of K 108 million represented new
development). The 1970s have seen INDECO continuing its rapid expansion.
In 1979 group not assets totalled K 406 million, the combined result of IN-
DECO acquiring majority shareholding in selected existing enterprises and of
new projects and expansions initiated by INDECO.

Party and government documents as well as national development plans
have envisaged the creation of an internally-balanced, diversified and com-

paratively self-sustaining economy in Zambia. In relation to manufacturing industry, official policy has emphasised the promotion of industries which are import-substituting, export-oriented, and employment-generating, relying as far as possible on local resources. The stated aims have also included the establishment of small-scale industries in the rural areas outside the line-of-rail urban centres in order to provide more geographically-balanced industrial development.[5] INDECO has been assigned the task of giving direct and concrete expression to such developments in manufacturing, and has initiated projects as varied as Zambia Clay Industries producing clay pipes, Kafue Textiles manufacturing cotton cloth, Livingstone Motor Assemblers assembling a range of Fiat passenger cars, Nitrogen Chemicals of Zambia making ammonium nitrate products, Mwinilunga Fruit and Vegetable Cannery, Kabwe Industrial Fabrics producing hessian bags and string, Kapiri Mposhi glass bottle factory, Kafironda explosives factory, Mansa dry-cell battery factory, and Metal Fabricators of Zambia using local copper to manufacture copper wire and cable. INDECO today holds controlling interest in over thirty companies that account for over 45 per cent of the turnover and earn about 40 per cent of gross profits of Zambia's manufacturing sector. These same subsidiaries in 1979 employed nearly 25,000 persons or over 40 per cent of the manufacturing sector labour force and contributed over 70 per cent of manufacturing gross domestic product.

Prima facie these appear to be impressive developments; on closer inspection, however, the record has been less commendable. Of the various criticisms that have been levelled against INDECO's contribution to the Zambian economy, two are of particular importance. First, it has been shown that the pattern of manufacturing development has, in many ways, been at variance with official party and government objectives. INDECO has preferred investments in industries oriented almost entirely to the production of consumer and intermediate goods, neglecting the development of the capital goods sector. Even in the consumer goods sector, many of the factories cater more for the "luxury" domestic market than for the provision of necessities. Nor has manufacturing development resulted in the generation of as much employment as might have been possible, and few small-scale industries have been set up in the rural areas. Moreover, imports of raw materials and intermediate inputs have continued to rise and manufacturing growth has not economised on foreign exchange as much as was hoped. Much recent manufacturing development initiated by INDECO has thus been judged to have been largely capital-intensive, urban-based, and directed towards the production of luxury consumer goods requiring the importation of a considerable volume of raw materials and intermediate products.[6]

Secondly, INDECO has undertaken projects that are not too profitable. Official documents have emphasised that state firms should be profitable with the intention of financing not only the investment requirements of the state-controlled enterprises but also the general development expenditures of the government. INDECO group profitability averaged only about 6 per cent of group turnover between 1970 and 1974. In 1975 it dropped to 1 per cent of turnover and further to net losses amounting to about 1.5 per cent of turnover in 1976. The figures for 1977, 1978 and 1980 show some improvement but the level of returns has, in contrast with official expectations, remained very low (around 2 per cent of total turnover).

If we use the policies as enunciated in official documents as a yardstick by which to assess to performance of parastatals, we can conclude that INDECO has not lived up to expectations. It is the main purpose of this chapter to examine the various factors − external as well as internal − that have contributed to INDECO not being as successful as was hoped. But we also seek to shed light on questions of more general interest and importance; what are the chief factors which retard the growth of manufacturing industry in African economies such as the Zambian one, and are parastatals such as INDECO, likely to be effective agencies for the state promotion of industry?

External Dependence

In examining public enterprises in a country such as Zambia, account has to be taken of the nature of the excessive dependence of Zambia's economy on foreign economic interests. The dimensions of dependence are various and include reliance on foreign markets, foreign capital, foreign technology and designs, and foreign managerial talents.[7] Zambia's immediate post-independence development plans placed considerable emphasis on foreign investment, particularly in manufacturing industry. By the late 1960s, however, the need to increase both control over and direct participation in the economy increasingly began to be felt. As we have seen, in the field of manufacturing industry the government began from 1968 to acquire partial ownership and some direct control over the most important industrial enterprises. "State participation," stated an important party document, "is designed to guarantee the control of the economy by the Zambian people (and) the reduction of the impact of foreign influence in shaping national destiny".[8]

But in all the take-overs of private companies, and in all the new ventures entered into after 1968, the acceptance of a considerable degree of continued dependence was acknowledged by the retention of minority shareholder administrative and technical management through contracts. Management and technical agreements were signed with resident expatriate and overseas companies, many of whom also possessed a share in the equity of the state-controlled company. Zambia did not yet consider she had sufficiently trained manpower to run the parastatal sector without the technical and managerial skills possessed by non-Zambians. To be sure, management agreements have been phased out in recent years and only two of the more than thirty INDECO subsidiaries still have management contracts. But large numbers of individual contract personnel have been recruited from abroad and, moreover, technical consultancy contracts have been concluded between at least a dozen INDECO subsidiaries and overseas companies.

Continuing dependence on foreign managerial and technical skills has had an important bearing on the pattern of manufacturing development that has evolved in contemporary Zambia. The structure of investments (choice of techniques, employment effects, location of plant, etc.,) has, as we have seen, not been in conformity with official policy declarations. Because of the constraints of sufficiently trained and qualified indigenous manpower, INDECO has been obliged to rely on foreign companies to provide advice, skilled personnel, and feasibility studies as well as machinery and equipment for carrying out investments. In other African countries, many investment decisions have been based on the existence of foreign companies willing to recommend and carry out a project.[9] The evidence for Zambia is limited by the paucity of research but Seidman's assertion that INDECO has operated "primarily to facilitate investments initiated by its foreign partners"[10] would appear to have some validity.

Zambia's industrialisation policy since independence has not led to the emergence of a new structure of production as could possibly have been the case if it had been centred around the concept of strategic basic industries using appropriate technologies and catering for the consumption needs of the majority of the people. Instead it has followed the classic import-substitution pattern.[11] Import-substitution, a major plank in Zambia's industrial policy, has encouraged the domestic production of previously imported goods, mainly consumer goods, which reflect and incorporate the technology (and management) of western, industrialized countries. Import-substitution has particularly catered for the consumption habits of the Zambian middle class (over 50 per cent of the manufacturing contribution to Gross Domestic Product is supplied by the food, beverages and tobacco industries) and, more importantly, has resulted in dependence on foreign technology. But western technology has been designed for conditions prevailing in developed countries where labour is expensive; its relevance for countries such as Zambia where labour is abundant and less expensive is therefore hardly appropriate. The not surprising consequence has been that manufacturing development in Zambia has not created jobs to any appreciable extent. Evidence on individual projects indicates that INDECO has set up various capital-intensive industries such as the car assembly plant and various grain milling plants. Even in cases where alternative technologies have been available, factories have been installed that are dependent on highly capital-intensive technology from abroad. Zambia Clay Industries, for example, set up two ultramodern brick factories at Nega Nega and Kalalushi in 1975 despite the existence of a number of older, labour-intensive operations scattered throughout Zambia. The bias of investment in favour of capital-intensive production is not therefore the result solely of technological factors. It has also ensued in part because the overseas firms "profit from the supply of equipment, components, and technical services which embody capital-intensive techniques".[12] Profits are often highest in the building of a plant and the supply and maintenance of machinery. Similar considerations have also been important in creating the bias against the development of a capital-goods sector in Zambia, particularly industries which will promote the employment of indigenous labour especially in agriculture (development of fertiliser, tractor, and processing concerns).

These structural biases have been reinforced by other areas of economic policy. Besides relying on foreign firms for the supply of machinery, INDECO companies have become heavily dependent on foreign finance. In recent years, just over 50 per cent of INDECO capital has been raised on international finance markets with likely repercussions on investment decisions. The availability of foreign credit for overseas projects which favour the use of foreign capital equipment has also been an important factor. In his foreword to the Third National Development Plan, President Kaunda made the following observation:

> It has been our experience in the past that foreign economic assistance has the tendency to distort our choice of technology for it has been invariably tied to purchases of machinery and equipment, etc., in the respective donor country. This condition has resulted in the importation of machinery and equipment which have generated very little employment for the local people.[13]

An exemplification of this is the construction of the extension of the plant at Nitrogen Chemicals of Zambia through suppliers' and buyers' credit from the German and French contractors. The cost of the extension (which was started in 1975 and is yet to be commissioned) is currently estimated at K 167 million[14] amounting to a debt/equity ratio of 15:1. The entire project, however, the most expensive in Zambia, will create employment for not more than five hundred persons when it is completed.[15]

The adoption of an import-substitution strategy within the framework of the economic structure Zambia inherited at independence has not led to import dependence being reduced but has simply resulted in a shift from dependence in the consumer goods sector to dependence on a variety of imported inputs in the capital and intermediate goods sectors as well as raw materials. With industrial growth since independence, such imports have increased absolutely, and have also increased relative to total imports. Capital and intermediate goods constituted 56 per cent of total imports in 1964 but today account for around 77 per cent. A policy of import-substitution merely shifted a range of manufacturing processes to Zambia from overseas while maintaining Zambian dependence on imports required for previous stages of production such as machinery and maintenance.[16] Zambian industry, including INDECO, is now excessively reliant on such imports with the consequence that there has only been a very minimal development of backward and forward linkages to local materials.

In such a dependent situation, the growth of industry becomes tied to fluctuations in foreign exchange earnings. Since 1974 with prices of Zambia's major export commodity — copper — fluctuating at the London Metal Exchange, and costs of imported goods continuing relentlessly to rise, a serious situation has developed in which falling foreign exchange earnings have failed to balance out with the growing demand. Shortage of foreign exchange resources has prevented most of the companies in the INDECO group from importing materials in sufficient quantities in order to maintain levels of production. Serious difficulties in procurement of sufficient foreign exchange has not only meant that the production capacities have been grossly under-utilised but also that some companies have been brought to a virtual closedown. INDECO companies have been severely affected because to a large extent they have been concerned with the finishing of imported materials rather than with planned, indigenous production. The scarcity of foreign exchange has made it difficult, for example, for Livingstone Motor Assemblers to import sufficient knocked-down sets from Italy as a result of which production of Fiat passenger cars has declined markedly in recent years. In this particular case the problem has been especially acute, as 95 per cent of the company's material requirements are normally imported from the Fiat mother company.

Finally, Zambia's land-locked position and ensuing transport problems have led to interruptions in the supply of imports and/or higher prices of imported inputs which have seriously affected most INDECO companies. These factors have prolonged completion time and also contributed to massive cost increases of the projects. Thus, for example, not only has the completion of the above-mentioned extension of Nitrogen Chemicals been delayed but the cost has soared from an original estimate of K 70 million to over K 167 million and probably to over K 200 million by the time the plant comes on line.

Transport and foreign exchange difficulties have brought to the fore the unbalanced industrial structure of INDECO as well as its acute vulnerability to external factors. The unbalanced industrial pattern — characterized by the predominance of consumer goods industries rather than those producing capital and intermediate goods; by reliance on capital-intensive imported technology rather than small-scale technological processes; and by dependence on imported supplies rather than processing of domestic raw materials – have resulted in Zambia becoming even more tied to overseas manufacturing complexes. The establishment of such a lopsided industrial structure with its virtually absolute external dependence is not unrelated to Zambia's dependence on foreign managerial and technical skills as well as inflows of foreign capital.

The Politics of INDECO

In connection with Zambia's parastatals, a commission of inquiry noted in 1974 that the "boards have complained of inadequate policy guidance, a confusion between social and commercial objectives, the lack of clear financing arrangements and excessive interference in day-to-day affairs".[17] These complaints persisted throughout the 1970s and remained the source of much of INDECO's contemporary difficulties.

INDECO was set up to be run on a business basis. Its activities were to be guided by commercial considerations and were expected to be profitable. But INDECO has also been urged to pay attention to the achievement of specific national goals such as employment generation. Many of the problems that have afflicted INDECO derive from this multiplicity of objectives. Not only is INDECO expected to be run at a profit and "in a proper commercial and businesslike way" but it is also to "keep the national interest in mind at all times"[18] by taking into account such social considerations as forward and backward linkages as well as effects on foreign exchange and employment of the projects it has initiated. The extent to which the attainment of such social objectives should be reconciled with the pursuit of profit has never been officially clarified and has continued to be one of the main uncertainties surrounding INDECO's role.

The government's industrial development strategy has not been of sufficient precision to provide INDECO with clear guidelines for its activities. Clearly defined and unambiguous criteria for investment and operating decisions have not been officially enunciated. In the absence of such criteria, as to what should be the relative weight assigned to the profitability as against the social criterion, becomes a matter of dispute. No definitive selection has been made from the range of objectives; nor have they been organised in order of priority. "You operate in the dark" has been the not surprising reaction of one INDECO managing director.[19]

The result has been that many of INDECO's investments have been questionable. Projects have been selected according to *ad hoc* criteria. It is not that little or no thought has been devoted to the relevance of these projects in terms of the government's development strategy but that since the government's industrial strategy has been vague and imprecise (comprising essentially a mere erection of targets and aims) it has been used to justify almost any conceivable project. The government's list of objectives for industrial development has not been of much assistance in specifying the type of industrial society Zambia should create and what its contribution to the economy should be.[20] In the absence of any overall strategy, the assumptions of government and parastatal officials are unlikely to be much different from those of the foreign partner or associate. For both parties, decision-making tends to be dictated primarily by short-term opportunity and local demand considerations (e.g., for beer, cigarettes, cars, etc.) rather than by questions of a self-reliant industrial strategy to restructure the economy. Thus although many projects have probably been initiated by foreign companies, they have not been contrary to the views of government officials and parastatal managers. But by adopting shortterm profit criteria, INDECO has preferred investments in importsubstitution industries producing more or less luxury goods as well as large, capital-intensive projects in the urban centres. It is not surprising, therefore, that the contribution of INDECO projects to employment has been limited and that they have failed to reduce the overall import bill.

Emphasis has been placed on INDECO showing a profit as a means of determining whether performance has been satisfactory.[21] But INDECO has only possessed limited autonomy and has been subject to a series of *ad hoc* political directives on specific operational issues. The government has greatly influenced INDECO through directives on key aspects of the operations of its subsidiary companies, including type and location of investments and pricing decisions.

Decisions regarding certain investments have been made by the government which has also issued directives regarding the location of projects. The location of Livingstone Motor Assemblers, Kapiri Glass Products and Mansa Batteries, all subsidiaries of INDECO, was decided on the basis of providing employment opportunities outside the major urban areas. These and similar projects have run into difficulty for various reasons but partly because many have been located in up-country centres situated at a long distance from the main markets and partly because some of these centres have had a poor infrastructure. There are several examples of enterprises whose viability has been undermined by poor siting. The manufacture of glass products, to take one example, is normally a market-oriented industry because of high transportation costs but the Kapiri Glass factory is located many miles from the main points of consumption. Or, to take another example, in the case of the multi-million brick factories set up under official directive in the rural areas at

Kalalushi and Nega Nega, to transport the bricks long distances to the construction sites raised the cost of the bricks to uneconomic levels with the result that the construction industry increasingly switched to the use of concrete blocks. On account of declining demand for its products, the brick works at Nega Nega was forced to close down in 1979. Yet despite such experience, the government has not devised alternative strategies, such as an efficient programme of incentives for decentralisation of industrial development. The result has been that state companies operating outside the main urban centres at some distance from their main markets have incurred substantial economic losses.

The government has also exercised control over prices of various commodities, goods and services. INDECO and its subsidiaries have not been able to set their own prices. The government has enforced price levels that have permitted little margin for companies to recover their costs of processing and, in some cases, the controlled prices have been lower than the landed cost of raw materials. Three food processing subsidiaries of INDECO engaged in grain milling and edible oil have suffered severe losses in recent years. As a result of government-maintained price ceilings, wheat flour in 1975 was sold by the milling companies at 40 per cent below the landed costs plus packing materials, whilst refined vegetable oil was sold at 15 per cent below cost of raw materials and packing. In 1976 INDECO ran at a loss for the first time, due mainly to price controls resulting in the three subsidiaries not being able to set prices sufficiently high to cover costs.

The financial viability of INDECO has thus been imperilled by the Government's pricing decisions. To be sure the Government has reimbursed companies for losses due to controlled prices. In 1975 subsidies amounting to K 13.7 million were paid to INDECO to cover past operating company losses arising from government-managed price controls. But as losses were estimated to be over K 25 million, the subsidies were clearly insufficient to cover losses.

There are few public enterprises in Zambia, INDECO included, which do not suffer from the effects of errors of omission and commission – in project conception and formulation, in the construction phase, and in the subsequent operational stages. Sound project planning and management practices are doubtless key conditions for the success of the public sector. The mushrooming growth of public enterprise in Zambia since independence has strained the supply of suitably qualified staff to run the parastatals. The acute shortage of administrative and management expertise has proved to be a recurring problem in INDECO.[22] According to a member of the Parastatal Bodies Service Commission, the causes of problems in INDECO companies have included the following managerial ones: "Ill-management supervision, lack of forward planning, complacency over success, serious financial indiscipline, over-employment and indecision to implement operational or administrative directives".[23]

But effective management in Zambia's parastatals has been adversely affected by political involvement. The parastatals have been characterized by an extremely high rate of transfers of middle and top management. The high rate of turnover of managerial personnel has stemmed from conscious government decisions to move managers between companies. Inevitably the result has been loss of efficiency. Management has also been affected by politically inspired appointments with the result that less than qualified managers have been appointed. Moreover, ministerial interference in the detailed, day-to-day administration of state-owned companies has been a common feature of the management of these enterprises.

Conclusion

High hopes were entertained that the state sector would evolve into a major focus for local initiatives to implement important structural change in Zambia. The industrial state sector, however, has not lived up to expectations. Shortcomings in INDECO may be understood as a reflection of various factors. One factor has been the dependence of INDECO on foreign economic interests entailing various consequences such as that development initiatives have originated in crucial instances from foreign promoters. Another factor has been the lack of clear industrial investment guidelines, making it difficult for INDECO to act in accordance with national development goals. Parastatal officials have adopted the selfsame business criteria as foreign businessmen with the result that public investment decisions have been based on commercial profitability rather than social considerations. As the same time, however, decisions regarding specific investments have been influenced by the government which has often forced state companies to deviate from the profit criterion. Finally, failures of planning and organisation, consequent upon the acute shortage of qualified managerial staff as well as political involvement, have also affected the performance of INDECO.

In spite of all the shortcomings, denationalisation has not been mooted as a solution to INDECO's problems in manufacturing industry. "Private companies", according to the Prime Minister," had not operated in the national interest, and the Government would remain committed to the establishment of a 'mixed economy' where public and private undertakings existed side by side."[24] But failures in the parastatal sector could not remain unchecked. In view of the variety of factors to which the failures of parastatals have been attributed, the government has adopted various approaches to improve the performance of INDECO.

First, the government has sought to develop a more effective machinery of control. Until recently, the government itself exerted control over the affairs of INDECO. Formal government control over INDECO was exercised through the power of appointment of the members of the Board of the Corporation as well as the managerial staff of the subsidiary companies. In addition, the decision-making powers of parastatal management were severely curtailed. Uniform terms and conditions of service within both the civil service and the parastatal sector limited the ability of parastatal managers to fix wages and salaries. Recruitment of employees was also withdrawn from the hands of managers and handed over to a central parastatal service commission in the fashion of the civil service. But since 1978 the government has sought to strengthen ZIMCO as a central holding agency by refurbishing its administrative capacity for coordination and control. The purpose is to improve overall direction of the affairs of parastatals such as INDECO while at the same time relieving the ministries and bureaucracies of the responsibility for various complex managerial tasks. Steps have also been taken to curtail the relative autonomy INDECO has enjoyed in its activities, as for example, in planning its projects, in arranging for foreign participation, etc., and then seeking governmental equity and loan finance. This is being changed. A corporate planning system is being instituted by ZIMCO within INDECO which it is hoped will be integrated with the national planning system thereby ensuring that INDECO's investment programmes are in accordance with government's objectives.

The government has initiated further means of ensuring control over INDECO investment policy. Management, technical and consultancy agreements with foreign firms have to be approved by the Government while ZIMCO has been empowered to examine periodically the effectiveness of the agreements as they relate to imparting management skills to Zambians and the transfer of technology generally. In addition, all contracts involving foreign exchange are subject to the approval of the Bank of Zambia, and all projects require an industrial or manufacturing licence from the Ministry of Industry and Commerce.

Yet, in spite of such control mechanisms, the government has recently decided to allow parastatals greater autonomy "to operate in a more truly commercial manner". Price decisions are being entrusted to individual companies (with only a few goods remaining under direct price control) as it has been realised that parastatals have been charging uneconomic prices. In return, the government expects such concerns "to pay substantial dividends on a regular basis".[25] But, to date, no further measures have been taken to permit parastatals to set their own prices and, indeed, the Cabinet has ordered state companies not to increase prices of their essential commodities in the interest of the nation.[26] The need to strike a balance between the social obligations of INDECO and its obligation to earn a reasonable rate of return on capital employed will be a difficult and continuing problem.

ZIMCO has also put all parastatal companies in the INDECO group on a so-called economic footing, in which the operative emphasis will be managerial efficiency and high productivity. In 1979 ZIMCO was granted powers to make managerial appointments on the basis of merit and was also directed to seek to curb the high rate of transfers and turnover of managerial personnel. Top management in INDECO has since then been asked to remain in posts for at least three years and is being given contracts for such time periods. In 1980 new conditions of service for all ZIMCO subsidiaries such as INDECO "have been introduced to attract and retain the right calibre of employees to achieve the highest standards of business management."[27] Moreover, in connexion with the new INDECO projects being planned, it is hoped that these will be based primarily on economic considerations. The Luangwa Industries bicycle assembly plant, which was to have started in 1981, may not fall within this ideal especially in view of its location at Chipata in the eastern corner of the country as well as because it is a pure assembly project relying heavily on imported materials. But other forthcoming projects such as the ceramic plant at Kitwe will, it is hoped, confirm the new emphasis being placed upon ensuring that INDECO is run on a business basis and at a profit.

The government has accepted that the "shoddy performance" of parastatal companies has been due to the shortage of skilled Zambian manpower such as financial analysts, technicians and engineers. "The need for external expertise remains acute" stated the Prime Minister recently and "the Government is seeking to recruit abroad".[28] This is especially the case as many projects are capital-intensive and technical expertise is sorely needed. The Government is also seeking to attract more foreign investment and foreign companies are being invited to enter into joint undertakings with INDECO. Under the Industrial Development Act of 1977, various safeguards and incentives are provided for attracting foreign investors to participate in joint ventures with parastatals. Indeed, any further industrial expansion is seen as entailing links with foreign capital and requiring financial and technical support.

Thus the position of INDECO is paradoxical — it was represented as a challenge to the inherited system of alien capital yet it is obliged to collaborate with that capital. A major concern often expressed about foreign capital is that by being an important source of finance for industrial development it can undermine any independent industrialisation.[29] The extent to which foreign investors have control over the use of their capital in Zambia is, as we have seen, fairly complete given their technical and other advantages. But this concern does not arouse undue worry in Zambia; reliance on foreigners is accepted as part of the process of transition from absolute dependence to eventual independent national development. Instead, claims are made that state ownership has "facilitated the process of increasing Zambian participation in building our economy and in controlling it for our benefit".[30] Moreover, even if foreign capital and enterprise are required, they can now be more effectively controlled than in the past. The government is clearly aware of the need to monitor the activities of overseas firms and prevent abuses. With effect from February 1978 the Swiss firm of consultants, Societé Générale de Surveillance has been engaged, as in Tanzania, to conduct inspection of shipment of goods to Zambia in order to check that qualities, quantities and prices are correct.[31] Since the introduction of the preshipment inspectorate, exchange control evasion through over-invoicing has, it has been claimed, "been brought under control".[32]

As the formal machinery of control is developed and refined, the need for a careful definition of development policies and goals will become urgent. In the absence of an industrial development strategy sufficiently precise to give the parastatals clear guidelines for their activities it will remain difficult for the Government to ensure that the parastatals act in accordance with national development to which INDECO can turn, the approach to the selection of projects and the choice of location and technology will continue to be piecemeal and arbitrary. And in the absence of clear investment guidelines, limitations will arise as to what the control machinery – aside from avoidance of abuses – is designed to achieve.

The economic reforms initiated in 1968 and which resulted in state ownership of industrial undertakings reflected strong nationalist sentiments. The state now has greater access to economic surplus and is able to retain profits which would otherwise have left the country. But although the manufacturing sector is now subject to much greater Zambian direction and control, state capital is still having to accommodate a good deal to foreign capital. Public ownership has done little to diminish dependence on foreign capital and know-how. In addition, the principles of Humanism as espoused by the Zambian political leadership have hardly been furthered: INDECO has remained strongly oriented towards capitalist relations (including wage/salary differentials; managerial prerogatives and/or the hierarchy of authority; limited worker control; and market determination or profit calculations). Most importantly, public ownership has not led to the emergence of a new structure of production. What has evolved in Zambia over the past decade has been a form of state capitalism with various joint stateprivate ventures which has accommodated the forces demanding less direct foreign control. Little consideration, however, has been devoted to the question whether capitalist development under state auspices can advance beyond the dependent type industrialisation of the Latin American economies.

Notes

1. *Report of the Commission of Inquiry into the Salaries, Salary Structures and Conditions of Service of the Public Services and the Parastatal Sector* (Lusaka: Government Printer, 1975), vol. 1, p. 130.
2. *ibid.*, pp. 130-4.
3. INDECO, *Annual Report* (Lusaka 1965), p. 14.
4. K.D. Kaunda, "Zambia's Economic Revolution". An address to the National Council of the United National Independence Party (UNIP) at Mulungushi – 19th April, 1968. Note should be made of the President's remarks that the "economic reforms" were "not aimed at foreign investors" but were "against resident expatriates".
5. UNIP, *National Policies for the Next Decade 1974-1984* (Lusaka: Government Printer, 1973), p. 26; Republic of Zambia, *First National Development Plan 1966-1970* (Lusaka: Government Printer, 1966), pp. 6-8, 33-6; Republic of Zambia, *Second National Development Plan 1972-1976* (Lusaka: Government Printer 1971), pp. 19-20, 93-4.
6. Alistair Young, *Industrial Diversification in Zambia* (New York: Praeger, 1973), Chaps. 7 and 9; Ann Seidman, "The Distorted Growth of Import – Substitution Industry: The Zambian Case" *Journal of Modern African Studies 12, 4* (1974): 601-631; International Labour Office, *Narrowing the Gaps. Planning for Basic Needs and Productive Employment in Zambia* (Addis Ababa: International Labour Office, 1977), Chap. 5; M.R. Bhagavan, *Zambia: Impact of Industrial Strategy on Regional Imbalance and Social In-equality* (Uppsala: Scandinavian Institute of African Studies, 1978), Chap. 3.
7. See, for example, Brian Van Arkadie, "Development of the State Sector and Economic Independence" in *Economic Independence In Africa* ed. Dharam Ghai (Nairobi: East African Literature Bureau 1973): 88-122.
8. UNIP, *National Policies, op.cit.*, p. 39.
9. See, for example, Issa G. Shivji, "Capitalism Unlimited: Public Corporations in Partnership with Multinational Corporation", *The African Review* 3, 3 (1973) 359-382.
10. A Seidman, *op.cit.*, p. 615.
11. *First National Development Plan, op. cit.*, p. 33, and *Second National Development Plan, op.cit.*, p. 93.
12. Giovanni Arrighi, "International Corporations, Labour Aristocracies, and Economic Development in Tropical Africa", *Imperialism and Underdevelopment: a reader*, ed. Robert I. Rhodes (New York: *Monthly Review*, 1970), p. 252. Note should also be made of the fact that low duties on capital goods and attractive investment and depreciation allowances have contributed to the bias in industrial development against labour intensive projects.
13. Republic of Zambia, *Third National Development Plan 1979-1983* (Lusaka: Government Printer, 1979), p. v.
14. *Times of Zambia* (Lusaka), 31 January 1978, p. 7.
15. *ibid.*, 24 April 1978, p. 2.
16. Young, op.cit., Chap. 5. Dependence on imports has increased because the strategy of import-substitution has been concerned exclusively with substitution of imports of consumer goods. Prior to independence the entire consumer commodity was imported, but after independence the capital goods required to produce the consumer item as well as intermediate goods and spare parts have to be imported on

account of the absence of basic industries in Zambia. See also, Robin Fincham, "Economic Dependence and the Development of Industry in Zambia", *Journal of Modern African Studies*, 18, 2 (1980), pp. 293-303.

17. *Report of Commission of Inquiry into the Salaries, op.cit.*, p. 131.
18. K.D. Kaunda, *op.cit.*, p. 46.
19. Talk by Mr. Leo Chileshe entitled "Opportunities of Parastatals and Threats to them" at the University of Zambia on the 13th February, 1979.
20. In preparing this ection of the chapter, I have benefitted in particular from John Loxley and John S. Saul. "Multinationals, Workers and the Parastatals in Tanzania" *"Review of African Political Economy* No. 2 (1975): 54-88.
21. INDECO, *Annual Report* 1973/74 (Lusaka, 1974), p. 9.
22. Government of Zambia, *Final Report of the Zambia Managerial Manpower and Training Needs Survey of the Private and Patastatal Sectors* (Lusaka, Government Printer, 1977).
23. Quoted in *Times of Zambia*, 25 April 1978, p. 1.
24. Prime Minister Daniel Lisulo, reported in *The Daily Mail* (Lusaka), 17 November 1978, p. 1.
25. *Ibid.,* See also the Budget speech of the Minister of Finance on the 26th January 1979.
26. UNIP Secretary-Geeneral Mainza Chona, reported in the *Times of Zambia*, 16 June 1979, p. 1.
27. ZIMCO excutive director for corporate planning, Mr. Ignatius Muchangwe, reported in the *Times of Zambia* 28 July 1980, p. 1.
28. Prime Minister Daniel Lisulo, reported in *Times of Zambia*, 17 November 1978, p. 1.
29. G. Arrighi, *op.cit.*
30. Address by President K.D. Kaunda to UNIP National Council at Kabwe – 1st December 1972, p. 12.
31. *Times of Zambia*, 19 January 1978, p. 2.
32. *Ibid.,* 12 July 1979, p. 1.

Chapter 5
The Process of Class Formation in Contemporary Zambia
by Gilbert N. Mudenda

Introduction

The concept of class is a controversial notion in the social sciences. The debate that surrounds this notion becomes more vitriolic when it comes to analysing social formations that have just emerged from colonial bondage. The source of this particular controversy has many and varied premises which are, unfortunately, confounded by the fact that there is a general denial of the existence of classes in African countries by both politicians and academics alike. The politicians deny the existence of classes in these countries by alleging that the nature of social development in Africa was uniquely humane and did not give rise to social differentiation as was the case elsewhere. As such, most African political leaders are generally suspicious of anybody who alludes to the existence of classes in African social formations, let alone the requisite notion of class struggle, however silent!

The academics, on the other hand, deny the existence of classes in Africa largely because the dominant bourgeois social science theory — structural functionalism — holds that society is composed of various social strata that live in "perfect" harmony with one another. As such the talk of classes, which implies social friction and conflict, is dismissed as being "ideological" and subjective. Of late, however, a small number of academics have rebelled against such "conventional wisdom" and have adopted more radical analyses of African societies which are class-based.[2]

It is the latter approach which is adopted in this chapter. We shall use the Marxist method of analysis to analyse the nature of class formation in contemporary Zambia. However, before we begin to unravel the intricacies of class formation in Zambia, we should try to explain our methodological preference. The reasons for our choice of this approach are many and varied; suffice it to say that the Marxist approach is the main, if not the only, approach to the study of social reality which begins by recognising that society comprises discrete social groups whose existence is founded on conflicting interests. Secondly, the Marxist approach is the only body of theory that regards social change as the outcome of the unfolding dialectic of class struggles. As Marx put it:

> The history of all hitherto society is a history of class struggles, Freeman and Slave, Patrician and Plebian, Lord and Serf, in a word, oppressor and oppressed stood in constant opposition to each other.[3]

It is largely for these reasons that we have chosen this mode of analysis in the hope that it will aid us in capturing fully the intricate dialectic of class formation in Zambia.

This chapter is divided into two parts. The first part addresses itself to some theoretical problems and considerations encountered when dealing with the nature of class formation in peripheral capitalist social formations. The first part comprises four sections. The first section deals with problems of definition and characterization of the notion of class. The second section endeavours to show the relationship between the notions of class and mode of production. In the third section we discuss the nature of the mode of production in peripheral capitalist social formation. The fourth section, which concludes the first part, discusses, more specifically, the nature of the mode of production in the contemporary Zambian social formation.

The second part of the chapter, addresses itself to analysing the process of class formation in the contemporary Zambian social formation. As such, this part comprises descriptions of the evolution of the various constituents of the major classes that obtain in Zambia today. The three sections that comprise this part of the chapter follow the major classes that obtain in the Zambian social formation and these are: the bourgeoisie, the working class and the peasantry. A proper understanding of this section can only be achieved through a thorough reading of the first part. This is so because it is in the first part that the theoretical framework is situated.

I. Theoretical Problems and Considerations

a. A Definition and Characterization of the Notion of Class

A definition of class from a Marxist perspective must, of necessity, begin by refuting the allegation that the founders of Marxism did not get round to defining the notion of class. A good reading of the "classics" readily proves that such is not the case. For example, Marx in his book: *The Eighteenth Brumaire of Louis Bonaparte* wrote:

> Insofar as millions of families live under economic conditions of existence that separate their mode of life, their interests and their culture from those of the other classes and put them in hostile opposition of the latter, they form a class.[4]

The above definition of class is central to any attempt at defining classes. However, it was Lenin who gave the Marxist tradition a more thorough definition of class. Lenin defined the notion of class in the following manner:

Classes are groups of people differing from each other by the place they occupy in a historically determined system of production, by their relation (in most cases fixed and formulated in law) to the means of production; by their role in the social organisation of labour and consequently, by the dimension of the share of social wealth of which they dispose and the mode of acquiring it. *Classes are groups of people which can appropriate the labour of another owing to the different places they occupy in a definite system of social economy.* [5]

From this definition a number of core characteristics and determinations of social classes come out very clearly. These are:

1) a place occupied by a group of people in a historically determined system of production;
2) a relation to the means of production;
3) an assigned role in the social organisation of labour;
4) a mode of acquiring and disposing a part of the social wealth; and
5) an exploitative and hostile relation to other classes.

The first characteristic underlines two very important methodological assertions. Firstly, it is posited that social being is essentially determined by man's productive activity. Secondly, it is asserted that the mode of production – a major determinant of class relations – is not constant but variable. In the light of these assertions, it becomes important to identify the time and specificity of the mode of production before analysing the nature of class formation in any given social formation. Furthermore, it should also be borne in mind that production does not only mean man's relationship with nature, but more importantly, production entails the relationships man enters into with other men in the process of production. Marx put it thus:

In the social production of their existence, men inevitably enter into definite relations which are independent of their will, namely, the relations of production appropriate to a given stage in the development of their forces of production. The totality of these relations constitute the economic structure of society, the real foundation, on which arises a legal and political superstructure and to which correspond definite forms of social consciousness. [6]

The place occupied by a group of people in a historically determined system of production ascribes to that group a "class place" and possibly a "class position". It is important to distinguish between these two concepts because they tend to be confused especially when analyses of class struggles are made. A class place is primarily and objectively ascribed by the relation of a particular class to the means of production and the concomitant roles in the social organisation of labour the members of that class play. The class position, on the other hand, is largely determined by subjective class alignments that issue in the process of class struggles. As such, a class position is largely a product of ideology. For example not all workers ascribe to the proletarian ideology despite the fact that, objectively, their "place" is within the working class.

The second characteristic, a relation to the means of production, underlines the point that a place occupied by a class is not predetermined by fate or luck; but rather determined by a relation to the means of production. In turn, a relationship to the means of production is, in the final analysis, determined by ownership or nonownership of the means of production. In a class-divided society, this relation accords one class the facility to exploit, dominate and subordinate another or other class(es). This is due to the fact that the dominant class has a monopoly over the means of production while the other classes have none or limited means of production of their own.

Thirdly, the relation to the means of production also implies that different classes will play different roles in the social organisation of labour. Marx put this point very succinctly when he observed:

> It is not that he is a leader of industry that a man is a capitalist; on the contrary, he is a leader of industry because he is a capitalist. The headership of industry is an attribute of capital, just as in feudal times, the functions of general and judge were attributes of landed property.[7]

Notwithstanding the current debate on the difference between ownership and control,[8] either way, in a capitalist society, the attributes of being without capital are, largely, those of being subjected to domination, oppression, exploitation and alienation by those who wield economic power.

The fourth characteristic, the dimension of the share of social wealth, is largely determined by the source of the mode in which that share is acquired. In his famous but uncompleted definition of class Marx had this to say:

> What constitutes a class? ... the reply to this question follows naturally from the reply to another question, namely: What makes wage-labourers, capitalists and landlords constitute the three great social classes?
> At first glance, ... the identity of revenues and the sources of revenue. There are three great social groups whose members, individuals forming them, live on wages, profit and ground-rent respectively, on the realisation of their labour, their capital and their landed property.[9]

What is important to note here is the fact that it is not the size of the income that is the defining principle of a class, but rather, the source of the income. Elsewhere Marx warns against the vulgarity of looking at the size of a person's purse as a way of determining his class. The source of income, is the only way of determining a person's class place. This is so because it is the source of one's income which is directly related to one's relation to the means of production.

The last characteristic of classes, hostility to one another, is a natural outcome of class relations which are, principally, based on a system of exploitation and domination. It should, however, be emphasised here that the exploitation and oppression of the dominated classes by the class that owns the means of production is not due to some grisely and atavistic capitalist ritual nor is it due to a propensity, on the part of those who own capital, for being callous and niggardly as it is usually alluded. On the contrary, exploitation and oppression are basic to any class society. The degrees of intensity vary according to the specificities of the mode of production. Hence, the antagonism that exists between classes, follows naturally from this objective class relation and constitutes the mainstay of class struggles which in turn are the dynamics of social change and revolutionary action. For it is in the struggle to realise its class interest that a class becomes a social force.

b. Class and the Mode of Production

In our definition of classes it was made very clear that classes are determined and bounded by the mode of production. It was also made clear that a mode of production is historically determined and variable. Since the mode of production is central to an understanding of class formation, it is therefore important that we try to define this notion and show how it relates to class formation. A simplified definition of mode of production would define the mode of production as the manner in which society organises its primary economic activity, namely, production, exchange and distribution of social wealth. As such, a mode of production is composed of two very principal elements. These are: the means of production comprise tools, techniques and resources – both natural and human. In other words, the means of production relate to the level of technology attained and used by a given society.

The relations of production, on the other hand, comprise those social relationships men enter into with one another in the organisation of production. As such, these relations are social and largely determined by property relations as well as the nature of the technology used in a given society. Hence, the technological level attained in a society will give rise to certain configurations of roles played by different social groups in the process of production. With the advancement of technology, new roles and classes come into being and when these can no longer be contained in the old structure, social changes of revolutional nature take place leading to an emergence of another mode of production. This process in usually referred to as the law of correspondence.

From the above, it should be understood that the mode of production forms the *structure* of society and contains the dynamics of societal change and development. Thus each mode of production will have social classes that are particular to that mode of production. However, owing to the fact that the mode of production is variable, no social formation can, at one time, have a "pure" mode of production. As such no social formation will comprise only those classes that are particular to one mode of production, however dominant. It is in this regard that it becomes imperative to take heed of what Bukharin said when he observed,

> ... a class does not descend full-grown from heaven but grows in a crude elementary manner from other social groups (transitional classes, intermediate and other classes, strata, social combinations.) ... a certain time usually passes before a class becomes conscious of itself through experience in battle, of its special and particular interest, aspirations, social "deals" and desires which emphatically distinguish it from all other classes in a given society.[10]

As such, for a given social formation, at any given point in time will comprise a configuration of sets of classes and other transitional classes. One set of classes would consist of those classes that are particular to the dominant mode of production; another set would compose those classes particular to the "future" mode of production; while yet another set would consist of those classes particular to the declining but still extant mode of production. Furthermore, and because of continuous development and change in both the mode of production and the class configuration, there could be groups of people that may not necessarily belong to any recognised class. In addition, it should be noted that a mode of production is merely the basic structure of a social formation while the social formation includes other features of social being which are political, ideological, cultural and spatial in nature. This being the case, some social groups in a social formation take the form of race, religion, nationality and in some extreme cases, professional groups. While it is important to take note of these many and diverse social groupings, it is equally important to guard against the tendency which mistakes these social differentiations for class distinctions. This is so because it is only class differences that are the most definitive and powerful social distinctions because they spring from the foundation of society. And as such, are the sole inspirers and makers of history.

So far, we have, in this section tried to show the centrality of the mode of production in the determination of social classes. We have also indicated that in any mode of production there is always a kaleidoscopic configuration of classes. In order to begin to unravel the constitutents of these configurations we shall use a method of social analysis which easily takes us to the core of class analysis while avoiding the *cul de sac* of static Parsonianism. This approach begins with the premise that society is divided into classes. Secondly, it is accepted that each class is composed of various sections, and fractions. As such, a social class constitutes a major and definitive social distinction. A section of a class, on the other hand is merely a discernible part of a class which could be composed of various fractions and elements.

A fraction is therefore a smaller part of a social differentiation. For example, the capitalist class is a very distinctive social class in contemporary society. However, the capitalist class is composed of people who own different "capitals". As such, one can talk of an agricultural bourgeoisie, or industrial bourgeoisie or a commercial bourgeoisie, etc. Similarly, the various sections of the bourgeoisie mentioned above could be further divided into more categories, and it is these further differentiations that we categorise as fractions.

This refinement is not a pedantic preoccupation but a very useful tool when it comes to analysing social formations whose class configuration is incoherent and distorted. Furthermore, this approach allows flexibility in following those fractions that, due to historical circumstance, switch from one section to another. This will become clear when we analyse the processes of class formation in Zambia.

c. The Mode of Production in Peripherial Capitalist Social Formations

What classes obtain in a country like Zambia? This question begs another question, namely, what mode of production obtains in a peripheral capitalist social formation? The answer to this question is as crucial as it is controversial. What is not controversial, however, is the fact that the Zambian social formation, as we know it today, is a product of the colonial experience. As such, Zambia's recent history is inextricably connected with the development of the capitalist world system and shares a lot in common with other countries that were similarly incorporated into the capitalist system. Having said this, we must add that the histories of countries like Zambia can not be reduced to a history of imperialism, for social formations have their own particular identity which is a product of circumstances, internal dynamism and response to external forces.

The world system in which most Third World countries find themselves is a capitalist system. Capitalism first developed and established itself in Western Europe. Its genesis could be traced back to feudal Europe; beginning with the rise of merchants, craft guilds, the expansion of world trade and these developments culminated, in the case of England, the first industrial nation, in the enclosure movement and the factory system. Unlike the development of capitalism in Europe, capitalism in the Third World was not nurtured in the "womb" of the previous mode of production but came as an imposition from outside.

The generalisation of commodity production, i.e. the capitalist mode of production, took place at a certain stage in the development of capitalism. This stage is designated by Lenin as imperialism which he defined as follows:

> Imperialism is capitalism in that stage of development in which the domination of monopolies and finance capital has established itself; in which the export of capital has acquired a pronounced importance; in which the division of the world among international trusts has begun; in which the partition of all the territories of the globe among great capitalist powers has been completed.[12]

From the above quotation we begin to understand that the generalisation of the capitalist mode of production by the incorporation of Third World social formation in to the capitalist system led to the establishment of an essentially capitalist mode of production in these social formations.

Having said this, we should note that the above statement has been a centre of debate and polemics.[13] Without getting into the debate, we need to state that a large part of the debate centres on the form rather than on the essence of the nature of the mode of production that obtains in Third World countries, thanks to imperialist penetration and incorporation. More specifically, the capitalist mode of production in Third World countries was instituted by a series of exogenous changes that dissolved and/or transformed the old *structure* of these societies. Secondly, a colonial bourgeois state was established in order to enhance the dominance of metropolitan capital.[14] However, the capitalist mode of production that resulted was an extraverted one in the sense that the structure of production as well as the circuit of commodity circulation thus instituted could only be completed via the metropolis. In analysing this process in India, Alavi had this to say:

> Thus we cannot grasp this aspect of the structure of colonial capitalism without simultaneously locating it within the matrix of imperialism...likewise, surplus value was drawn off from the colonial economy by metropolitan capitalism so that extended reproduction of capital occurred but only via the metropolis; capital accumulation took place in the metropolis where it raised the organic composition of capital whereas the surplus value was created in the colony. Thus here again the structural condition of the capitalist mode of production was realised but in a specifically colonial form, the form appropriate to colonial capitalism....[15]

In the light of the above, one can speak of colonialism as the initial stage in the establishment of the capitalist mode of production in Third World countries and neocolonialism as the more advanced form of the capitalist mode of production in contemporary peripheral capitalist social formations. It was Nkrumah who first discussed this phenomenon creatively. He called it the worst form of imperialism because:

> ... for those who practice it, it means exploitation without any responsibility and for those who suffer from it, it means exploitation without redress.[16]

Neocolonialism is currently the dominant form of capitalist production in Third World countries, which manifests itself as state capitalism. According to Mafeje the salient attributes of state capitalism are as follows:

1) Increased domination of the economy by foreign monopolies and the continued loss of domestic income to them;
2) Increased discrepancy between resource use and domestic demand, as foreign capital concentrates on extractive industries which produce commodities that are not consumed locally, e.g. mining and export agriculture;
3) Increased technological dependence on foreign supplies and retardation of domestic capability;
4) Monopolisation of the local market through import substitution industries and further losses of added value due to inducements offered in order to secure licences and capital; and
5) Increased imbalances in income between those engaged in the modern sector . . . usually capital intensive and those engaged in the neglected sectors always technologically backward and inhabited by the great majority of the population.[17]

From the above observations, it is possible to say that most Third World countries that have not taken a definitive choice for scientific socialism, are largely part of the capitalist world system and have a mode of production which is essentially capitalistic. The exact form and the way the capitalist mode of production manifests itself, in these countries, might display a few minor differences and peculiarities. In some cases state capitalism is the dominant form while in others the extremities of capitalist exploitation are let loose on both the polity and the economy. These differences in form are what is implied in the adjectives used to qualify Third World states as either being "moderates" or "radicals". This characterisation has often led to faulty categorisation of these social formations, in the sense that "radicals" are dubbed socialists while the "moderates" are hailed as capitalists. In essence, most of the so-called socialist states, say in Africa, are part and parcel of the capitalist world system.[18]

d. The Nature of the Mode of Production in Contemporary Zambia

The nature of precolonial modes of production in Zambia is not part of this study. Suffice to say that this is an area in Zambia's historiography that has not been adequately subjected to critical analysis. This oversight or lack of discourse on this era is not due to a lack of scholarly interest in the study of Zambia's precolonial history but rather due to the prevailing empiricist tradition which dominates historical research in Zambia. More especially this predominance is more pronounced in the precolonial era. Our concern in this chapter is confined to the contemporary period which begins with Zambia's incorporation into the capitalist world system.

The manner in which Zambia was incorporated into the capitalist world system provides a very good illustration of Lenin's description of the highest stage in the development of capitalism, namely, imperialism. Zambia's colonisation was initially undertaken by a commercial company, the British South African Company (BSACO) which secured a Royal Charter to annex and administer territories lying north of the Limpopo River on behalf of the British Crown. These territories became known as Southern Rhodesia, Northern Rhodesia and Nyasaland; now known as Zimbabwe, Zambia and Malawi, respectively.

Effective Company Rule in Zambia started a few years before the beginning of this century and lasted until 1923. During this period, the company was in complete charge of whatever took place in the country. The BSA Company among other things, took possession of all the mineral rights in the country, alienated large tracts of land, set up an inexpensive but rapacious administrative system and began to nurture a capitalist-oriented system of production. Having nurtured a capitalist system of production, and secured control and ownership of some of the vital means of production in the country, i.e. mineral rights, land and labour procurement systems, the company ceded its administrative functions to the British Colonial Office.[19]

The subsequent colonial government which took over from the BSA Company was also notorious for giving monopoly capital a lot of concessions to an extent that Zambia was dubbed as Company territory by both administrators and settlers at the time. This does not however deny the existence of some conflicts and contradictions among company officials, government functionaries as well as the champions of settler interests.[20] What is important to note, however, is the fact that these conflicts and contradictions were nonantagonistic and did not go as far as to challenge the necessity of the capitalist system.

However, the three protagonists, mentioned above, did not exclusively dominate the political sphere for a a very long time. Towards the end of the 1940's "colonial capitalism" had also nurtured its own contradiction in the form of African Nationalism.[21] It was this new element in Zambia's political sphere that brought the demise of colonial rule and ushered a "new era" of national independence.

The seventeen-odd years that constitute the era of national independence can be, for the purposes of analysis, be divided into four phases. These are:

1) Classical neocolonial phase: 1964-1967
2) Nationalist assault phase: 1968-1971
3) Nationalist consolidation and atrophy phase: 1972-1977
3) Multilateral neocolonial phase: 1978.

Obviously this periodisation is very arbitrary. Its purpose is merely that of highlighting the motifs of the evolution of Zambia's neocolonisation. The first phase is characterized as the classical neocolonial phase because this was the time when the independent Zambian government pursued a *laissez-faire* attitude towards monopoly capital. During this period the government believed or seemed to believe that the management of the national economy was largely the preserve of private businessmen. This period came to an abrupt end when the government failed to enjoin private business to rise up to the nation's expectation following the Unilateral Declaration of Independence, (U.D.I.) in Rhodesia and the economic problems that issued from that act which impinged on Zambia's development expectation.

The second phase issued from the disappointment described above. The government realised the folly of its credo and responded in a rather nationalistic manner by initiating a programme of nationalising what it believed to be the "commanding hights" of the economy. This phase was heralded by the Mulungushi Reforms of 1968 which were quickly followed by a series of other economic reforms which together brought most of the economic activities in the country under the "ownership" of the State.

To back this initial economic move politically, Zambia inaugurated the second Republic in 1972 in the form of a One-Party Participatory Democracy. Further reorganisations and takeovers were announced to buttress the state's foothold in the economy.[22] This phase is characterized as that of consolidation and atrophy largely because the efforts made to enhance state participation in the economy also created the backdrop for the atrophication of economic nationalism. This is due to a number of reasons which are many and varied. The most important being that: economic nationalism was not backed by political and ideological commitment to national development. As a result, the national aspiration was sacrificed on the altar of personal enrichment and careerism, albeit without professionalism. We shall return to this point later in connection with class formation during this particular period.

Towards the end of the 1970s, it became very clear that the initial energy of economic nationalism had been spent. The combination of ideological confusion and political inertia together with the world economic crisis which took the form of *stagflation* and recession created the condition for the advent of multilateral neocolonialism, characterized by the penetration of the IMF and its corequisites into the Zambian economy.[23] In Zambia, this phase of neocolonisation was manifested by negative economic growth rates, rising unemployment, graft and corruption, as well as beginnings of the "dissident movement."[24]

The above, albeit schematic, narrative of the contemporary Zambian situation is a mere reflection of the manner in which the capitalist mode of production was nurtured, established and functioned. What follows is a very brief characterization of the capitalist mode of production in Zambia, beginning with the initial penetration in the form of colonialism to present day neocolonialism.

We indicated, earlier on, that Zambia was initially colonised by a commercial company. The period of Company Rule was mainly devoted to the establishment of a capitalist economy in Zambia. This endeavour was accomplished by the destruction of the natural economy — precolonial modes of production — through the imposition of taxes and forced labour, alienation of land, mineral rights and the introduction of capitalist property relations. Furthermore, a governmental/administrative system was established to defend and sanction these new practices. Through the labour migration system, the rural economy was made completely inadequate to sustain the population and thereby the whole country was turned into a huge labour reservoir which was put to "good use" in the mines and plantations in Zambia and beyond.

The colonial government which took over from the BSA Company continued with the same practices, maybe with reduced zeal. However, to say that capitalist exploitation was proscribed by the colonial government would not be correct, witness the number of concessions that were granted to monopoly capital and the persistent policy of depressing the prices of land, labour and capital.[25] With the development of the mining industry in Zambia, the labour reservoir proved invaluable. The mining industry acted as the growth sector in the economy and stimulated growth in other sectors of the economy, such as agriculture, transport, power, construction and other service industries. What is interesting to note about these other industries is the fact that most of them were either subsidiaries of the giant mining companies or subsidiaries of other multinational companies, mostly based in South Africa. In other words, most of the economic activities in the country were owned and/or controlled by monopoly capital. The developments and the contradictions they introduced in the Zambian social formation provided the conditions for the rise of the nationalist movement and gave fuel to the struggle for independence.

The attainment of national independence which followed the period of the struggle for independence heralded the transition from colonial capitalism to neocolonialism. This statement does not, however, suggest that the attainment of national independence was nothing but a big joke. On the contrary, the attainment of national independence and democratic rights are very important landmarks in the history of any nation. However, the point that is made is this: the attainment of national independence in Zambia represented a superstructural change that did not run very deep. In other words, the political changes that were brought about by independence did not affect or transform significantly the dominant mode of production established by the colonial imposition. On the contrary, postcolonial developments in Zambia have tended to buttress and enhance the reproduction of the capitalist mode of production. As such, one can speak of the development of a neocolonial situation during the postcolonial period in Zambia.

The story of the way monopoly capital conducted business before nationalisation is ably narrated elsewhere.[26] However, after nationalisation, monopoly capital abandoned the use of more crude forms such as under-capitalisation and high levels of profit remittance and evolved a more so-phisticated and complex battery of mechanisms and conduits for expro-priating the huge amounts of surpluses from the Zambian economy. These range from joint ventures, "Zambianisation of Companies", transfer pricing, licensing, consultancy and through to contractual arrangements and a host of other mechanisms and conduits such as the use of the I.M.F. in collusion with the state.

Lately, this point has become very clear and more pernicious. A quick glance at the various investment scenarios used in most nationalised com-panies in Zambia reveals that these companies get most of their capital from the state, either as a loan or grant, as well as from West European bank con-sortia via the mediation of the World Bank, I.M.F. and the Zambian state. It is this scenario and phenomenon that Nabudere calls multilateral imperi-alism.[27]

What is happening in Zambia was very succinctly summarised by Petras when he wrote:

> The transfer from imperial to state ownership occurs without any radical shift in the social relations of production (including wage/salary differentials, managerial prero-gatives and/or the hierarchy of authority) market determinations or profit calculations. State ownership does not in any fundamental way transform the conditions of ex-ploitation of labour but rather reflects a shift in the surplus (a greater percentage is reinvested in productive facilities within the nation instead of the metropolis).[28]

In other words, monopoly capital continues to dominate the Zambian economy with the mediation of the state. However, this should not be understood as saying that nationalisation *per se* leads to some sort of state capitalism. On the contrary, and in the Zambian case in particular, state capitalism is largely a result of the incomplete and the haphazard manner in which nationalisation was done. As such, it could be said that the Zambian state, wittingly or unwittingly, actively participated in creating the conditions that have enhanced the neocolonisation of the Zambian social formation and by facilitating capitalist reproduction and thereby the capitalist mode of production in Zambia. It is in the light of such an analysis that one could say that the dominant mode of production in contemporary Zambia is the capitalist mode of production.

II. Description and Analysis of Class Formation in Contemporary Zambia

So far, we have argued that the Zambian social formation is part of the capitalist world system and that the capitalist mode of production is the dominant mode of production in the country. We have also argued that classes are basically determined by the mode of production that obtains in a social formation. From the above, we can surmise that the configuration of classes found in Zambia will consist of those major classes that comprise the capitalist mode of production. Namely the bourgeoisie, the proletariat and the peasantry. Having said this, we should again be reminded that these categorisations do not form homogeneous groups for they abound in intra-class distinctions and segmentation. Our general categorisation is merely meant to emphasise the need for us first to see the whole forest before concentrating on the individual trees.

Furthermore, it is important to bear in mind that the notion of class formation is not static but dynamic. As such, and in order for us to appreciate the configuration of the contemporary classes and their constituent elements within the Zambian social formation, it is important we analyse the processes by which these classes came into being, identifying their genesis, their evolution and their transformation, as the case may be. We shall proceed by first discussing the bourgeoisie, then the working class and lastly the peasantry.

a. The Bourgeoisie in Zambia

To say that Zambia is part of the world capitalist system is merely stating a very well known fact. However, an attempt at analysing the nature and form of the bourgeoisie in Zambia poses problems of a theoretical and analytical nature. Notwithstanding the traditional divisions within the bourgeoisie based on ownership of different "capitals" and the relative hegemony of the "capital" they represent, the Zambian bourgeoisie has further complications: the most important being that the various sections and fractions that comprise the Zambian bourgeoisie have very different and at times very unconventional "genealogies" which have tended to vary over time. In spite of these complications, however, it is still possible to discern three distinct sections within the Zambian bourgeoisie. These are: the imperial/comprador bourgeoisie, the bureaucratic/managerial bourgeoisie and the petty bourgeoisie.

The imperial and comprador section of the Zambian bourgeoisie is a very illusive category to analyse for it is composed of several discrete fractions. The most important of these fractions are: the imperial, the comprador and the national fractions. Admittedly, such a characterization sounds rather inelegant but so is reality, and any attempt to portray an elegant picture that does not correspond to the messy reality would, at best, be a fascinating waste of time. We shall proceed by describing the nature and formation of these fractions individually.

The imperial fraction of the bourgeoisie in the Zambian social formation is composed of that group of people which owns and controls the monopoly capital that dominates the Zambian economy. What is very characteristic about this group of people is that the persons who comprise it are not domiciled in Zambia. This is so because in colonial and neocolonial situations, the owners of finance or monopoly capital do not have to be physically domiciled in the dominated social formation but reside in the metropolis. Despite this physical absence, this fraction of the bourgeoisie plays an inordinately vital role in the life of the dominated social formation through an elaborate network of local representation. This applies to both colonial and neocolonial situations, the only difference being, the colour of the representatives. However, in both cases these local representatives work very closely with the state in promoting the interest of monopoly capital.

The comprador fraction of the Zambian bourgeoisie comprises those people who are the local representatives of the interests of monopoly capital. The members of this group are mainly directors of the local subsidiaries of the multinational corporations and their associated companies. The evolution of this fraction is very interesting. During the period of Company Rule, this fraction constituted the colonial government as well as being employees of the B.S.A. Company. In colonial times, members of this fraction were divested of political power but continued to act as the representatives of monopoly capital as well as being the ungazetted advisors to the colonial government. During the postcolonial period the constitution of this fraction underwent and is still undergoing major changes, in the sense that there is a growing number of Zambians being enlisted in the ranks of the comprador fraction of the bourgeoisie in Zambia. This process has evolved through two phases. In the first phase, Zambians were merely appointed to sit on the boards of directors. And in the second stage, which is more recent, Zambians are in fact given nominal ownership and executive chairmanship of these subsidiary companies. Sometimes this package comes complete with a change in the name of the company!

The social origins of the Zambian members of this fraction is also interesting and revealing in the sense that most of the members of this fraction were once members of the bureaucratic/managerial bourgeoisie and the petty bourgeoisie. Their recruitment into the comprador fraction is both a reflection of the fact that the "nationalist assault" on monopoly capital was coming to an end and that monopoly capital was readjusting itself in the face of the changing situation. It was under such circumstances that "the men on the spot" were recruited into the service of monopoly capital.[29] Their principal function is to facilitate the exploitation of the country's resources by monopoly capital while allaying nationalistic revulsion to an otherwise ugly face of foreign monopoly domination by presenting indigenous "faces". In cases where monopoly capital grants nominal ownership and executive chairmanship to a Zambian (who then claims to have bought out foreign interests in the company), monopoly capital uses this ploy to enhance the chances of using that company as a means of securing an entry into the Zambian market, because the "Zambian company" has more chances of securing contracts. It is therefore not surprising that it is mostly the engineering and service industries that employ this stratagem. Some of the members of this fraction were, not so long ago, accorded the title of being "good capitalists".[30]

Closely connected to the comprador fraction of the Zambian bourgeoisie is another fraction we shall call, for lack of a better term, the national fraction. This categorization is both confusing and controversial. The confusion is largely due to two factors. Firstly, this fraction displays relative autonomy from both monopoly capital and the state, and presents a more nationalistic posture when dealing with monopoly capital and the neocolonial state. Secondly, the so-called Kenyan debate which is centred on a study which claims to have "discovered a national bourgeoisie" has led a lot of scholars to begin looking for national bourgeoisie in neocolonies.[31] The debate is now well-known, and apart from raising a lot of confusion regarding this fraction, it is now generally accepted that a national bourgeoisie which is strong enough to begin challenging monopoly capital and its lackeys in a neocolony, is a contradiction in terms. Our national fraction of the bourgeoisie in Zambia has no such grandiose pretentions.

In general terms, this fraction of the Zambian bourgeoisie is largely engaged in: import-export trade and commerce; transport; commercial farming; small scale construction; manufacturing and mining. In most cases their businesses and operations are confined to various regions of the country and are usually owned by individuals in conjunction with members of their family. In Zambia, this group of people was predominantly of foreign origin during the colonial period. However, postcolonial developments, namely, the Mulungushi and the Matero Reforms of 1968 and 1969, respectively, contributed in introducing a "Zambian" element in the national fraction of the bourgeoisie. However, due to the pervasive dominance of monopoly capital in coalescence with state capitalism in Zambia, it is not possible to envisage a situation in which this fraction would some time, in future, dislodge the hegemony of the imperial, comprador and bureaucratic fractions. This statement does not deny the fact that members of the petty and bureaucratic bourgeoisie continue to join the ranks of the national bourgeoisie.

We have chosen to call this fraction "national" because this fraction is the Zambian counterpart of the national bourgeoisie elsewhere. Were it not for the neocolonisation of the Zambian social formation, it is this fraction that could have spear-headed the development of capitalism in Zambia. Unfortunately, history has robbed them of this endeavour. As such, some of its members have been forced to turn to more iconoclastic oppositional politics. The most vocal members of this fraction are now dubbed dissidents. We have described their struggle as iconoclastic because their continued existence in Zambia, ironically, depends on providing services to monopoly capital and state capitalism. While one may say that the members of the comprador fraction comprise those who have sold their hearts to the devil for a small share of monopoly profits; the members of the national fraction of the bourgeoisie could not be lionised as being lone rangers defending the integrity of a national economy.

The second section of the Zambian bourgeoisie is the bureaucratic/managerial bourgeoisie. Again this section poses some theoretical problems. The extent of the confusion surrounding this section of the bourgeoisie is reflected by the plethora of names and characterizations that are given to it in the literature. [32] Having said this, we still retain the term bureaucratic because it helps to clear a conceptual problem by directly associating this section with its source of power – the state. The bureaucratic section of the Zambian bourgeoisie is composed of three fractions, and these are: the top-level party and government functionaries; the toplevel executives in the state-owned corporations; and the topranking officers in the defence and security forces. These fractions only describe functional differences because the origins of their constituents are very similar and there is often horizontal mobility across these fractions.

There is a debate as to whether this section could be properly said to be part of the bourgeoisie. [33] We shall not go into that debate; suffice merely to indicate the outlines of the debate.

The argument advanced as to why this section of the bourgeoisie should not be regarded as being part of the bourgeoisie is a very simple and basic one, namely, the individual members of this group do not own any capital. However, the counter-argument acknowledges the charge but goes on to say that while individual members do not own any capital of their own, as groups, the members of this section of the bourgeoisie control the state which owns vast amounts of capital, thanks to state participation in the economy. It is further argued that as a result of their control of the state, it becomes possible for members of this group to appropriate, for its members, some of the surpluses that accrue to the state in the form of huge salaries, allowances and fringe benefits. [34] This does not include "scandal money".

Historically, this section of the Zambian bourgeoisie came into being after the attainment of national independence and its consolidation began to take a discernible form after the promulgation of the Second Republic in 1972. Notwithstanding the rumour in the chic circles of Zambian society that there are forty-four families that rule Zambia, the bureaucratic section of the bourgeoisie recruits its members from the ranks of the petty bourgeoisie where it originated. Because it works in close cooperation with the other sections of the bourgeoisie, some of its members leave this section to join the ranks of the comprador and national fractions. As such, its major function in society is that of maintaining the *status quo* while waiting to join the more rewarding fraction of the bourgeoisie.

The petty bourgeoisie constitutes the third section of the Zambian bourgeoisie. Again this section is illusive and conceptually problematic. For analytical purposes it is helpful to divide this section into two fractions. To do this we shall use the Poulantzasian categories of "the old" and "the new" petty bourgeoisie.[35]

The old petty bourgeoisie is that fraction of the petty bourgeoisie that is engaged in petty commodity production and retail trade. In this fraction, the units of production are usually based on family run workshops and family owned and run retail shops. This fraction is characterized as "old" because it retains the traditional characteristics of the petty bourgeoisie. In the colonial situation, this group of people was almost exclusively composed of people of Indian and Greek origin. However, since independence, and especially after the Mulungushi Reforms of 1968 a "Zambian" element has been added to this fraction.[36] The Zambian element mostly comprises bar-owners and the small commercial farmers.

The new petty bourgeoisie comprises the people that are usually referred to as the "middle class". It is different from the old petty bourgeoisie because it owns no material capital but owns specialised skills and knowledge which it sells for its livelihood. As such it enjoys a better standard of living than the working class and the peasantry. It is called "new" largely because its functions are a result of the new administrative and regulatory requirements of contemporary capitalism. In Zambia this fraction is composed of a large number of discrete groups and these are: middle level, government, party, military and security functionaries, members of professional groups, senior staff personnel in parastatal organisations and business institutions, etc. The common denominator of all these constituents of this fraction is the fact that all the people in these elements are products of a modern educational system.

The origin of this fraction of the petty bourgeoisie is closely connected with the advent of a modern educational system during the colonial era. In other words, due to the requirement of monopoly capital for a servicing cadre together with the expansion of the state sector and the bureaucracy, especially after independence, there has been an inordinately fast growth in the numbers of this fraction. This fraction has been growing faster than the old fraction of the petty bourgeoisie. It is from this fraction that the other sections and fractions of the Zambian bourgeoisie recruit. It could be said that the Zambian bourgeoisie, apart from the old petty bourgeois fraction, is largely a "meritocracy".

Together, both fractions of the Zambian petty bourgeoisie play a very critical part in helping to reproduce Zambia's neocolonial status. The old petty bourgeoisie fraction provides and, to an extent, helps in managing local market outlets for monopoly capital and running small lines of business that monopoly capital and/or the state sector cannot run efficiently and profitably. The new petty bourgeois fraction is charged with helping in the maintance of the *status quo* by carrying out administrative and regulatory functions in both the Zambian economy and polity and thereby enabling the reproduction of the neocolonial situation.

So far we have endeavoured to analyse the nature and formation of the Zambia bourgeoisie. In this effort, we have tried to show that the Zambian bourgeoisie is composed of three sections and each section comprises many fractions whose genealogies are diverse and constantly changing. Also implied in the above analysis is the fact that the Zambian bourgeoisie is a class without a historical mission because it is dominated by monopoly capital. In other words, we are restating Fanon's indictment when he wrote:

> Seen through its eyes, its mission has nothing to do with transforming the nation; it consists, prosaically, of being the transmission line between the nation and a capitalism, rampant though camouflaged, which today puts on a masque of neo-colonialism. The national bourgeoisie will be quite content with the role of the Western bourgeoisie's business agent, and will play its part without any complexes in a most dignified manner. But this same lucrative role, this cheap-jack's function, this meanness of outlook and this absence of all ambition symbolise the incapability of the national middle class to fulfil its historic role of bourgeoisie. Here, the dynamic, pioneer aspects, the characteristics of the inventor and of the discoverer of new worlds which are found in all national bourgeoisie are lamentably absent. In the colonial countries, the spirit of indulgence is dominant at the core of the bourgeoisie; and this is because the national bourgeoisie identifies itself with the Western bourgeoisie, from whom it has learnt its lessons. It follows the Western bourgeoisie along its path of negation and decadence without ever having emulated it in its first stages of exploration and invention.... In its beginning, the national bourgeoisie of the colonial countries identifies itself with the decadence of the bourgeoisie of the West. We need not think that it is jumping ahead; it is in fact beginning at the end. It is already senile before it has come to know the petulance, the fearlessness or the will to succeed of youth.[37]

We have quoted at length because this passage is an apt summary of the nature of bourgeoisie in a neocolony. Furthermore, this indictment helps to dispell any illusion about the neocolonial bourgeoisie which is prevalent among some elitist groups in Zambia and beyond.

b. The Working Class in Zambia

Zambia is one of the very few African countries that have a relatively large working class. The genesis of the Zambian working class is very much connected with the advent of colonialism and the establishment of the capitalist mode of production. Historical parallels concerning the proletarianisation of the Zambian worker could be drawn with a similar process which took place in Europe more than two centuries ago. Marx described the proletarianisation of the European worker in the following manner:

> Thus were the agricultural people, first forcibly expropriated from the soil, then driven from their homes, turned into vagabonds, and then whipped, branded, tortured by laws grotesquely terrible, into the discipline necessary for the wage system.[38]

Similar practices were used to turn Zambia's cultivators and pastoralists in order to turn them into migrant labourers and later into a modern working class. The main instruments used in Zambia to accomplish this exercise were: the imposition of taxes; the alienation of land; forced labour and labour recruitment bureaux. It was, at the time, alleged that these practices were aimed at excorcising the idleness that was inherent in the African and to make him work for the love of wages alone. These grotesque practices had a brutalising effect on the Zambian population and an equally devastating effect on the natural economy. In short, all of these capitalist machinations led to the genesis of the Zambian working class.

The process of proletarianisation in Zambia has evolved to a point where it is now possible to discern three distinct sections which constitute the Zambian working class. These are: the urban or modern sector proletariat; the rural or agricultural worker; and workers in the informal sector. These sections of the Zambian working class are not exclusive and homogeneous categories. The sections comprise a number of fractions and there is mobility across sections and fractions.

The urban or modern sector proletariat is the most important and easily recognisable section in the Zambian working class. This section comprises mostly workers who appear in labour statistics. For analytical purposes, the various fractions that constitute this section are classified according to the general industrial classification. And these are as follows: mining, manufacturing, construction, transport and power, distribution and catering, financial and government services.

The history of the Zambian working class, like most other developments in Zambia, is closely connected with the development of the mining industry. The mining industry was the first big employer of labour in the country. However, it was not until the late 1920s that large concentrations of African mine workers appeared on the Zambian Copperbelt. Before that, most of the migrant workers from Zambia went to work in mines and on farms in South Africa, Zimbabwe and Zaire. With the development of the mining industry in Zambia, especially after the commissioning of the first copper mines during the first years of the 1930s, more and more Zambians took up employment within the country. Because of the similar conditions of work, and the concentration of the mines in one part of the country, the mine workers in Zambia are the most homogeneous fraction of the Zambian working class. At one time the mining industry used to be the biggest employer in the country, but of late, this is not the case. In addition, the number of jobs in the industry have been declining. For example, between 1975 and 1979 about 13,000 jobs have been lost in the industry.[39] Over the years this fraction of the Zambian working class has evolved an organisational structure which has been able to defend working class interests, albeit and at times in a very confused manner. Having said this, we must hasten to add that the mine workers have, both in the past and the present, been the examplars of working class discipline, organisation and consciousness in the country.

The workers in the manufacturing industries in Zambia form another fraction of the Zambian working class. This group of workers is relatively new in the country, largely due to the fact that the manufacturing industry in Zambia only got going after the Rhodesian U.D.I. in 1965. Since then, the industry has become one of the largest employers in the country. In spite of the large number of people employed in the manufacturing industry, this fraction of the working class remains relatively weak owing to intra-industrial elements that constitute the fractions. Furthermore, the workers in the manufacturing industry are spread over the whole length of the line-of-rail and as such they lack both homogeneity and geographical concentration which the mine workers have.

The construction workers form the third fraction of the modern Zambian proletariat. This group of workers is very unstable and at times the most poorly paid and the most unskilled group of workers. The number of workers in the construction industry rises and falls depending on whether there is large-scale infrastructural developments or not. This instability holds true for both the colonial and the postcolonial periads. However, it should be mentioned that during the early part of the colonial period major infrastructural projects like the building of the rail line, roads and similar public works, a large section of workers were usually forced labourers and their employment lasted as long as the project lasted. In 1972 there were about 73,000 workers employed in the construction industry. However, the number of jobs, in the industry, fell to about 40,000 by 1979.[40] To date, the construction workers have not established a strong organisation that is strong enough to defend the workers' interests and fight the redundancies so common in the industry. Characteristically, the major employers in the construction industry are private, and in most cases foreign firms.

The fraction consisting of workers in the transport and the electricity industries is employed by the parastatals. The transport workers are largely composed of people employed in the railway companies and the road transport companies. The Zambia Railway employees are one of the oldest groups of workers in the country and date back to colonial times. On the other hand, workers in the Uhuru Railway (TAZARA) have only less than ten years of existence and comprise people from two countries with different industrial traditions. Similarly, the workers in road transport are of recent origin and enjoy relatively different conditions of service depending on the company they work for. In general terms, however, workers in the transport sector have the advantage of easy mobility despite their lack of geographical concentration. Unlike the transport workers, the workers in the electricity industry are relatively small in number and tend to be more of office workers. Over the years, this fraction of the working class has not increased in number significantly.

The workers employed in the distribution and catering services comprise two elements. One element consists of people employed in the trading sector of the economy and the other comprises people who work in restaurants and hotels. The elements that work in the trading sector, despite the long history of employment, remain unorganised. This is largely due to the fact that a large part of this group is in the employ of the old petty bourgeoisie as shop assistants and as such the conditions of their employment are of a personal nature and are characterized by isolation. On the other hand, the workers in the catering industry have the advantage of being concentrated in large numbers and have since organised themselves in a relatively strong union.

The workers in the financial sector of the economy form a fraction which consists of elements from the banking, insurance, real estate and other similar business services. Characteristically, this group is composed of people who have had the benefit of higher education and are mainly employed by private firms. Despite the fact that this group of people has a large element of what we called the new petty bourgeoisie, their poor conditions of service have driven them to militancy in the defence of working class rights.[41]

Lastly, the state employees form another fraction of the working class. However, this fraction needs very careful disaggregation because a large section of the state employees are part of the new petty bourgeoisie. The fraction that we are interested in here consists of the lower part of the civil service, namely, the clerical staff, technicians, drivers, orderlies, cleaners, security guards, etc. Such elements are notoriously lowly paid by the state and have almost inhuman conditions of service. Unfortunately, this fraction of the working class has been mystified by the top civil servants into believing that it is part of the public service and not part of the working class. Of late, it has become relatively difficult to sustain this hoax and the lower sections of the civil service have come to know that they are part of the exploited and oppressed groups in the country and are beginning to fight for their rights, albeit in a rather *ad hoc* manner.[42]

The second section of the Zambian working class is composed of agricultural workers. This section of the Zambian working class comprises two fractions: plantation workers and seasonal workers. In the past, agricultural workers used to be one of the biggest groups of workers in the country. Of late, however, their numbers have been declining very fast due to four major reasons. Firstly, there has been a gradual decline of the agricultural industry in the country especially those that employ such labour.[43] Secondly, there has been a gradual mechanisation of agriculture in the country. Thirdly, the minimum wage has been increased and farmers claim that they can no longer employ as many farm hands as they used to do previously. Lastly, the abolition of poll tax has relieved the poorer sections of the Zambian population from paying any taxes and as such they are not forced to seek wage employment; more so, agricultural work.

The largest fraction of the agricultural or rural workers consists of plantation workers. Zambian agriculture is dominated by a relatively large plantation sector which could be divided into two parts, large scale plantations and large commercial farms. While the plantations are of recent origin, the commercial farms dominated the agricultural industry during the colonial period. The commercial farms were notorious for the low wages, that they paid their workers. However, due to isolation and the relative lack of education, agricultural workers have always found it difficult to organise themselves into a strong union that would fight for better conditions of work and better pay. On the other hand, plantation workers have, in spite of being new-comers, already established a relatively strong organisational structure. Furthermore, there is a strong possibility that plantation workers will soon increase in number and strength. This new input is likely to come from the people who will be employed on the plantations that will be established as a result of the Operations Food Production Programme which was launched a few months ago.[44]

Seasonal agricultural labourers form the second fraction of the agricultural workers in Zambia. This group of workers is composed of several elements. The most important of these are: migrant workers, seasonal farm hands and itinerant rural workers. Migrant workers are almost a historical category and are no longer a significant group of workers in Zambia today. However, during the early part of the colonial period, this group of workers was the largest one, but with the abolition of poll tax, this group was drastically reduced. The group that is still of great significance is that group of workers who are employed to do agricultural work during harvest time. The largest element in this group consists of sugar-cane cutters who are brought in to cut sugar-cane during the cutting season and are sent home after the season. The itinerant rural workers are another element usually composed of people from depressed areas who cannot subsist from the land and are forced to look for casual work on the farms of more prosperous farmers. Again, this group of people is slowly disappearing and giving way to formal employment. The third section of the Zambian working class comprises of a number of highly discrete and marginalised fractions and elements. Euphemistically known as workers in the informal sector of the Zambian economy, but otherwise known as the lumpen-proletariat. Fanon gave a graphic description of these people when he described them as:

> that horde of starving men, uprooted from their tribe and clan. . . (who when they did not find a market for their labour took to stealing, debauchery and alcoholism. . . the pimps, the hooligans, the unemployed petty criminals. . . the prostitutes too, and the maids who are paid two pounds a month, all the hopeless dregs of humanity, all who turn in circles between suicide and madness. . . The constitution of a lumpen-proletariat is a phenomenon which obeys its own logic, and neither the brimmings of the missionaries nor the decrees of the central government can check its growth. This lumpen proletariat is like a horde of rats; you may kick them and throw stones at them, but despite your efforts they'll go on gnawing at the roots of the tree.[45]

The above quotation gives a good description of the lot of a large number of people who live in the shanty townships of all Zambia's urban centres. There are two fractions that are discernible in this section of the Zambian population. One fraction comprises the people who live on the fringes of society but not degraded enough to engage in criminal activities. The main elements in this fraction are composed of those people in domestic service, market vendors and the so-called self-employed craftsmen. The other fraction is mostly composed of criminal elements such as pimps, prostitutes, black-marketeers, shebeen queens, petty thieves and members of organised crime. This fraction of the lumpen-proletariat is on the increase and Zambia is at the moment overwhelmed by a rising tide of crime and the blackmarketeering of essential commodities.

What is common to all of the three sections of the Zambian working class is the fact that all the members of these sections, fractions and elements discussed above are people who have been divorced from the means of production by a process of proletarianisation. This process began with the advent of colonial rule which introduced the capitalist mode of production into the Zambian social formation. Despite the different processes that have led to the formation of the various sections, fractions and elements of the Zambian working class, the Zambian working class comprises those who have nothing to sell, to ensure their existence, but their own labour. Marx described a similar process very succinctly when he wrote:

Hence, the historical moment which changes the producers into wage workers, appears, on the one hand, as their emancipation from serfdom and from the fetters of the guilds, (read tribal society), and this side alone exists for our bourgeoisie historians. But, on the other hand, these new freemen became sellers of themselves only after they had been robbed of all their own means of production, and of all the quarantees of existence afforded by the feudal arrangements (read tribal society). And the history of this, their expropriation, is written in the annals of mankind in letters of blood and fire.[46]

This history of the Zambian working class is now about eighty years long and it continues to be written daily with "blood and fire".

c. The Peasantry in Zambia

The third social class in Zambia is the peasantry. The peasantry, as a class in an African social formation is full of both misunderstanding and confusion. The confusion is mainly due to the mistaken notion that the peasantry as a social class is a feudal phenomenon, complete with the manorial system. As such, the peasantry is not supposed to engage in a money enomony. The advocates of this view are of the opinion that in Africa there is no peasantry but rather "husbandmen". Another group of social scientists, on the other hand, are of the view that anybody who is engaged in "primitive agriculture" is a peasant, and from this general statement it is concluded that Africa is teeming with peasants since the majority of people in Africa practice primitive primitive agriculture. Reality, however, is more complex than what the advocates of both points of view would have us to believe. First, it is recognised that the African peasantry is an integral part of the capitalist system.[47] Secondly, it should be accepted that not all rural dwellers and agriculturalists are peasants. Thirdly, a proper understanding and analysis of the class nature of the people who live in rural areas requires disaggregation and a more sensitive analytical framework which takes into account the nature of capitalist penetration that is specific to the social formation of the region in question.[48]

As has already been pointed out, the prime concern of capital in Zambia was not aimed at extracting surpluses from peasant production but to create a labour reservoir for the capitalist enterprises which were being set up in the region. Furthermore, since the move towards labour stabilization and the influx of people into urban areas after independence, the concern of both capital and the state has been that of trying to keep people out of the urban centres because the labour that is required for capitalist production no longer needs to come from the rural areas. In other words, as far as capital is concerned, the rural areas are no longer the place where labour is reproduced and all who live in the rural areas in Zambia are, to put it mildly, a surplus population. With the above reservations in mind, it is now possible to isolate the various sections and fractions that constitute the peasantry in Zambia. To do this we shall use Mao's scheme which divides the peasantry into three sections: the rich peasants, the middle peasants and the poor peasants.[49]

The rich peasants are those peasants that own their means of production and employ labour. In Zambia, this section of the peasantry is composed of two fractions: the lower or poor stratum of commercial farmers and the improved farmers. During the colonial period, the former fraction comprised of poor white farmers. After independence, a number of Zambians joined this fraction including the element known as the weekend farmers.[50] The improved farmers are very similar to the former fraction except that their farms are in the (tribal) Trust Reserve Land. In spite of the fact that these farmers do not own any title deeds for the land they work, they own enough capital to be able to farm commercially. A large number of these farmers are those that have benefitted from the agricultural loans that were made available to Africans after independence. So far the section of the rich peasantry in Zambia is a transitory category because some of its members make enough money to turn into capitalist farmers, while others may be ruined and join the ranks of their poorer brethren.

The middle peasantry in Zambia consists of those farmers that are referred to as the emergent farmers. Almost all of these farmers work on the land that is in the Trust Reserve and own their means of production, but largely depend on family labour for most of the work and on occasion employ seasonal labour. This group of farmers came into being during the latter part of the colonial period and its members are mainly found in the Central, Southern and Eastern provinces of Zambia. Since independence, the emergent farmer has been the target group for most of the agricultural development strategies that have been devised in all the three development plans. To date, however, this group of farmers has defied the expectations of the development planners in the country and has not delivered the goods of an agrarian revolution. The reason for this failure, however, is not due to laziness as it is often alluded but rather due to the agricultural finance companies which, in Zambia, play a role similar to that of the legendary oriental money lender.[51]

The overwhelming majority of the people in the rural areas in Zambia constitute the poor section of the Zambian peasantry. This section of the peasantry is composed of a number of fractions. However, what is common among all these diverse groups of people is the fact that almost all of them do not own any means of production and are marginally involved in the Zambian economy. The fact that they get their livelihood from the land is largely due to ecological and survival reasons because, given the chance, most of them could turn to gathering and hunting. Some members of this section work as seasonal workers on the farms of their more prosperous neighbours while others live on stipends from their relatives who are in employment. In other words, this section of the Zambian peasantry leads a very precarious life because its members have been marginalised: first, by colonial policies and now by current government policies which have enhanced both neocolonialism and rural underdevelopment.

Thus, the peasantry as a class in the Zambian social formation has its origin thanks to the penetration of the capitalist mode of production. However, the various sections and fractions that comprise the peasantry in Zambia have different histories and possibly equally different destinies. What is evident at the moment is the fact that their destiny lies outside the known proclivities and interests of monopoly capital and neocolonialism. So far, the peasantry has been the most gullible class in Zambia because of the deplorable living conditions and cultural backwardness which constitute peasant reality. And as such the Zambian peasantry remains open and vulnerable to manipulation and machinations of monopoly capital and its local lackeys.

A Concluding Note

In this chapter I have tried to do two things. First, I endeavoured to throw some light on some of the theoretical problems encountered when analysing class formation in a Third World country dominated by monopoly capital. These problems range from those that are of a definitional and conceptual nature to those that are more of a derivative and associational nature. In our quest for a simple but clear theoretical framework, we have evolved and used one which sees classes as groups of people which are bounded and determined by historical developments and are constituted by sections and fractions which are in constant state of flux. In addition, the development and transformation of these sections and fractions is governed by the laws of motion, the laws of social change and development.

My second task was that of describing and analysing the nature of class formation in contemporary Zambia. In this endeavour, I have argued that the Zambian social formation, like most peripheral capitalist social formations is composed of the three dominant classes of peripheral capitalism, namely, the bourgeoisie, the proletariat and the peasantry. These classes are constituted by sections and fractions, some of which are unique and specific to the Zambian situation, and as such their objectification is bounded within the logic of Zambian history and development.

If this study has achieved these limited aims then my task has been accomplished. It should be mentioned, however, that this study did not explore a very rich and sometimes the most dramatic and important aspect of class existence; namely, class struggle. Our plea for this, seemingly, gross omission is that any meaningful attempt at understanding the unfolding dialectic of class struggles ought to begin with a clear understanding of the nature of the actors themselves, and the context of their objectification. In addition, such an endeavour ought to be grounded within the nature and logic of the determining laws of motion, i.e. the laws that determine societal change. It is from this launching pad, we believe, that one could with relative facility delve into the intricacies of class struggles and the explanation of the alliances that classes forge in the act of struggle. Unfortunately, such a very fascinating endeavour is beyond the confines of this chapter.

Notes

1. In most of what has been written by African leaders concerning African socialism there is an attempt to show that African societies were classless. See: G N Mudenda: "Problems and Prospects of Class Analysis in the Study of African Social Formations" *Journal of African Marxists,* issue 1 Nov. 1981 pp. 67-71.
2. The radical trend in African scholarship began with minor "rebellions" within various disciplines in the social sciences. These departures culminated in a call for an interdisciplinary approach to the study of the situation in Africa. This new breed of scholars contribute to more radical and committed journals like the *Review of African Political Economy* and the *Journal of African Marxists* to name but two.
3. Marx, K. and Engels, F., *The Communist Manifesto,* Penguin Books 1967, p. 79.
4. Marx, K. *The Eighteenth Brumaire of Louis Bonaparte,* George Allen & Unwin, 1926 p. 133.
5. Lenin, V.I. *Collected Works,* Vol. 29 Progress Publishers 1965, p. 421 Emphasis added.
6. Marx, K. *A Contribution to a Critique of Political Economy,* Progress Publishers 1970, p. 20.
7. Marx, K. *Capital,* Vol, I, Progress Publishers, 1975 pp. 314-315.
8. There is a debate on ownership and control of a business enterprise. Traditionally, ownership was closely associated with control. However, some argue that since the managerial revolution, the two are not identical. Our attitude is that the debate borders on the pedantic and we see no point in trying to split a very thin hair in the name of erudition.
9. Marx, K. *Capital* Vol. III Progress Publishers, 1975 p. 886.
10. Bukharin, N. *Historical Materialism: A System of Sociology,* Allen & Unwin, 1926 pp. 292-293.
11. Poulantzas, N. *Political Power and Social Classes,* New Left Books, 1973, and *Classes in Contemporary Capitalism* New Left Books 1976.
12. Lenin, V.I. *Selected Works,* Vol. I, Progress Publishers, 1970, p. 737.
13. Forster-Carter, A. "The Modes of Production Controversy", *New Left Review* No. 107 1978, pp. 47-77.
14. The colonial state is known for having preserved some old and pre-colonial structures like chieftaincy and put them in the service of capital. As a result, if one does

not look at this transformation of functions one may miss a very important societal change.

15. Alavi, H. "The Structure of Colonial Social Functions", a paper presented at the Conference on *Underdevelopment an International Comparison,* University of Bielefeld, July 1-7 1979 p. 9. We have in this text omitted the phrase "Colonial mode of Production" because it might introduce undue misunderatanding of the text.

16. Nkrumah, K. *Neo-Colonialism: The Last State of Imperialism,* Panaf Books 1970. Unfortunately much of African scholarship is still in the pre-history of this seminal work.

17. Mafeje, A. *Science, Ideology and Development: Three essays on Development Theory,* Scandinavian Institute of African Studies, 1978, p. 19.

18. The radical/moderate typology has led to more confusion than clarification, for example countries like Zambia, Tanzania and Somalia are regarded as socialist because of radical rhetoric. One should not judge a country's orientation by what that country says or might have said but by what that country does in political, economic and ideological practice.

19. It is interesting to note that the granting of "huge" and exclusive prospecting concessions to big financial interests, i.e., the Nkana Coneession (466,200 hectares) and the Rhodesia Congo Border Concession (12,946,000 hectares), was done before handing over administrative functions to the Colonial Office.

20. *Proceedings of the Northern Rhodesian Legislative Council.* These documents provide very interesting reading to a student of colonial Zambia. It turns out that the most vocal and articulate member advocating settler interests was Leopold Moore who saw nothing in the colonial administration but an attempt to perpetuate aristocratic privileges. He was contemptuous of the arrogance of those who stayed at home and knew no better, but who wanted to run the show from the comforts of Whitehall and exercise altruism by proxy. Moore was equally bitter about monopoly capital. To him the company (BSA Company) represented a grotesque and unholy combination of financial monopoly, social privilege and political absolutism responsible for holding up the country's wealth and development. Abstracted from J. W. Davidson; *The Northern Rhodesian Legislative Council,* Faber and Faber, 1946, p. 71.

21. The more virile strand that went into the making of the Nationalist movement in Zambia came from the Trades Union. Ironically this link seems to have been weakened if not broken after the attainment of national independence.

22. In 1973 the President announced the abrogation of management contracts with the former owners of the nationalised mining companies, the formation of MEMACO, and appointed Zambian Directors of NCCM, RCM and MEMACO. In the Watershed Speech in 1975, the President announced that all land was to belong to the state.

23. For an explanation and analysis of the role of the I.M.F., I.B.R.D., etc. see Nabudere D.W. *The Political Economy of Imperialism,* Zed Press, 1977.

24. The dissidents are those Zambian businessmen who have been vocal in critising Kaunda's economic policies. They were called that by President in mid-1980 in contrast to the "good capitalists".

25. The colonial government had a policy of attracting settlers by making land very cheap. The price of labour was kept low by, inter alia, making the price of food cheap. Some aspects of this policy are still contentious in Zambia today. See *Times of Zambia,* Vol No. 5,656 February 4, 1982.

26. See Martin, A. *Minding Their Own Business,* Penguin African Library, 1972, and Lanning, G. & Muller, M. *Africa Undermined,* Penguin Books, 1979.

27. Nabudere, D.W. *The Political Economy of Imperialism* op.cit., and *Essays on the Theory and Practice of Imperialism*, Onyx Press, 1979.
28. Petras, J. "State Capitalism and the Third World", *Development and Change*, Vol. 8 No. 1 1977, p. 7.
29. A large part of the members of the comprador bourgeoisie were men who held high positions in the parastatal and government sectors. As such, it could be adduced that, previous to their present position, they had dealings with their "new master" who found them suitable to echo the master's voice because they were locally well placed and well connected.
30. President's speech, op.cit.
31. See "Capitalist Accumulation in the Periphery – The Kenyan Case Re-examined" in the *Review of African Political Economy* No. 17 Januara-April, 1980.
32. Leys, C. *Underdevelopment in Kenya: The Political Economy of Neo-Colonialism*, Heinemann, 1977.
33. This could be called the Dar-es-Salaam debate which was sparked off by I. Shivji's *Class Struggles in Tanzania*, Tanzania Publishing House, 1975.
34. Top executives in Zambia enjoy a lot of benefits, such as huge salaries, allowances, free transport, accommodation, servants, etc. It has been mooted that they constitute an aristocracy which dares not speak its name. What is interesting about most of these privileges is that they are not provided for under the published conditions of service.
35. Poulantzas, N. *Social Classes in Contemporary Capitalism*, op.cit.
36. The areas of business that were affected by the Mulungushi Reforms of 1968 were mainly retail trading, construction, and a reorganisation of fiscal policies in relation to those aimed at lending credit to small businessmen.
37. Fanon, F. *The Wretched of the Earth*, Penguin Books, 1980, pp. 122-123.
38. Marx, K. *The Genesis of Capital*, Progress Publishers, 1974, p. 32.
39. Central Statistical Office, *Monthly Digest of Statistics*, Vol. XIV, Nos. 1-3 Jan-March 1980 p. 5.
40. ibid p. 5.
41. For example, employees in the banks have to secure their own housing and, as a result, the majority live in poorer accommodation than their counterparts employed in the government and the parastatal sectors.
42. A good number of people, especially in the lower ranks of the civil service have taken to individualistic forms of protest such as being drunk on the job or being deliberately, rude insubordinate and inefficient.
43. A good example of this is the collapse of the tobacco industry despite the fact that Zambia has an ideal climate for growing tobacco.
44. Republic of Zambia, *Project: Operation Food Production*, State House, 23rd May 1980.
45. Fanon, F. op.cit (passim) pp. 103-104.
46. Marx, K. "Primitive Accumulation" quotes from McClellan, D. *Karl Marx: Selected Writings*, Oxford University Press, 1978 p. 485.
47. Historically-speaking, feudalism is associated with serfdom, while the peasantry was an Anglo-French phenomenon, the two countries in which capitalism developed at an earlier stage. For further discussion refer to the "Editorial" in the *Review of African Political Economy*, No. 10.
48. Amin, S. "Underdevelopment and Dependence in Black Africa: Origins and Contemporary Forms". *Journal of Modern African Studies*, Vol. 10 No. 4 1972, also see Lenin V.I. *Development Capitalism in Russia*, Progress Publishers, 1976.

49. Mao Tse Tung, *Selected Works:* Vol. 1, Foreign Languages Press, 1969, pp. 13-19.
50. The weekend farmers are mostly "leaders" who bought farms for prestigious reasons without using the farms productively; instead the farms were turned into venues for parties on weekends. The more unkind commentators claim that these farms have produced more of debauchery than agricultural produce!
51. A number of telling exposes have been written on the rapacious nature of ADMARC, the Malawian counterpart of Zambia's Agricultural Finance Companies. Apart from a few journalistic news releases, the Zambian companies still remain *terra incognita*.

Chapter 6
The Sexual Division of Labour in the Urban Informal Sector: A
Case Study of Lusaka*
by Raj Bardouille

Introduction

This paper is intended to examine the economic participation role of the
urban poor in the townships of Lusaka who have become marginalised from
the dominant productive sectors of the Zambian economy. More specifically
the study attempts to identify and examine the nature of the sexual division of labour of the so-called labouring poor, whose dominant means of
survival is poorly paid work, and then to an analysis of women's activities in
the retail sector in which the majority are forced to seek refuge. It focuses on
the determinants, such as sex and age, of different scale activities, the different degrees of autonomy over the production process and the extent of
the subordination of informal sector operators to capital. In an effort to
understand how the urban poor get by in informal sector activities, we analyse
the nature of structural, technical and cultural constraints and furthermore
whether such constraints affect women and men differently; the scope for
upward mobility of informal sector operators and the extent to which such
upward mobility is determined by the sex of the individual in the informal
sector. As such, the analysis here is less concerned with women and men
who earn their living in secure wage/salary employment in the capitalist in-
dustrial/commercial sectors.

I argue that the external and internal processes over time have structured
and shaped the productive relations and the social division of labour not only
by class but also by sex. The case study material, covering four different
residential areas in Lusaka, is utilised to illustrate that sex becomes a critical

* This contribution is part of an ongoing project on "Women's Economic Contribution
in the Urban Informal Sector: A Case Study of Some Townships of Lusaka". The
project is funded by the University of Zambia and it is being carried out under the
auspecies of the Manpower Research Unit of the Institute for African Studies, University of Zambia.

variable in determining differential work opportunities of women and men both in formal and informal sectors. Data analysed in this paper are not necessarily representative of the entire urban poor in Zambia or for that matter Lusaka, but they are also not unrepresentative of the majority of the urban poor, particularly women.

In tackling the question of employment one must consider broadly how people are involved in the economic process and what type of work they are brought to do; under what conditions and circumstances people work and whether the nature of work done by women and men differs, what induces women to seek income-generating activities and what alternative opportunities exist for women and men in the sphere of work. Some of these issues can be understood better when placed in the context of the socioeconomic formation of a given society. For this purpose, I briefly examine the nature of structural changes that over time have taken place in the Zambian economy with particular reference to he status of the formal sector employment and sexual division of labour among the employed work force. A vast majority of the urban people (and in particular women) who are unable to find formal wage employment must seek alternative income-generating activities in the less formal (or so-called informal) sector. The case study illustrates that even in the less formal sector, the survival strategies of the marginalised people can be clearly distinguished on the basis of the sexual division of labour.

Structural Changes in the Zambian Economy and Status of Formal Employment

The economy of Zambia like most Third World countries may be characterized by the phenomenon of dualism, both economic and social. Economic dualism may be understood in relation to the coexistence of two sectors or systems comprising a small modern sector and a large rural sector within one economy. But implicit in a dual economic structure is the parallel development of a dual social structure comprising the vast majority of rural communities in the traditional sector and urban masses in the informal sector. The traditional sector (including the urban informal sector) is relatively inpendent of the modern sector and rather peripheral to the dominant productive sectors. The connection between the two sectors is the flow of the cheap labour force from the traditional to the modern sector which has had very damaging consequences for the former.

The foundation of a dual economy in Zambia was laid by colonialism, aimed at the disruption of a simple and subsistence-oriented economy and the integration of a section of the population into Western capitalist economies.

This was initially achieved through the introduction of a migratory labour force to the neighbouring mines. With the discovery of workable deposits in Northern Rhodesia, the demand for cheap labour for the mines increased. Consequently, both internal and external migration became widespread. It should be remarked that the migratory labour force comprised exclusively young and able-bodied men. The introduction of plantation agriculture further increased the demand for cheap wage labour and turned more peasants into wage workers. The imposition of but and poll taxes by the colonial administration served as an effective mechanism which forced Africans to earn cash through wage labour. Colonial policies systematically undermined precapitalist agricultural and trading systems in Northern Rhodesia and forced Africans into providing cheap labour for the mines and plantations.

The loss of tens of thousands of young men who were forced out of the villages in search of wage employment meant that agricultural activities had to be left to women, children and older people who were left behind in the villages. Such colonial regulations had both economic and social consequences. Africans were forced off the best lands and these were turned over to white commercial farmers. Because of the relatively inferior quality of lands given to Africans combined with the low level of productive forces (as young men left the villages in search of wage employment) in agriculture, it became increasingly difficult to maintain levels of agricultural productivity previously attained. This brought about a productivity gap between men employed in the modern sector and women and old men in the traditional agricultural sector. The previous status of women as independent producers was thus undermined. The families were disintegrated as a result of the migration of men. Women and older men had to bear the entire burden of sustaining their dependents. (The implications of colonial policies on women are discussed elsewhere: R. Bardouille, 1981).

Although villages became well integrated into the international capitalist system through the sale of labour power in the mines and plantations and purchase of imported commodities (because of colonial restrictions on local productive activities including handicrafts and trade to some extent destroyed African handicraft industries) manufactured in the Metropole, the rural economy was left very much out of any benefit from the development of the mining enclave. Apart from industrial projects, such as railways, roads, electricity etc., directly required in facilitating production and export of copper and imports of manufactured goods, the colonial administration had no intentions of diverting copper earnings to the general industrial development of the country.

The formation of the Federation in 1953 further retarded the establishment of a wider industrial base in Zambia as the colonial administration chose the cities of Salisbury and Bulawayo (in Southern Rhodesia) as the centres of industrial development for the region. Restrictive laws hindered the advancement of native African population in Northern Rhodesia despite the country's advanced mining industry. With respect to technical training, it should be remarked that no African was permitted by law to be apprenticed in Northern Rhodesia (Govt. of the Republic of Zambia, 1966). The educational system which Zambia inherited was utterly inadequate (with some 1200 secondary school graduates and about 100 university level graduates) to serve the needs of the newly independent country. Thus, on the eve of independence Zambia inherited a dual socio-economic structure characterized by a technological modern mining enclave in the midst of a rural and traditional agricultural economy.

The introduction of wage labour set up a basis for class formation in Zambia. The class relationships became increasingly dependent on the dominant institutions, such as the international finance capital, technology, commerce, banking etc., of the export enclave. A few entreprenenual Africans succeeded in establishing small stores or a bar/tavern to serve the village community. A few who benefited from the limited educational facilities managed to obtain jobs as lower level clerks or petty administrative officials or teachers. But it was men who strove into these jobs because of sexist policies of colonials which precluded women from the limited educational as well as work opportunities. Although commercial farming made it extremely difficult for African cultivators to sell their produce in the open market, some "progressive" farmers managed to expand their output by extending their land area on which the low-cost hired labour of neighbours was used. These emergent progressive farmers gradually accumulated wealth. In this way, new class relationships emerged with a few well-to-do traders, farmers and low-level civil servants benefitting from the dominant export enclave, while the vast majority of the native population was turned into a reservoir of cheap labour even though international capital did not need all of it.

Soon after political independence the government of the Republic of Zambia became increasingly aware of the dependent nature of the Zambian economy. Something had to be done to achieve some measure of autonomy and control over the most productive sector – mining in this case. The Mulunguhsi economic reforms announced in 1968 were aimed at attaining rapid expansion of the manufacturing sector through partial state participation. The strategy chosen for general industrial development was basically oriented towards import-substitution. A general industrial development programme as well as the expansion of social and economic infrastructure – i.e. schools, hospitals, roads, electricity, etc. – meant that government had to commit large investments in the planned programmes. Since copper was the only productive and promising sector in relation to the generation of reinvestible resources, the government, in 1969, chose to nationalise the mining industry through equity participation (a 51.0 % interest in industry). Partial nationalisation was to provide means to control the conditions and effects of mine production. Consequently, joint ventures were formed between an agency of the state and two multi-national corporations, the Anglo American Group and the Roan Selection Trust. A parastatal organisation, the Industrial Development Corporation (INDECO), was placed in charge of partially-nationalised mining companies. In 1971, the Mining Development Corporation (MINDECO), placed under the Ministry of Mines, was delegated to oversee the mines operations. MINDECO had on its staff some technically competent people who felt obligated to the operations of the mines. This brought about conflicts between the technical class and the local political/bureaucratic class (INDECO) whose interests are protected through the mediation of the state (Bardouille, 1981a). Consequently, the overseeing operations of the mines were removed from MINDECO and placed under ZIMCO. As more parastatal companies were formed, the demand for local executive and managerial personnel also began to increase. The Civil Service was also increasingly Zambianised. Consequently in the few years after independence, Zambia experienced a burgeoning bureaucratic class manning the Civil Service and the parastatal sector including the mining complex. The political class, be that the bureaucratic bourgeoisie in the public sector or executive and managerial bourgeoisie in the parastatal sector, acts as a mediator between international capital and the state and through the latter it is able to preserve the interests of local elites and international capital.

The attainment of political independence in Zambia and likewise in Central and Southern Africa has done little to alter the fundamental institutions and class relationships which emerged during colonial rule. Against that background, I examine the status of formal employment and in particular the Lusaka labour market and work opportunities of women and men at the national and Lusaka level. This will provide a basis for understanding work opportunities for women and men at the micro-level, i.e. the case study level.

Status of formal employment

Although the basis for wage employment was laid during the colonial era, the working population of Zambia at the time of independence was predominantly in rural occupations. After the attainment of political independence, migration controls were removed and Zambia experienced an unprecedented rate of urbanisation between 1964 and 1974. Although the drift of the population to urban areas since 1974 has been somewhat slower, population estimates until 1984 suggest that urbanisation will continue and by the end of this period, approximately 45.0 % of the population will be in the urban areas mainly in the narrow "line-of-rail" in Central and Copperbelt provinces (C.S.O., 1979).

The implications of an ever-growing urban population due to migration and the natural growth of the population are serious in relation to the provision of employment, housing and related social services. Over the First National Development Plan period, i.e. 1966-1971, wage employment increased from 233,000 to 310,000 or at an average annual rate of nearly 6.0 %. The expansion in employment was mainly due to Zambianisation of the Civil Service sector, increased government expenditures on education, health and related social services. Additional employment was also generated as a result of the establishment of import-substitution industries. However, during the Second National Development Plan period, i.e. 1972-1976, growth in wage employment was negligible, i.e. only 2820 additional jobs were created as opposed to a target of 20,000 jobs annually. The inability of the economy to generate additional wage employment may be attributed to its structural dependence on international capital and its close links to external capitalist economies.

The operations of the mining industry are geared towards the needs of metropolitan countries. The capital intensive nature of imported technology utilised in this industry restricts employment generation potentials and this is further aggravated by the fact that interindustry linkages are weak. The productive sector is closely linked to external capitalist economies and lacks the internal dynamics to effect development within the raw material producing country. Similarly, the import-substitution strategy adopted in the manufacturing sector in Zambia is also unable to generate sufficient employment for the growing labour force. The failure of this sector to spread increased productivity in all sectors of the Zambian economy may be attributed to the nature of products manufactured for which not only technology is imported but in some cases even raw materials utilised are also imported. Thus the distorted nature of the manufacturing sector is unable to stimulate and spread employment through the establishment of interindustry linkages in the wider economy (Seidman, 1974). The problem of development in the context of Zambia seems to lie deep within the system itself and that is the lack of direction in national development goals and a clear development strategy (Turok, 1980).

Zambia is heavily dependent on capitalist enterprise for development, expatriate manpower, capital intensive nature of imported technology and imported raw materials used in productive sectors of the economy. Because of the capital-intensive nature of imported technology, all new workers are unable to find wage employment. Moreover, the great majority of the population lacks the kind of training, skill and prior work experience required in an industrial economy. Those who cannot be absorbed in the formal wage sector are forced to seek alternative avenues for making a living. Some become absorbed in the low-paid service jobs and self-employment, e.g., petty trading, small scale manufacturing etc. As capital-intensive industrialisation continues, the absorption capacity of this less formal (or informal) sector comprising lowpaid service jobs, such as domestic servants, security guards, selfemployment etc., is also likely to decrease. Thus certain sections of the population, women and men, who have been precluded from the dominant sectors of the economy also face the possibilities of a further squeeze from the informal sector.

The latest statistics on the gainfully employed population in Zambia relate to the 1969 Population Census. Although the data as such is indeed out-dated, in the absence of alternative statistics it nevertheless serves as a useful guideline in examining the proportionate distribution of the employed work force by sex. At the national level, approximately 57.4 % of the adult male population and merely 13.0 % of the adult female population in the 1969 Census were recorded as gainfully employed. The fact that official statistics tend to underestimate the actual economic contribution of women is a universal phenomenon. That just over one-tenth of the working-age female population is officially recorded as gainfully employed mystifies the reality of work situations of the majority of women otherwise considered as full-time housewives. The work of a majority of rural housewives on family plots as well as their individual plots is vital to the sustenance of family. Similarly, work of the urban poor housewives through a wide range of nonfarm and in many cases subsistence-oriented informal activities is vital in meeting the immediate needs of family. If this is not work, because it is performed outside the normal labour market environment, then we need to redefine the concept of "work".

Examination of data on the formal sector employment by sex indicates that women represent a very small proportion (i.e. only 7.0 % of total economy (C.S.O., 1970). It may be observed that not only a few women feature in the formal wage sector, but they are also disproportionately represented in a few economic sectors, e.g., social and personal services. The concentration of women in the tertiary sector suggests that a few occupations, e.g., teaching, nursing, clerical and related activities etc., open to women in formal sector, are somehow akin to their general image as providers of services, be they unpaid private household services or paid services in public life.

The characteristics of the Lusaka labour force suggest that women and men seem to have differential access to economic work opportunities. Distribution of the work force by sex showed that out of total male workers of 67292, approximately 88.0 % were in some form of wage employment, 8.0 %

in self-employment and only 4.0 % as unpaid family workers; while out of total female workers of 18989, some 58.0 % were in wage employment, 10 % in self-employment and 32.0 % as unpaid family worker (C.S.O., 1970). It may be observed that out of the total formal sector employment (of 56134 persons) in Lusaka, women constituted only 9.5 % (or 5351). This is only slightly higher than their share of employment of 7.0 % at the national level. Figures on urban self-employment of men and women appear to be grossly underestimated. This is mainly due to the fact that the sector is rarely enumerated in official statistics.

That approximately one third of female workers in Lusaka were recorded as unpaid family workers as compared to only 4.0 % of their male counterparts in this category suggests that even in the urban work situation, a significant proportion of women's labour continues to be unremunerated. Much of this is commanded by men whose authority and power to appropriate women's labour is legitimised through the relations of kinship and marriage.

Percentage distribution of workers by broad occupational category and sex (see Table 1) reveals that out of total female workers, approximately 35.0 % are sales workers; 18.0 % service workers and about 13.0 % professional, technical and related workers mainly in the teaching, nursing and clerical areas. These three categories of occupations are basically service-oriented and as such don't require technical skills utilised in the modern sector. Although a significant percentage of men out of all employed men is also represented in sales and service-related occupations, women seem to be disproportionately represented in such tertiarised occupations. It is a fact that due to shortages of local high-level manpower, only a few African men are recorded in production and skill-oriented occupations, but women are virtually nonexistent in such modern industrial occupations. This suggests that men are more integrated into wider economic opportunities than women are.

The basis for differential access of women and men in the spheres of education and employment was no doubt laid during the colonial era; sexist attitudes of the labour market continue to prevail despite the fact that government official policy discourages such differential treatrent. With the opening up of educational and training opportunities to women, the younger generation of women is gradually stepping into clerical, secretarial, teaching, administrative and even managerial occupations. These are Schuster's *new women* of Lusaka (Schuster, 1979). But the majority of Zambian women, particularly the older generation and those without clerical or secretarial skills have to overcome the drawbacks of colonial policies pertaining to education and work and, more importantly, the prevailing sexist attitudes of employers (who are almost entirely men) which restrict and regulate their access to economic work. In the pages that follow, I use data from four urban case studies completed recently to illustrate the survival strategies of the urban poor (and particularly the poor women) who have become economically marginalised due to the failure of the modern sector to create viable economic opportunities for the relatively unsophisticated labour force.

The Case Study

The previous section attempted to situate the problem of employment in the context of a dependency framework. That is to say that the Zambian economy is closely linked to central capitalist countries and the development strategy chosen has failed to fulfill some fundamental socioeconomic objectives such as employment, income equality, housing and related social services. The effects of development in the dominant productive sectors have not reached the majority of the population in relation to increasing the level of productive forces. This section examines the nature of the survival strategies of the marginal population in some townships of Lusaka.

Urban squatter settlements, popularly known as periurban areas or townships, sprang up during the course of a rapid rate of urbanisation experienced in Zambia during 1964-74. Lusaka received a large proportion of migrants from the rural areas. Consequently, the demand for housing and employment began to increase. The initial crop of migrants with modest levels of formal education and training could not be easily absorbed in the modern sector. Those who were able to find jobs were restricted to only the low-income type.

The case study material relates to four communities in Lusaka. These comprised two high-density areas of George compound and Chaisa; 1 medium-density area of Chilenje (including Old and New Chilenje and Chilenje South); and one low-density area of Woodlands.[1] The communities were selected on the basis of their social class position. The main objective is to examine the determinants of work opportunities of women in different class positions. A woman's social class position is usually determined by that of her husband (in the case of married women) or kin. This is due to women's subordinate economic status within the wider society and their private dependence on men. It is hypothesised here that regardless of their class position, the sphere of work allowed to the majority of women is indeed confined and limited to only those areas similar to daily household chores. Since independence, the government's efforts to indigenise employment has resulted in the inclusion of women who possess relevant skills in jobs formerly restricted to men. Women with such marketable skills are indeed few (as the case study reveals) and the options open to them are even fewer (see Table 1).

Data in the four communities were collected through the household survey.[2] Approximately 1,730 women were interviewed. Besides the general particulars of respondents such as age, marital status and education/training, information was also collected on the migration history, occupational record, income from economic activities and women's attitude to economic work.

The majority (53 per cent) of women in the sample were above 30 years of age. Women in this category have virtually no formal education or training whatsoever.[3] The remaining 47 per cent of women are young (below 30 years of age) and the majority of these have had some exposure to formal education (less than Grade 7), but no training — with the exception of a few who trained as nurses, teachers, secretaries or hair dressers.

Table 1 Economic Participation by broad occupational groups and sex, Lusaka Urban, 1970*

Occupations	No.	Male % total male	No.	Female % total female	Total No.	% total
Prof./techn. and related workers	853	4.9	238	13.2	1091	5.7
Adm./manager and Clerical workers	198	1.1	16	0.9	214	1.1
Sales workers	2864	16.6	639	35.5	3503	18.4
Service workers	1546	9.0	325	18.0	1871	9.8
Agr./forestry and related workers.	2691	15.6	243	13.5	2934	15.4
Produ./manuf. and related workers	1308	7.6	94	5.2	1402	7.4
Packaging/ storage workers	2154	12.5	35	1.9	2189	11.5
Workers not elsewhere classified	5639	32.7	212	11.8	5851	30.7
Total	17253	100.0	1802	100.0	19055	100.0

Source: Cited from K. Hansen (1980). Original source:
Republic of Zambia, Population Consus, 1969 adapted from census tapes.

The urban lower class in the three communities (excluding Woodlands) may be divided into two groups: the blue-collar unionised workers in wage employment; often at the low income level — and the subproletariat (the majority being women). These are, in McGee's (1974) interpretation as "proto-proletariat", a diverse group of small-scale artisans, traders, transporters, repairers, hustlers and workers in personal and domestic services. With moderate and, in some cases, little education, men are able to find wage employment in the formal sector. Education is not the only determinant to job entry (as the case study reveals); there seems to be a middle area of office work, e.g., general workers or "office orderlies" as the respondents say, lower clerical or messengers and other related activities where other factors such as personal networks are equally important and through the exploitation of such contacts men do succeed in finding wage employment.

Distribution of the economically active work force by sex in the three communities showed that approximately 90-95 per cent of married women's husbands were engaged in some form of income-generating activities; while some 45-70 per cent of female respondents belonged to this category. The latter figure is in contrast to that recorded in official statistics at the national and Lusaka levels. According to the 1969 Population Census, only 13 per cent of the adult female population at the national level and some 48 per cent at the Lusaka level were recorded as gainfully employed (wage and self-employment). This brings us to the question of the circumstances under which women must seek income-generating activities. In the high and medium density areas, the average household income is low and as some of my respondents remarked, the "husband's income has never been adequate to support the entire family". Moreover, the husband expects the wife's (wives') contribution to the upkeep of family.

In the case of urban poor women, it is not necessarily the husband's low income but the amount contributed to the upkeep of the family which determines whether women must seek income-generating activities. The average monthly contribution of a husband to the family as reported by respondents rarely exceeds K 50, though this ranges from as little as K 20 to a maximum of K 150 per month. Therefore, the main determinant of women's need to work is then the amount they receive for housekeeping.

The case study of poor townships suggest that the majority of women hardly get enough money for the sustenance of family. In what type of incomegenerating activities are women and men from these communities involved? Data relating to the status of the gainfully employed by sex show (see Table 2) that approximately two-thirds of men and less than one-tenth of women in low income urban areas of George and Chaisa depend for their livelihood on wage employment. On the other hand, in the medium and high income areas of Chilenje and Woodlands, some 80-100 per cent of men and 36-54 per cent of women are engaged in wage/salary employment. These figures suggest that there appears to be some degree of relationship between

Table 2 Income-generating activities of households in selected townships by sex; 1981

Townships	Formal sector						Informal sector						Total					
	M (2) No.	% H	W (3) No.	% W	T (4) No.	% M	M (5) No.	% W	W (6) No.	% M	T (7) No.	% W	(8) % T	M No.	W (9) No.	% T	T No.	(10) % T
George Compound	294	62.0	15	7.0	264	43.0	154	38.0	192	93.0	346	57.0	66.0	403	207	34.0	610	100.0
Chaisa "	305	68.0	17	5.0	322	41.0	142	32.0	315	95.0	457	59.0	57.0	447	332	43.0	779	100.0
Chilenje "	535	80.0	80	36.0	433	65.0	87	20.0	145	64.0	232	35.0	66.0	440	225	34.0	665	100.0
Woodlands "	167	100.0	49	54.0	216	84.0			41	46.0	41	16.0	65.0	167	90	35.0	257	100.0
Total	1074	74.0	161	19.0	1235	53.0	383	26.0	693	81.0	1076	47.0	63.0	1457	854	37.0	2311	100.0

Source: The Household survey, Manpower Research Unit.

the social class of individuals and the likely sector of their employment. But the social division of labour offers differential work opportunities to women and men presumably belonging to the same social class (cf. Hansen, 1980). Although a majority of men in the low social stratum have little education and training, they somehow manage to enter wage employment.

Table 3 Occupational distribution of female respondents in selected areas.

Occupation	Selected areas											
	George				*Chaisa*			*Chilenje*			*Woodlands*	
	No.	%	Total	No.	%	Total	No.	%	Total	No.	%	Total
1. Professional	–	–		–	–		–	–		2	2.2	
2. Managerial/ admin.	–	–		–	–		–	–		2	2.2	
3. Teaching	–	–		–	–		18	8.0		14	15.5	
4. Nursing	3	1.4		5	1.5		13	5.8		10	11.1	
5. Lower techn/prof.	–	–		–	–		4	1.8		5	5.5	
6. Clerical/ secretarial	3	1.5		5	1.5		14	6.2		16	17.8	
7. Service/ casual workers	9	4.3		7	2.1		31	13.8		–	–	
8. Petty traders/ self-employed in home crafts	192	92.8		315	94.9		145	64.4		41	45.7	
Total	207	100.0		332	100.0		225	100.0		90	100.0	

Women in poor townships resort to a variety of income-generating activities in the so-called informal sector. Out of a total of some 1,050 women interviewed in George and Chaisa, approximately 50 per cent are engaged in some form of economic activity. Of these, about 85 per cent are concentrated in petty retailing, mainly in food and related items (see Table 4) and the remaining in some other service-oriented activities, e.g., sewing, knitting, hair dressing, beer brewing and the like.

The concentration of the majority of women in low-income petty trading must be viewed in relation to their marginalisation from the rest of the productive sectors of the economy. Occupational distribution of the gainfully employed people (see Tables 1 and 2) reveals that the main sources of income-generating activities at the national, urban and case study level for women are clearly divided between skilled and unskilled categories. A clear sexual division of labour exists between these skilled categories. Women who work primarily in petty trading and to a lesser extent in domestic service are likely to be unskilled. It is on retail-selling activities of women in these selected areas that I wish to focus.

Table 4 The nature of women's economic activities outside the wage-sector in selected areas.

	George No.		Chaisa No.		Chilenje No.		Woodlands No.	
1. *Retailing*								
—Vegetables	54		72		45		9	
—Fish	27		41		18		2	
—Dry goods	10		19		14		8	
—Meat/poultry	17		6		16		4	
—Scarce Comm.	25		39		15		1	
—Fuel	19		54		10		1	
Cooked food	20		32		20		2	
Sub-total	172	90.0%	263	83.0%	138	95.0%	27	65.5%
II Home crafts —Sewing/ knitting	1		5		1		11	
—Hair dressing	—		—		2		1	
III Rent collection	13		33		—		1	
IV Illegal e.g. beer brewing	6		14		4		—	
Sub-total	20	10.0%	52	17.0%		5.0%	13	32.0%
Total	192	100.0%	315	100 %	145	100.0%	40	

Retail-selling Activities of Women

Female retailers in the urban areas are relative newcomers and for that matter the history of petty trading itself is a postindependence phenomenon in Zambia. Nyirenda's (1957) study on African vendors in Lusaka showed that very few females were engaged in retailing activities in Lusaka. Subsequent studies (Beveridge and Oberschall, 1972; Todd, 1980; Bardouille, 1980) revealed that this was no longer the case. In fact, women predominate in retail-selling activities. For example, the present case study shows that approximately 80 per cent of all retailers are women. The characteristics of retail trading are somewhat complex because they are dependent on the type of product sold, e.g., cooked food, uncooked food, and other durables, and the location where it is sold — front-yard stalls, fixed location outside the home, e.g., market stalls, street vending.

i. Front-yard stalls

Women who sell in the home are basically of two types: 1. they are usually younger than their counterparts operating from market stalls, and 2. they usually sell small portions of items such as vegetables, eggs, dry fish (kapenta), charcoal, cooking oil, etc. Their regular clientele is from the neighbourhood vicinity. Those who carry out retail selling in the home are able to combine their economic activities with household chores and childcare. Their profit margin is invariably small because of the nature of goods and the small quantities of items sold. Capital is necessary even to start a small business and it is more often women with capital, provided either by savings, other kin, or husband, who set up home retailing in this way. Such front-yard stalls are open most of the day and throughout the week including weekends. The extent to which women see this as "work" depends largely on the scale of turnover and the number of hours spent on it. A woman with a large number of children is primarily involved in domestic chores and sees the small-scale selling of vegetables, etc. as a "bit on the side". Even though the profit margin from such small-scale retailing is small and indeed inadequate to support the family, doing without such small amounts for certain groups of women may mean sacrificing the immediate needs of the family, i.e. a meal.

ii. Fixed-location shops/stalls

Women operating from a fixed location, i.e. a shop or stall in the township market, are mainly retailers of fresh vegetables, fresh and dried fish, chickens, cooked/prepared foods, e.g., fat cakes, roasted groundnuts, etc. On the other hand, the larger shops selling dry goods, e.g., grocery items, clothing, toiletries and a variety of diverse items, are predominantly owned by men and operated mainly as household enterprises but sometimes with wage labour. Such enterprises require much larger capital than vegetable selling and as such very few women own and operate these shops because of the lack of working capital. Some division of labour occurs in so far as the man does the wholesale buying in town and deals with commercial distributors, while the woman does the majority of selling in the shop. Her labour of course is not remunerated as this is commandeered by her husband through the relations of marriage, in which the wife becomes the private property of the husband.

Bars/taverns, a lucrative business in low-income communities, are predominantly owned by men because of their association with drinking and, above all, prostitution. A few older women with the necessary capital manage to enter this business, but this is generally considered unrespectable by the community. Women engaged in this business are seen as prostitutes and immoral. I asked my female respondents to state their views on the worst economic opportunities of women in the townships. The majority held the view that work in or *even outside* a bar/tavern and prostitution were the worst possible options of women. One woman remarked, "I will die rather than see my daughter become a bar maid." In this context, both the structural, i.e. capital, and cultural constraints keep women out of high-profit businesses.

iii. Street vending

In the poor townships a few women sell small portions of seasonal fruits, prepared foods, cigarettes, etc. on the roadside. The location chosen often depends on the volume of traffic, i.e. clientele, in a particular area. Street vendors usually operate in places near the bus stop, outside the township market, the township school, etc. They often become victims of police harassment. Sometimes they are fined heavily and/or their goods seized and destroyed. Despite the risks involved in street vending, for a certain group of women the options are indeed limited.

iv. Other nonwage activities of women

Retailing activities appear to be one of the few options open to women in the townships. A few women also do sewing, knitting, embroidery, etc. This activity requires much larger capital, tools, materials, and also some level of training (formal or nonformal) than retailing of vegetables and related food items. In the poor townships, dressmaking and tailoring are monopolised by men because of large capital requirements. On the other hand, in the high-income area of Woodlands, approximately one-third of the selfemployed women are engaged in this activity. Women in this area, by virtue of their husbands' economic status, belong to a high social class. Capital is provided by husbands, either from savings or loans. But for the majority of poor women, capital is a serious constraint in carrying out viable economic activities.

In the poor townships, women are forced to resort to a diverity of survival strategies. Beer brewing is one of such strategies. Inputs, basically maize, are of the low-cost nature and capital is rarely a prerequisite to undertaking this activity. Some fortunate ones with a steady clientele do manage to get a handsome profit from this activity. Risks are high because of the illegal nature of this activity.

Rent collection is another form of survival strategy of poor women in high-density townships. In view of shortages of the low-cost housing, a few women with their own houses are able to exploit this situation by renting one or two rooms of their living-quarters. The presence of multiple households within a single housing unit, commonly observed in poor townships, is another important survival strategy of the urban poor. Living in invasion squatter settlements and/or sharing a single housing unit with other families is an important means of reducing economic dependence on the money economy.

The case study suggests that for the majority of poor women in the townships, the retail-selling activity is one of the few outlets open to them. What is so common about retailing and furthermore why do women predominate in this activity? The petty trading in these townships basically involves retailing of food and related items, an activity akin to women's general domestic tasks. Capital requirements are modest and formal education and training not necessary. A majority of poor women have neither the large capital nor the necessary skill to run an entrepreneurial-type enterprise. They have large families, their husbands' income is low and the contribution to the family upkeep is grossly inadequate. Under the circumstances, there are indeed few exploitable niches available to a majority of women in this category. On the other hand, female retailers who are single, divorced, widowed or separated and thus the sole supporters of their families do manage to earn much larger profit margins than the majority of their married counterparts who live with their husbands.

Despite small profit margins from retailing activities, recruitment into the township markets for the majority of women may be not the most obvious solution, frequently it is the *only* solution. An alternative to retailing for the unskilled women in the townships is perhaps domestic service, a low-paid occupation, unprotected in relation to the conditions of service, arduous and above all monotonous. Women in retail activities (like other informal sectors) provide a valuable service to sectors of the population at a cost below their labour power and thereby covering at least some of the subsistence needs of the poor which would otherwise have not been met by large-scale capital-intensive enterprises.

What are the prospects of urban informal sector operators in relation to their upward mobility? It would be incorrect to generalise that among the urban poor none are upwardly mobile and that none manage through skill, initiative and hard work to break out of this level of informal activities. The advantage of micro studies is that they demystify certain generalisations regarding the homogeneity of the urban working poor. The case study is instructive in that it shows that even within one township the urban poor are by no means economically a homogeneous groups. Factors such as age and sex together with the accompanying level of capital resources are important determinants of upward mobility of individual operators in the urban informal sector. These factors not only affect the type of informal occupations that individuals choose to move into but also the constraints under which they are forced to operate and ultimately the potential of achieving some measure of upward mobility.

It may be argued that the level of accumulation of an individual operator in the informal sector determines the extent to which she/he can achieve upward mobility either through the expansion of the informal sector business or breaking out of the informal sector and moving into the formal sector. Having examined the circumstances under which the majority of urban poor women are forced to depend on petty trading activities, their possibility of accumulating some capital is remote. These women are primarily of the middle-age group (over 40 years) and have large families (sometimes as many as 11-14 members) to support. Their family commitment increases rather than decreases as the school-going children must be provided with uniforms, books, lunch money, bus fare, etc. This does not imply that men do not contribute towards their children's education. But what it does mean is that the contribution is rarely adequate and hence the need to supplement the meagre means necessitates women's economic work. Women in retailing remain economically static and with a progressively competitive marketing system as they grow older, they are also likely to be downwardly mobile.

Only five women in my sample in George, Chaisa and Chilenje are large-scale sellers, basically of charcoal. They operate their businesses with the financial and practical assistance of their husbands. Similarly, women in large-scale businesses (e.g., sewing, knitting, grocery stores, etc.) in Woodlands also depend on their husbands for capital, transport, business contacts, etc. They are relatively younger than their counterparts in petty retailing in the townships. The women covered in the Woodlands sample are wives of executives, managers, professionals and related top-rank officials. These women are not economically hard-pressed and thus unlikely to look for petty economic activities as compared to their poor sisters in the townships for whom petty trading is one of the few possible viable options. Although business-women in the Woodlands area have better chances of upward mobility (because of access to capital, contacts, and the relatively higher level of education and some training) than poor women in the townships, however, the nature of their activities, e.g., sewing, knitting, trading, etc., in itself is a constraint to achieving high levels of capital accumulation. It is in this respect, I argue, that sex becomes a critical variable in determining the level of upward mobility.

Turning to the men, retailing it seems does not attract young and middle-aged men because of its low-income prospects. The few men who do retailing are the older ones. They enter this activity at the end of their most productive lives and do not intend to seek alternative employment in the formal sector. The small-scale elderly male retailers see this level of their activity as permanent and they are likely to remain at this or perhaps even below this level for the rest of their lives. They have no intentions of expanding their businesses since the low level of accumulation barely covers the reproduction of their labour power and thus the reinvestible potentials are virtually nonexistent.

Younger men are in manufacturing activities, e.g., carpentry, tailoring, tin-smithing, electrical/mechanical and related repairs, welding and in large-scale retailing. Their level of accumulation from their present businesses is promising as compared to alternative possibilities in the formal sector. They are interested in expanding their present businesses and hope to move out of this level of operation.

The micro study suggests that the informal sector provides different levels of mobility to individual operators depending on their age and sex. The elderly men and the majority of women are downwardly mobile and unlikely to accumulate adequate capital even to sustain the competitive informal sector market, far less moving out of the low level of their businesses. The upwardly mobile young men are the only operators who come into the informal sector in the hope of returning to better economic levels though not necessarily through formal wage employment. They use the informal sector as an entry point and have no intentions of spending the rest of their lives in subsistence-oriented levels of operation. As for the majority of female retailers (younger and middle-aged), they are likely to remain static in the middle, i.e. neither upwardly nor downwardly mobile. At the bottom end of the mobility scale are the elderly women and men who, as they get older, are likely to be downwardly mobile and possibly phased out of economic operations as they are unlikely to cope with the competitive marketing system.

Some Tentative Conclusions

It is important to emphasise that conclusions at the outset can only be made at the micro level, though the likelihood of wider trends at the national level can also be discerned.

In Zambia, as in advanced capitalist countries, a selective nature of labour absorption exists. This is based on both a social and sexual division of labour. A majority of jobs in the capitalist sector require formal education and skills and those who lack such prerequisites are forced to seek alternative income-generating activities outside the formal sector. Within the social division of labour there also exists the occupational segregation based on the sexual division of labour. Although women with professional, managerial and clerical skills are increasingly being attracted into the labour force in Zambia, this is a fairly recent phenomenon. Women in these occupations are not only numerically few but they are also disproportionately represented in only a few occupations. The nature of formal occupations (i.e. service-oriented) in which educated and trained women are employed affords only limited upward mobility.

The majority of women and men who have become marginalised from the dominant productive sectors are forced to seek refuge in so-called urban informal sector activities. Such activities range from petty manufacturing to providing cheap services (i.e. petty trading, electrical/mechanical services, etc.). Even at this level of economic activity, there also exists a clear pattern of the sexual division of labour. In certain informal activities such as petty manufacturing and medium- to large-scale retailing men, young and middle-aged, seem to predominate and women irrespective of their age are precluded from such activities, particularly in petty manufacturing.

In petty trading activities, on the other hand, a rigid sexual division of labour does not exist. Although women of all ages predominate in petty retailing, in the case of men it is only the older ones who opt for this activity. Petty retailing offers only low-income prospects as it predominantly serves low-income groups in the townships who can afford neither the transport costs nor the scale of buying from the down-town shopping area. Petty retailing provides a low level of accumulation and consequently this activity has become unable to generate growth but only to reproduce the existing conditions and scale of operations.

The sexual segregation of occupations (both in formal and informal sectors) is an effective mechanism aimed at regulating and monitoring different spheres of work of women and men. The ideology of "sex-typing" legitimises differential and unequal access of women to spheres of education, training and employment. Such cultural constraints manifest themselves in structural constraints such as access to credit facilities, development of productive forces (i.e. technology), material inputs and related productive infra-structure. As such, these constraints militate against women's full partici-pation in social, political and economic arenas.

The existence of a large reserve army of labour ensures that wages are kept below the value of labour power. It is this value of labour power which determines the extent to which women must seek income-generating activi-ties. The continued existence of cultural and structural constraints discrimi-nates against women's opportunities to make a decent living. Since the husbands' contribution has never been adequate to the upkeep of family, women by sheer economic necessity resort to a variety of survival strategies. Living in shanty towns and overcrowded houses on the periphery of the city, without the basic infrastructure, is one way of reducing the living costs, on the other hand poor diet, consisting mainly of staples such as mealie meal, is another way of keeping the subsistence costs down.

Empirical evidence shows that the urban poor do not constitute a homo-geneous economic group. Although the majority of the population in poor townships is indeed poor, a few individuals are able to move out of the petty production level by accumulating some capital. These are young men engaged in petty manufacturing; electrical, mechanical and building repair services and medium- to large-scale trading activities. Despite individual cases of upward mobility, the majority of low-income informal sector operators and particularly women are likely to be downwardly mobile as the marketing system becomes competitive and new entrants especially the young ones seek refuge in those activities which require a low level of working capital. The possibility of even further marginalisation of the low-income urban poor is likely to create the conditions of increasing poverty (if the level of employ-ment generation is not increased) in peripheral urban areas of Lusaka.

Not all informal sector operators see their present activities as a stop-gap measure in the process of finding formal wage employment. To the majority, the informal sector is no longer a "refuge" occupation. They are likely to stay in these activities because the alternative is not necessarily a better one. The extent to which they are able to break out of the low level of activity depends largely on their age, sex and marital status as these are important determinants of the level of capital accumulation and hence the possibility of upward mobility.

Notes

1. Field work was conducted in April, 1981 by a team of research assistants including myself as a principal investigator.

2. Housing units in each of the areas were selected randomly. In order to have a representative sample, housing units were selected from different sections of thses communities. For this purpose, aerial photographs were used in order to facilitate the selection of residential blocks and finally the households for interview. This survey was basically to list the households on the basis of women's economic activities and served as a basis for selecting a small sample for a comprehensive household survey.

3. The household survey in Woodlands is not yet complete. However, for the purpose of this paper, I have decided to include the information relating to the respondents' income-generating activities and their husbands' occupations.

References

Bardouille, R. (1980) Women marketeers in the township of Chawama, Lusaka. Manpower Research Unit, Working Paper. University of Zambia (mimeo).

– (1981) Women's economic contribution in the urban informal sector. *Manpower Research Report No. 7.* University of Zambia (mimeo).

– (1981a) Background to the mining industry in Zambia: A study of local technological capability. Paper presented at a Conference on East African Science and Technology, Sep. 16-20, 1981. Arusha, Tanzania (to be published in the Proceedings of the Conference).

Beveridge, A & Oberschall, A. (1979) *African businessmen and development in Zambia.* Princeton: Princeton University Press.

Central Statistical Office (1970) *Population Census, 1969. First Report.* Lusaka: C.S.O.

– (1979) *Monthly Digest of Statistics.*

– (1979a) *1974 Sample Census of Population. Second Report.* Lusaka: C.S.O.

Government of the Republic of Zambia (1966) *Manpower Report.* Lusaka: Cabinet Office.

– (1966a) *First National Development Plan.* Lusaka: National Commission for Development Planning.

– (1972) *Second National Development Plan.* Lusaka: N.C.D.P.

Hansen, K. Tranberg (1980) When sex becomes a critical variable: Married women and work in Lusaka. *African Social Research, 30.*

McGee, T. (1974) *The persistence of the proto-proletariat: Occupational structures and planning for the future of Third World countries,* Los Angeles: University of California, School of Architecture and Urban Planning.

Nyirenda, A. (1957) African market vendors in Lusaka, with a note on the recent boycott. *Rhodes-Livingstone Journal, 22.*

Schuster, I. Glazer (1979) *New women of Lusaka,* Palo Alto, Cal.: Mayfield Publishing Co.

Seidman, A. (1974) The distorted growth of import-substitution: The case of Zambia, *Journal of Modern African Studies, 12.* Also published in B. Turok (ed.), *Development in Zambia: A reader.* London: Zed Press.

Todd, D. (1979) Small-scale manufacturing in Lusaka: A comparison of markets and small-scale industry sites, *Urban Community Research Report No. 4* University of Zambia (mimeo).

Turok, B. (1979) The penalties of Zambia's mixed economy. In his *Development in Zambia: A reader.* London: Zed Press.

Chapter 7
Survey of Recent Inquiries and their Results
by Klaas Woldring

Introduction

By the end of 1981, the state of Zambia's system of public administration left much to be desired. I am assured by scholars who have recently worked in Ghana, Nigeria and Kenya, however, that the situation is not as bad in Zambia as it is in those countries, especially as far as corruption is concerned. That is a hopeful observation. On the other hand, these colleagues report that you can "get things done there" if you play the game and offer suitable bribes to appropriate persons. Not so in Zambia. Bribery is not, to my knowledge, widespread in Zambia, and one attempts to work with and through the bureaucracy. This task is arduous, time-consuming and sometimes simply impossible. Frequently, I felt that Kafka's Castle had come to Zambia; one goes round in circles, has to wait long periods for services and must fill in numerous forms all for a minimum of output. The impression the visitor gains at times is of a bureaucracy understaffed or of officials too frequently absent; but the reverse, in fact, is true. There are far too many clerks and far too many administrators, but they are unproductive, and, further, there are far too many administrative steps to be taken before any service is delivered. There are, of course, exceptions. It is a hopeful sign, too, that the long awaited Report of the Commission of Inquiry into the Civil Service is soon to be released (July, 1983?). All the same, over recent years, several reports have cited large-scale mismanagement and inefficiency, so that a pressing question must be: What happens to the recommendations?

When gathering data for his *Second Report to the Government of Zambia on Incomes, Wages and Prices in Zambia*,[1] Prof. H.A. Turner found that the problem of actually finding the data was a great obstacle in the way of his inquiry. He complained to the Minister for Finance:

> There are several points I should like to make on statistics. It is a repeated difficulty with this kind of policy problem that, although everybody feels strongly that the situation is serious and something should be done, it is impossible to make precise suggestions because one does not know exactly – or even approximately – what is actually happening. *Which means statistics: and especially, as up-to-date statistics as*

possible. . . . There have certainly been some substantial improvements in economic data generally since then, but it is sad that in respect of the vital matters with which the present Mission is concerned, it should arrive to find the Government little better equipped than in 1969.[2]

In 1969, Turner had recommended certain policies for increasing employment and raising productivity, especially in rural areas. But in 1978 he noted that the reverse had happened "largely (but not entirely) because of external circumstances". To the extent that it was seen as an internal problem, however, para. 3 of the Introduction is revealing:

The other central message of this report, however, is that a main reason for the delays in dealing with these problems since 1969 was the complacency and inefficiency induced in leading circles by another development. Since 1969, Zambia has become what we would call a "social bureaucracy".[3]

When I was teaching at the University of Zambia (mid-1979 to mid-1981), I found that, in spite of the serious economic and security problems Zambia was confronted with during that very period, the students were keen to learn and were unquestionably intelligent. Almost all were extremely concerned with their country's deteriorating administrative and economic situation. The brightest were seeking scholarships abroad rather than join a complacent, inefficient and sometimes corrupt bureaucracy or parastatal organisation to which they would have to conform. A few still believed that the malaise could be contained and improved from within; most students, under such conditions, naturally tend to favour radical solutions, based on radical explanations. But this tendency was tempered by the realisation that, wherever this had been attempted in Africa, the aftermath had been painful and productive of further instability. In addition, the radical left at UNZA, throughout the 1970s, could not be regarded as the vanguard of a popular movement of the left. The attempted coup in October 1980 was not inspired by the left, but seems to have been an attempt by persons with quite solid entrepreneurial, managerial and professional backgrounds to remove a sluggish administration unable to promote true development in Zambia. Their backgrounds and statements suggested a strong capitalist orientation.

The reasons for Zambia's sluggish administration and the resulting very imperfect implementation of policies are complex and manifold and I shall not attempt to explain them fully. Before briefly surveying the most glaring examples of bureaucratic and parastatal misdemeanours, however, I would like to offer four comments.

First, the problem has little to do with the ideological orientation of the Government (whether one wishes to call that socialist, humanist or *de facto* capitalist) except that that orientation has led to a degree of unproductive confusion.

Second, the tendency for some Zambian intellectuals to blame historical and external factors (colonialism, imperialism and the liberation wars etc.), while essentially justifiable, is not helpful. Solutions to these problems require long-term, external strategies. There are, however, several domestic problems that can be tackled, at least in the short run, without reference to them.

Third, to the extent that Zambia can alleviate the present situation internally, management skills, attitudes and financial practices must be greatly improved if better use is to be made of existing resources and possibilities. Among major problems Zambia can tackle immediately are those to do with management; particularly the management of manpower utilisation and that of finance. Certainly, the *Zambia Managerial Manpower and Training Needs Survey of the Private and Parastatal Sectors* (April, 1977) revealed great gaps that still needed to be filled. I was surprised to learn on my arrival in Zambia, therefore, how few students had graduated in the natural sciences and, in particular, from the School of Mines − mining being Zambia's bread-and-butter industry. The majority of graduates, indeed, were from the Schools of Humanities and Social Science, and from Education. The restriction of intakes into natural science appears to have been aimed at the achievement of high academic performance. Yet, one may ask: Why did this argument not apply to the other Schools? The policy involved is both mystifying and suspect, especially in the light of persistent complaints by Zambian graduates in the mining industry who allege discrimination vis-a-vis salary by top expatriate management. Again, it is to be hoped that, during the 1980s, the university is stepping up its intake into the natural sciences, including Mining and Agriculture.

Fourth, the first postcolonial development phase has been dominated by the nationalist leaders who delivered political independence to Zambia. The dominance of such men has continued rather longer than elsewhere in Africa because the pre-1964 liberation drive was externalised to the whole of Southern Africa. But these men, who were then approximately 40 years of age, are now 60; their day is drawing to an end. Their values, experience, age and skills are, in the main neither conducive nor suited to the promotion of successful development. As developers, indeed, they have largely failed. They did their best, of course, assisted by the mere 100 graduates that Zambia could boast in 1964, but without any great awareness of the problems they had become involved in. The early years of independence really did not test them and when the test did come (from about 1974 onwards), they faltered on all sides as administrators and financial managers. Their lifestyle had, in part, been modelled on that of the previous colonisers (what other model was there?) and, for a developing country, it was most inappropriate. It is not strange therefore that, in the independence struggle, President Kaunda had to divest himself, (most reluctantly), of the services of some of his most brilliant lieutenants on account of inefficiency and/or scandal. It was not merely a case of their complacency and self-seeking practices being obstacles to the promotion of successful development strategies. They were also a hindrance to the promotion of a new generation of development-oriented, bright young men and women because they blocked the top positions. The result has been that, where young people have risen to prominence, they have found themselves in a context of nonsupportive incompetence. This situation has been compounded by a cultural component which dictates, that younger personnel should not take issue with their seniors, especially not those who had successfully delivered Zambia from colonial bondage. This cultural factor is also frequently mentioned as the cause of failure of Zambia's experiments in Industrial Democracy. During my two years at UNZA I did gain the impression, however, that Zambia is reaching the end of this first postcolonial phase. This manifested itself in the strong urge, even impatience, of many students to get to the top and to put matters right. Doubtless, they will invest much energy in that effort and, given half a chance and support they will succeed.

This catalogue of irregularities and inefficiencies makes sad reading, but they were aired quite openly and extensively by the highly critical press. Several leaders also persistently called for inquiries and action to be taken against culprits.

Corruption and Inefficiency — the State of Mismanagement

"Is the Government of Zambia slowly disintegrating?" This leading question was put in a Sunday Special of the *Sunday Times of Zambia,* early in February 1981.[4] A week later, the Speaker of the National Assembly (Mr. Robinson Nabulyato) revealed that the Budget had been passed unconstitutionally, and that the Secretary to the Cabinet had to cancel the announced milk price because it had not been gazetted. Such machinery-of-Government errors were, in fact, only a symptom of a grosser malaise. Hence, not surprisingly, the Speaker felt justified in calling for the resignation of incapable Ministers.[5] Backbenchers, all Government Party UNIP members supported him, shouting "Sack the lot, fire the Government". Conceivably, by this time the situation had become so untenable that President Kaunda had already decided to change his Numbers Two and Three (Party Secretary Mainza Chona and Prime Minister Daniel Lisulo) and replace them by appointing Humphrey Mulemba and Nalumino Mundia, respectively. By all accounts, these changes proved to be positive, and thereafter some confidence in the government returned.

Speaker Nabulyato was not the only one who repeatedly urged the resignation of what he called "dead wood" with which, he believed, Zambia was well endowed. This questioning of incompetence and corruption went on continuously in the period during which I observed Zambian government in action. For example in a speech on Zambian Humanism, Mulala Sikota, a National Guidance Political Secretary, stated:

> The Civil Service, the Parastatal Organisations and the lot are all beginning to squeak. There are signs of rust. All of us must find answers to this malice. What has gone wrong with us?[6]

And veteran politician Reuben Kamanga, the respected Chairman of the Political and Legal Affairs Subcommittee of UNIP's Central Committee, remarked:

> True enough, corruption, nepotism, tribalism and such forms of behaviour exist at every level in Zambian life. It is also equally true to say that, when those at the top have something to hide, it becomes increasingly difficult for them to check on the activities of those at lower ranks. For indeed, another reality of life is that an administrator who is himself corrupt would find it hard to declaim the same fault in someone else.[7]

The President, too, has frequently deplored corrupt tendencies amongst Zambians. In May, 1980, for example, he disclosed, that some hospital staff members were stealing medicine to sell to private practitioners:

> Whoever is involved in this dirty behaviour, I say, please stop this corrupt practice. Corruption in the Civil Service, Parastatal Companies and quasi-Government institutions should be fought with vigour.[8]

In October, the President stressed the need to amend the law "to make it more effective in dealing with corruption, tribalism and nepotism now sweeping the nation". This law (The Corrupt Practices Act) was passed in October 1980 (its provisions will be discussed briefly later).

High Commissioner to Nigeria, André Mutemba, is one who recognises the shortcomings of the older nationalists. In an Open Letter to the *Times of Zambia* (May 6 1981), the envoy argued that some party and government leaders had outlined their usefulness and should retire. Mutemba (then 52) considered that he himself was over his peak and that "failure by some leaders was one of the reasons why this country was facing problems". In his view:

> The Party and its Government are too sensitive to simple criticism even if the criticism is constructive and as a result most of our mistakes which we should have rectified have been swept under the carpet. I was not in a position to see this mistake until I was out of very active central power corridors. I feel guilty, honestly, about this discovery. The coordination is very poor, the right hand seems not to know what the left hand is doing. Accountability is negligible. Some of us are too hypocritical.[9]

The French agronomist Dumont was reported as saying that President Kaunda "had the right ideas for his people but that he was hampered by a clique of profiteers who surrounded him".

> There is an urban elite of Party officials cruising the road in chauffeur-driven Mercedes and peasants working two days to afford a bag of salt. 20 % of Zambia's gross national product goes to the 2 % of the population who wield power.[10]

Speaking to the *Voice of the Arab World* newspaper, he was reported as having recommended Arab leaders not to give President Kaunda any more loans under these circumstances.

I turn now to some particular cases which were widely reported. The first major inquiry into corruption and inefficiency was that conducted by the Commission of Inquiry into the Affairs of Zambia Railways under the Chairmanship of the Hon. J.C. Mumpanshya, M.P. (then Minister of State for Power, Transport and Commerce). Initially, Zambia Railways' Political Committee had strongly requested that such a Commission be established to look into the following malpractices: tribalism, corruption, people rising on false integrity, favouritism, frustration, oppression, suppression, unwarranted sacking, the promotion of favoured staff members to positions above their capabilities, and so on. The Commission had been sought in 1975, but it was not until 1977 that the Zambia Railways Amalgamated Workers Union pushed for its establishment on the same grounds that the Commission was actually instituted. The Executive Committee of the union (as explained in Chapter 1, sections 2 and 3 of the Mumpanshya Report) had received very disturbing reports of tribalism, nepotism, corruption and thefts from employees late in 1976 and throughout 1977, which they found to be essentially correct. It was then that they called upon the Minister urgently to institute an inquiry in terms of the Inquiries Act.[11] The Commission presented a comprehensive and revealing Report (March 1978), which confirmed virtually all the allegations. Indicative of the highly unsatisfactory situation it found were its following comments:

> Wherever we went, we received repeated allegations of the practice of tribalism in Zambia Railways. We received widespread complaints to the following effect:

> a. that in Zambia Railways it is not what you know but whom you know that counts;
> b. that merit and qualifications do not count for appointment in Zambia Railways;
> c. that certain tribes were entrenched in certain departments on Zambia Railways;
> d. that members of "small tribes" who were without "full-backs" had no future on the Railways;
> e. that disciplinary measures were corrupted by tribal favouritism;
> f. that advertisements for vacancies were mere formalities while positions and promotions were filled by unfair preferment;
> g. that certain allegations were born of malice on the part of certain tribes who considered themselves aggrieved by the dismissal of their tribesmen.[12]

The conclusion left no room for doubt:
Our recommendation presupposes that since we have found that –

(a) tribalism, nepotism and corruption are practised in Zambia Railways;
(b) the incidence of thefts in Zambia Railways is alarming;
(c) Mr. Mwale's dismissal was not effected on sound principles of management;

positive remedial action should be taken to –

(i)   undo what has been done through the practices of tribalism, nepotism and corruption;
(ii) check the incidence of thefts;
(iii) settle the Mwale affair in pursuance of sound administrative principles. [13]

The generally unsatisfactory performance of Zambia's parastatals was first investigated by the Kayope Committee on Parastatal Bodies which was appointed on 31 January 1978. Its term of reference were:

(a) to examine reports and accounts of the parastatal bodies;
(b) to examine the reports, if any, of the Auditor-General on parastatal bodies;
(c) to examine, in the context of the autonomy and efficiency of the parastatal bodies, that they are being managed in accordance with sound business principles and prudent commercial practices; and
(d) to exercise such other functions vested in the Public Accounts Committee as are not covered by paragraphs (a), (b) and (c) above and as may be allotted to the Committee by the Speaker from time to time. [14]

In its investigations, the Committee restricted itself to a number of "Familiarisation Tours", in the first instance, to selected Parastatals, eg., *Zambia Daily Mail*, Cold Storage Board, National Agricultural Marketing Board, Rural Development Corporation and United Bus Company. In almost all cases, losses were largely attributed to poor management practices. Subsequent Reports by the Auditor-General[15] and by the Committee itself (reconstituted)[16] confirmed this. In 1979, the Committee, which had conducted 29 Familiarisation Tours, drew attention to some extra-ordinary difficulties it had to content with:

(a) late presentation by the Executive of the Action-Taken Report on the Report of the Committee on Parastatal Bodies for the Fifth Session of the Third National Assembly;
(b) non-presentation by the Auditor-General of a report on parastatal bodies on which the Committee could firmly base their inquiries;
(c) failure by most parastatal organisations to present their annual reports to Parliament as required by provisions of the Standing Orders;
(d) victimisation of employees by certain parastatal organisations such that they were afraid to give evidence before the Committee;
(e) the belief of some top executives that they could not be disciplined for their misdeeds in their companies because of the support they enjoy from top leadership in the Party and its Government hierarchy and in some cases interference by some top

officials in the work of your Committee and apparent lack of understanding of the Committee's terms of reference, powers and privileges.[17]

A great number of problems concerning the inefficiency of Government Departments and Local Authorities were aired in the press during the period of research, among which were the following:

(a) More than 5000 government vehicles were reportedly off the road in January 1981 because of lack of spare parts and poor maintenance. This represented about 32 % of all government vehicles, including the Mercedes Benz and Peugeots used by Ministers and other top party and government officials. According to Mr. Patrick Chiwenda, Permanent Secretary of the Ministry for Works and Supply, more than 400 Government vehicles were discarded each year on account of accidents, lack of spare parts and old age.[18] The dismissal scene of the government wreckyard along Old Mumbwa Road in Lusaka confirms this sorry tale. Why is it that, 17 years after independence, Zambia should have a shortage of motor mechanics as is claimed?

(b) There was evidence of wastage of funds by the Ministry of Foreign Affairs (contained in the Report of the Auditor-General for the year ending 31 December 1979)[19] which must have been exceptionally disappointing to the President. Clearly, some Zambian diplomats had a totally irresponsible attitude towards public funds and property, and their lifestyle appears to have been even more out-of-step with the situation in Zambia than that of some party leaders. There are several entries recording substantial staff advances which apparently could not be recovered, expenses for long-term hotel accommodation without a warrant, unnecessary or extravagant property deals and free transport for party leaders to tour missions. In March 1981[20] *The Sunday Times* reported that "the Ministry of Foreign Affairs had failed to tell the Auditor-General what progress was being made to receover nearly K 500 000 owed by diplomats in loans and salary advances". At that time only K 14 000 had in fact been recovered. The most damaging blow concerned the illicit dealings of the Zambian diplomat, Mr. Marshall Khulila. Reportedly, in January 1981, he provided two British journalists, who were posing as nongovernment arms dealers, with a bogus "end-user certificate" to collect a £1000 bribe. The envoy was suspended (June 1981) while "investigations were being continued".[21]

(c) The mess of Lusaka's telephone system is a case of quite unbelievable confusion and speculation. When I arrived in Zambia, it was obvious that, in some parts of Lusaka, the system did not work at all, and, in other parts, ineffectively. During 1977, backed by a K 32 million World Bank loan, the International Telephone and Telegraph Corporation (ITT) was contracted by Zambia's Post and Telecommunications Corporation (PTC) to install a new advanced telephone system in Lusaka. By December 1980, it had become clear that the new system could not be made to work, and PTC sued ITT for K 320 000 in lost revenue.[22] By mid-1981, the new system was still not working and a part-return to the old system, however inadequate and difficult, was recommended. I have been unable to discover the reason for this delay; many conflicting opinions were offered but no official explanation. "Kapelwa Musonda on Tuesday" suggested that it could be a multi-national trick to ensure that Zambia remained dependent on ITT for additional high technology parts for many years to come; or that (as this gifted and humorous commentator argued) it was a result of the curfew (December 1980), in that security agents would now have fewer telephone calls to handle and this would facilitate their work. Alternatively, it was asked whether it was the work of political malcontents who wanted to create industrial chaos in Zambia in order to justify the overthrow of the Government.[23] Most informed commentators attributed the chaos to the complexity of the new equipment. If they were right, a pertinent question would be: Is it wise to introduce such advanced equipment into a developing country? Does it not guarantee technological dependency? If Zambia has such difficulty in maintaining a fleet of government cars, how is it going to maintain a complex telephone exchange?

(d) A similar drama is presented by Lusaka's Mass Media Complex which, when finally operational, would no doubt be of great benefit in that the area of broadcasting would be much widened and qualitatively improved. The aim is virtually to cover the whole of Zambia. The Japanese backed project was to have started in 1970, but its foundation stone was actually laid only in 1979. The original estimate of K 11 million, blew out to K 50 million in 1980. By mid-1981, the project was still far from completion because of interminable delays caused by transport, staff and management difficulties, and this in spite of frequent inspection tours by Ministers and their aides.[24]

(e) In March 1981, the so-called Thomas Alexander Wood (TAW) Scandal came to a head. Backbenchers wanted to know the details of the abortive contract with that American leasing company as a result of which the Zambia Government had to pay K 4 million compensation after cancelling the contract without giving sufficient notice (the trucks arrived regardless). The Special Investigations team for Economy and Trade (SITET), which handled the controversy up to the point, uncovered irregularities committed by civil servants in 1973 which had eventually resulted in the loss.[25] Legal Affairs Minister Chigaga, under pressure, disclosed that the Education and Culture Permanent Secretary (Peter

Siwo) and former Legal Affairs Ministry Permanent Secretary (Sebastian Zulu) had "connived to swindle the Government over the TAW contract". According to Chigaga's statement in the National Assembly, Siwo had signed two waiver letters sent to Wood (in 1973/4) confirming the contract and even dispensing with a delivery deadline. This action was taken contrary to government instructions which had been to rescind the contract forthwith. This extraordinary behaviour leaves much to be explained in a court of law, though at the time of writing the case appears still to be *sub judice.*

(f) An instance of attempted personal corruption was provided by the "Winegate" scandal, which came to light when 10 000 cases of South African wine, worth K 250 000, suddenly arrived at the Lusaka airport. Apparently, an attempt was being made to import this wine, without licence, in the name of M.P. John Kalenga. SITET investigated this matter and even went to South Africa to talk to the exporters, who claimed there were two other dealers involved and that the profits were to have been shared among the three importers.[26] Wine being an extremely rare and expensive commodity in Zambia at this time, Kalenga and his partners in the venture would have made substantial profits. Since he knew he could not import the wine without a licence and, moreover, would have to pay the South African exporters in foreign exchange, one can only conclude that he intended to use his public office for irregular purposes.

(g) More serious was the TIKA affair. TIKA (Technical Industrial Kulumbila Associate Ltd.), planned for Mumbeje in Solwezi from 1972, was to have been a K 122 million iron and steel complex providing up to 1000 jobs. It never got underway, but it did cost Zambia at least K 15 million. This matter was also brought to a head when M.P.s began to ask probing questions about Zambia's reported obligation to compensate the various partners and consultants. It was not publicly known until December 1979[27] that the TIKA venture had come to nothing. A long series of penetrating questions had been asked on the subject in the National Assembly (1974 and 1975), which revealed that the consultants were Swindell Dressler, an American company. Construction was to have been undertaken as follows:

Mining, beneficiation and pelletisation of areas would be carried out by Energoprojekt of Yugoslavia; reduction plant by the Swindell Dressler Company; Electrical furnaces would be constructed and installed by Denag of West Germany; other jobs such as soil tests, building of townships, site-clearing and foundations would be undertaken by local contractors on tender basis.

By 1979, the then Minister for Mines, Newstead Zimba, stated in Parliament[28] "that TIKA was too sensitive to be discussed and that some of the partners would be sued by the Zambian Government". Furthermore, mysteriously, "the Government knew fully that feasibility studies which had been conducted on TIKA advised the authorities not to go ahead with the project because it was not going to yield any benefits for the nation". There was much speculation in Zambia as to why the project would not have been feasible and one suggestion was that oil as an energy source had become the problem. Robby Makayi, an investigative Zambian journalist argued, however, that the plant could easily have been converted to electricity, which is cheap and readily available in Zambia. Makayi concluded "that it could not have been completely written off had it not been for political intrigues in Zambia and international business manoeuvres". By mid-1981, Energoprojekt, the Yugoslav company (with long experience in Zambia) as well as the Zambian partner and subcontractor ZECCO still had not been paid for their services. What seems to have been most lacking in this venture was the political will and ability to succeed.

(h) Many smaller cases of corruption can be cited, among them

  (i)   The Kanyama Fund, had been set up by President Kaunda in 1978 to help people whose homes had been wrecked by floods. Virtual misappropriation of part of this fund ensued. Items donated to the fund by the public were "bought" at give-away prices by party leaders, these being a Cabinet Minister, a Provincial Secretary, a Governor and a District Secretary.[29] An attempt was made to recover the shortfalls.

  (ii) The Barnett affair came to light after Titus Mukupo alleged in Parliament that the First Secretary of the Zambian Embassy in Bonn was one of the leaders involved in an international scandal in which pay-offs were being demanded on aid intended for Zambia.[30] He said that an international broker/financier involved was being detained in Zambia because he had asked to be paid his fee. That man turned out to be Constantine Joel Barnett, a Jamaican-born British citizen, who (reportedly) claimed that he had organised a loan of 500 million French Francs (K 83.6 million) towards the K 400 million Operation Food Programme. He further claimed that he had been promised one per cent "finder's fee", half of which he would surrender to two top leaders in the party and its government – in clear violation of the Leadership Code laid down by President Kaunda. Attorney-General Chigaga disputed the claim publicly[31] and announced that the government had not in any way sought the services of Barnett and that he would not be paid. Barnett, who spent four months in detention and claimed not to have been charged with anything, retorted that the loan had been released by the Banque Français du Commerce Exterior whose executives had visited Zambia late in 1980 to finalise the arrangements. When President Kaunda announced "Operation Food Production" in October 1980, he did list Barnett's Technology Transfer Consult firm as one of the organisations to be involved in the ten-year programme. Further investigations revealed that another eight companies had been promoted and formed by Barnett between December 1978 and February 1980, all of which were registered with the Ministry of Commerce and Industry.[32] Several Zambian leaders were listed as Directors of these companies as well as Barnett, eg., Dr. Leonard Chivuno (Director of the National Planning and Development Commission), Fred Mwananshiku and Dick Litana (the diplomat in Bonn). Chivuno and Mwananshiku subsequently publicly dissociated themselves from involvement in these companies. Allegation in the press centred on the suspicion that Zambian leaders were trying to use these loan funds, raised ostensibly for the Food Programme, for private commercial purposes.

A further inuendo was that some of the leaders had made a deal with Barnett which was seemingly official (presumably so that finder's fee could be paid from public funds) but which was not, in fact, official at all. The Barnett case was to be heard in open court later in the year. Why it was necessary to keep Barnett four months in detention was not cleared up.

What is the situation vis-à-vis crime and the police in Zambia? It is to be expected that, given an increasing unemployment rate, crime, too, will increase. In Zambia, the correlation between unemployment and crime appears to be positive. Urbanisation and poverty on the fringes of cities have given rise to highly organised gangs of robbers and thieves from whom little is safe. During the first three weeks of my contract, I heard first-hand of 12 burglaries in staff houses on campus, two of which were virtually emptied of furniture, equipment and personal belongings. Mr. Wilted Phiri, Minister of Home Affairs, informed Parliament (August 7 1980) that "the crime rate in the first half of 1980 had risen between 150 and 500 per cent".[33] Compared with the same period in 1979, felonies rose by 300 per cent, ordinary robberies by 400 per cent and white collar crime by 500 per cent. Similar evidence for armed robberies and theft of motor vehicles made it clear that Zambia was in the grip of an unprecedented crime wave with all urban enclaves showing extremely high increases. The Minister advanced the following as causal factors: High unemployment, increasing numbers of grade seven school leavers, and the continuing rural-urban drift. The availability of guns left behind by the Zimbabwean freedom fighters, the unfavourable economic climate in neighbouring countries and police understaffing were also held to be responsible for the increase in crime.[34] By all accounts, this situation did not improve during 1982 and, unless the employment situation eases, the 1980s will probably continue to present great security difficulties. The incidence of corruption amongst leaders can, of course, only have acted as an encouragement to potential law-breakers and criminals. People will put up with poverty as long as they trust their leaders and believe in them, but trust was seriously lacking in Zambia during this period, An entire generation, in fact is growing up and becoming accustomed to a life of robbing or being robbed. It is not surprising that nearly all houses of any consequence are barricaded behind high walls, burglar bars, security guards and dogs. It is sad to comment that the security industry in Zambia is one of the few that are flourishing and that, not unlike the whites in South Africa, the Zambian elite, as well as most expatriates, are living in a virtual prison. By July 1980, according to Commissioner of Prisons, Jonathan Mwanza the Prison Department was locking up an average of 10,000 inmates a day.[35] Mwanza compared this with the figure at independence, which was "less than 2500". Naturally, the Police Force has come under great strain. It is understaffed and continuously plagued by transport difficulties.[36] Morale in the force is not helped by corrupt practices at the top. In December 1979, for example, Commissioner of Police Jeffrey Munalala was suspended for alleged misconduct. In October 1980, Munlala was found guilty of stealing a K 1100 Toyota Land-Cruiser gearbox donated to the Police Force by the Japanese Overseas Corporation Volunteers, and sentenced to seven years imprisonment. In May 1980,[37] five more Police Chiefs were suspended (amongst them a Deputy-Commissioner) and put on half-salary. A year later investigations were still going on. In May, 1981, Crispin Katukula, former Inspector-General and newly appointed diplomat, was sentenced to three years' imprisonment for theft while a public servant. (He was accused of having stolen a steering rack worth K 2000 from a government car).[39]

One may well ask why it is that such highly placed public servants engage in this kind of petty pilfering? Are their salaries so poor or are they merely the tip of the iceberg that just happens to be visible (or exposed and brought to justice by envious careerists)? The fact is that, although the salaries of top officials are, by Western standards quite moderate, together with government service benefits they are sufficient to allow a relatively comfortable lifestyle, certainly as compared with the rest of the population. There should be, therefore, no need to pilfer.

The university also came in for its share of criticism. UNZA's relatively congenial atmosphere hides a very slow-moving and top-heavy bureaucracy. While there are some outstanding administrators in UNZA, they have to carry the burden of many incompetent supervisors and clerks. What is incomprehensible, therefore, is the authorities' reluctance to discipline inefficiency and wrong-doing. I remember the case of the petrol money clerk whose only input for months on end, was to hang his coat over his chair at about 8 a.m. and then to disappear for the rest of the day. It was sheer luck to catch him in the act and to get him to process a claim.

In August, 1981 UNZA auditors Coopers and Lybrandt revealed that nearly K 10 million could not be accounted for by the university authorities. A month earlier, President Kaunda, who is also Chancellor of UNZA, had appointed a Commission of Inquiry into the affairs of UNZA.[40] According to its terms of reference, the Commission would inquire into the effectiveness of the administration and administrative structures under the (new) federal organisation of the university (there being two campuses, one in Lusaka and one in Ndola). Several other matters were included in the terms of reference, such as staff and student attitudes and the effective utilisation of resources. Students were quick to welcome the new inquiry. They criticised the deteriorating condition of the student residences, threats to academic freedom by the presence of Special Branch men on campus, and the irrelevance of the new posts of Principal on each campus.[41] They also requested vacation employment for every student and a course in political economy in all faculties. The Inquiry does not seem to have had much immediate impact since, in April 1982, students protested strongly about the administration of the newly established Institute of Human Relations as well as about conditions generally. Initially this led to the expulsion of some of the students, followed by new demonstrations by others, but just when the administration was ready to compromise on the proposed disciplinary action, the police and the military suddenly moved in. Six foreign lecturers were searched, some taken for questioning and four deported for what were regarded as subversive activities. The university was closed and reopened only in June 1982.

With the efficiency and integrity of civil servants so much in question, it is not surprising that in November 1980 the general public, although politically rather powerless, hardly welcomed the substantial salary increases for several categories of civil servants. These were recommended by a Committee of Inquiry comprising top public servants, after sitting for a mere four months.[42] Furthermore increases were back-dated to 1 August 1980. The two main terms of reference had been:

1. To make recommendations on salaries, salary structures and conditions of service. . . having particular regard to:
   (a) the rise in the cost of living since the last review which set the present salary levels and conditions of service;
   (b) the effects of the Turner Report;
   (c) the need for stability, efficiency and continuity in the Public Service;
   (d) the need to provide adequate incentives to professional and technical categories of staff and to persons serving in rural areas;
   (e) the need to re-adjust salary structures in order to allow for flexibility and rationalisation; and

(f) the date of implementation of the recommendation.
2. To examine ways and means of meeting the increases that may result from any recommendations under the first terms of reference with special emphasis on the need
   to reduce the size of the Public Service without impairing operational efficiency.[43]

Apart from the relative upgrading of a few of the lowly-paid categories
of jobs, wage differentials in the service and in Zambia as a whole, either
remained the same (in effect, were restored) or were actually increased. The
recommendations of the First and Second Turner Reports, therefore, were
ignored. Even within the service itself, the highest paid servant receives nearly
20 times as much as the lowest paid before tax. When a comparison is made
with rural workers, the gap is wider still.[44]

Three of the principal recommendations (there are 116 altogether) should
be noted here:

1. Efficiency has fallen to an unacceptable level. Government should therefore institute
   an in-depth study of the operational efficiency in the Public Service;
4. There is no need to introduce incentives for persons serving in rural areas;
5. The Public Service is not overstaffed in view of the increasing demand for professional and technical staff. However, a manpower audit of posts should be carried out
   to determine its optimum size.[45]

Recommendation 1 led to the formation of the Civil Service probe teams,
which completed their report at the end of 1982.

Recommendation 4, to my mind, is in grave error. It was argued that, in
rural areas, there were already incentives, such as cheaper food, lower costs
(eg., for housing and land) and less hectic and dangerous living conditions.
Yet, the rural-urban drift continues, and continues to add to the problems
of unemployment, poverty and crime. In 1979, of 20 UNZA scholarships in
Medicine, only three were taken up because students were required to practice
for some years in rural areas. What would happen, on the other hand, if a
loading of, say, 25 % to 50 % were to be paid to civil servants and professionals who moved to rural areas? Not only would candidates fall over themselves trying to get out of the cities (especially Lusaka) but after arriving in
their rural abode they would also stimulate local purchasing power and inject
new ideas into the rural scene. They would, moreover, create new demands
and attempt to import more sophisticated lifestyles. To my mind, nothing
would be more effective in stimulating decentralisation and the economy
while at the same time alleviating, possibly eliminating, the overwhelming
problems now poisoning urban life.

Recommendation 5 also runs counter to the Turner Report. An argument
against reducing the size of the Civil Service often heard in Zambia is: What is
to be done with the rejects, given the fact that the private sector is small and
far from buoyant at present? Further arguments are that it would have an
adverse effect on spending power, and add to the problems of unemployment
and crime.

I wish both to take issue with these arguments and to emphasise the applicability of my counter-arguments to most developing countries, where the Civil Service and the Parastatals together are frequently by far the most important employers.

There are two quite opposite positions or models to be identified in this matter:

Model 1: In this model (which applies to Zambia) the government sector is seen primarily as an employment agency whose hierarchical structure functions to reward party faithfuls. Merit is of lesser signfficance than are reward for party loyalty, the provision of employment and the maintenance of fractional (and tribal) harmony, all of which govern appointment and promotion policies. When misdemeanours occur and are brought to light, there may, at first, be much concern expressed, but there is an overriding tendency not to punish too severely, (if at all). Instead, personnel are moved laterally or re-appointed after the dust has settled. In this way, the same people are kept in employment and gradually the merit principle and general performance are very adversely affected. The incentive to do well in such a system is very weak, and officials easily fall prey to foreign companies and unscrupulous profiteers. Mediocre personnel drift to the top, and so-called leaders tend to become agents for their interests rather than the nation's.

Model 2: In this model, the Government sector is seen as primarily an engine of growth, taking command of developing the country and stimulating the economy. It ruthlessly adheres to the merit principle and does not operate as an employment agency. It tolerates neither inefficiency nor corruption. Its size is no greater than it needs to be, since it is realised that unproductive or idle workers are, in fact, counter-productive elements. Such a sector is guided by a strict and strictly enforced leadership code, and leaders project a very independent and tough negotiating position with foreign interests.

In spite of the shortcomings of some of the recommendations of the Committee of Inquiries into Salaries, there is perhaps reason to believe that Zambia is in transition from Model 1 to Model 2. The Civil Service probe may reveal such a trend, and the Corruptive Practices Act (No. 14 of 1980) hopefully also suggests this. Understandably, having had no experience with the workings of bureaucracy in a developing country, prior to 1964, and being persistently altogether short of skills, the first postindependence phase could only have yielded the results it did. The colonial administration, although the only model to follow at first, represented the very opposite of a respected indigenous meritocracy aiming at balanced national development. Neither can Western bureaucracies and parastatals be models, because these are still largely appendices of and supports for the private sectors in which 80 % of the workforce is employed. The general level of skills in such bureaucracies, moreover, is much higher than in a developing country. Undoubtedly, the socialist models offer more relevant experience to draw on, although the extensive interaction with multi-national companies and the aftermath of the colonial experience (common to most developing countries) were absent in those models. The situation, therefore, is unique, and progress can only be made by experiment and, inevitably, by making mistakes. The socialist models, however, demand a high degree of discipline if they are to produce engines of development. Such discipline levels, however, have not always been achievable or acceptable.

I am not at all convinced that developing nations should be entirely bureaucratised or that the private sector should remain insignificant or at least dominated by parastatals. The experiences in Mozambique and the change in direction achieved by President Samora Machel by 1980 strongly suggest that there is scope for a flourishing private sector, provided it is largely in the hands of domestic entrepreneurs. I do believe, however, that the state should always remain the main instrument of control of the economy and represent the people rather than foreign interests. Economic independence, I suggest, is not incompatible with an enterprising domestically owned private sector. This may be achieved more effectively by a small productive bureaucracy, very efficiently organised, which is not encumbered by unnecessary and/or incompetent staff. It is therefore much more desirable, even for Zambia now, to reduce the size of her government sector and pay the redundant staff a full salary for, say, five years and thereafter 80 % of full salary for another five years, and so on, than to continue in the present fashion. This scheme could also assist in stimulating the private sector, especially the development of small business enterprises by ex-Civil Service personnel who, having been provided with the security of an income for ten years, would be in a favourable position to redirect their careers.

Now that so many glaring mistakes have come to light, the time has come not just to improve the efficiency of the Government sector, but also to reorientate quite drastically its character and direction. If this were to happen, the 1980s may turn out to be the decade of the Management Revolution!

The provisions of the Corrupt Practices Act, thoughtfully put together after considerable research by SITET overseas, are encouraging in this respect. The *Zambia Daily Mail* drew attention to an important novel feature of the legislation:

> Under the Corrupt Practices Act, new rules of evidence have been considerably changed: The accused will have to prove his innocence unlike previously when the prosecution had to prove the accused guilty beyond all reasonable doubt. And if a person is convicted of corruption, he shall be liable to a five-year mandatory sentence.[46]

The introduction of this Roman/Dutch procedure (in section 46.4) has potentially strengthened the hand of the Executive, at least in corruption cases.

Part II of the Act outlines the establishment of an Anti-Corruption Commission "which shall be a Government Department under the control and supervision of the President". Only those qualified to be Judges of the High Court may be Commissioners.

Part III deals with the extensive functions of the Commission, which include even the active education of the public to counter corrupt practices.

Part IV provides a comprehensive list of punishable offences.

The passing of this Act nevertheless had a somewhat lukewarm response in the Zambian press. The *Zambian Daily Mail* article sounded this warning:

> However, much as some legal experts say about its success, some laymen show hopelessness in the effectiveness of the Act. It is feared that the Act will affect only those at the nadir of society as it is alleged that people in the top hierarchy of the Party and its Government will not be affected; rather have been exempted. This conclusion that certain leaders have been exempted stems from what has been happening lately. It is argued that several leaders and leading figures in the country, despite having committed offences, have allegedly escaped trial just because of their status in society.[47]

Political Activity

The multiplying economic and management problems which the Zambian government was facing by the end of the 1970s resulted in two kinds of political action (in 1980 and 1981), aimed at shifting the balance of power in the country. In October 1980, there was an attempt to overthrow the government, and, throughout the period, there was heightened strike and other political activity by the Zambian Congress of Trade Unions (ZCTU) under the leadership of Frederick Chiluba.

The first rumblings were heard in April 1980, when the then Chairman of the Standard Bank Zambia (Ltd.), Elias Chipimo, publicly expressed the view that the "multi-party system was the surest way of avoiding coups and eliminating the disgraceful tendency of presidents ending up with bullets in their heads".[48] The President responded at some length, stating that: "dissidents led by former Cabinet Ministers are behind a plot to incite the army into overthrowing the Government and to assassinate me".[49] Dr. Kaunda named the dissidents as Elias Chipimo, Valentine Musakanya (a former Minister for Technical Education and Vocational Training, and Governor of the Bank of Zambia) and Andrew Kashita (former Minister of Mines and Industry). Others implicated in "this vicious and deliberate campaign against the Party and its Government" were Barclays Bank Zambia Manager Francis Nkhoma, and former Minister of Education and Finance John Mwanakatwe. Chipimo, an old adverdary of "KK", later resigned his post and, after the accused had publicly reaffirmed their support for the President, there the matter seemed to rest.

On 16 October 1980, Zambian security forces exchanged fire with a group of about 50 Zairean mercenaries on a deserted farm at Chilanga, 15 km south of Lusaka.[50] Two of the mercenaries were killed and, after some days, most of the others were captured, together with substantial quantities of AK 47s and ammunition. Within a week, seven prominent Zambian citizens were arrested: Chipimo, Musakanya, Patrick Chisanga, Edward Shamwana (a lawyer, former High Court Commissioner and Manager of ITT) as well as three senior army officers. At a press conference held on the lawn of State House (October 27), President Kaunda revealed how the alleged coup had been staged but had folded 24 hours before it was to take place.[51] He explained that the plot had been hatched "by a clique of Zambian elements aided by mercenaries and fascist South Africa". The link with South Africa was attributed to contacts that South African forces had attempted to forge in Sesheke (Western Province), but what bearing this was supposed to have on the coup was not clear. Many details of the plot were also left unexplained because "the matter was under investigation", the President said. Chipimo and Chisanga were soon released, but several others were arrested subsequently and, on May 28 1981, thirteen people, four of them army officers, were committed to summary trial on treason charges.[52] It was alleged that the core of this group (9) conspired with a Lusaka lawyer, Pierce Annfield, to overthrow the Government (Annfield left Zambia, escaped arrest and was tried *in absentia*). The trial dragged on until January 1983, when eventually six were found guilty of the main charge and convicted to the mandatory death sentence.

A trial of strength has furthermore developed between the ZCTU and the party and its government. Basically, this has happened because the ZCTU leadership is convinced that the government has consistently failed to respond to workers' demands to improve their standard of living, although several secondary issues have emerged as well. This clash is likely to dominate Zambia's political scene through the 1980s because the ZCTU has a substantial power base of 16 affiliated unions, including the Mineworkers Union of Zambia (MUZ) which represents some 55 000 Copperbelt miners who produce 95 % of the country's exports. Although formerly a branch of UNIP, the ZCTU has, in fact, adopted the rôle of an opposition party outside the parliamentary sphere. In September 1980, ZCTU Chairman Frederick Chiluba announced that "industrial workers had to brace themselves for industrial action" and that he was "ready to press the button at any time for a national strike before the end of the year." "It is time for us all to unite", he urged, "and be prepared to die." Denouncing the high crime rate, deteriorating economic conditions and the privileged lifestyle of the elite, Chiluba added that "we must be prepared to suffer, to be prosecuted and to be jailed to bring about improvements."[53]

The strike threat seemed to surprise the Government and was portrayed as "political" by the Minister of Labour and Social Services, Joshua Lumina. The immediate issue at stake was the rejection in its entirety by the ZCTU of the controversial Local Government Administration Bill. Although it was ostensibly aimed at more effective decentralisation of power, the ZCTU argued that it would, instead, take away the voting rights of the people and, in particular, would mean the government's paying salaries and allowances to 20 more councillors and local administrators in each district, amounting to more than K 500 000 a month.[54]

The first round of industrial action occurred when 600 railway men struck (1 October 1980) in Kabwe, Zambia's main railways depot. The Railways Workers Union of Zambia (RWUZ) demanded the removal of the Works Manager, David Chibula, who, it claimed, "had been sacking people indiscriminately". Minister Lumina rushed to the scene but the RWUZ refused to see him, on instructions from the ZCTU. At the same time, the Zambian National Union of Teachers (ZNUT) threatened to strike on the Copperbelt and in Kabwe over promised better conditions and salaries. A national teachers' strike, however, was averted.

In a major *Times Review* article, Zambia was then publicly lectured by Basil Kabwe, a former General Secretary of the ZCTU, on the rôle of the trade unions.[55] He claimed that the ZCTU leadership "was going too far in ridiculing the Party leadership". Their constant criticism of Party leaders was unfair and divisive. Why should the ZCTU leadership fear to be arrested, he wanted to know? Perhaps Chiluba's expectations were more realistic than Kabwe's rhetoric. In the first week of November, the Party probed ZCTU activities to see "if there was any foreign infiltration", and this was followed soon by the withdrawal of the passports of Chiluba, General-Secretary Newstead Zimba and assistant General-Secretary Chitalu Sampa. Further probing led to the expulsion (January 16 1981) from the party of 17 ZCTU and MUZ leaders by the government. The Central Committee claimed that through this action the party had asserted its supremacy over the ZCTU with a view to preventing antiParty and destabilising activities by ZCTU leaders. In the same breath it assured the labour movement that it had no intention of interfering in trade union affairs.[56]

The response was quick. On January 20, more than 5000 miners from Nchanga Consolidated Copper Mines (NCCM) downed tools, and production at No. 1 Shaft came to a halt. The strike spread next day to Mufulira, Chibuluma, Chambeshi, Ndola Copper Refinery and Rokana Mines. Reuben Kamanga (senior Member of UNIP's Central Committee) warned the 'disgruntled labour leaders" that the strikes were "illegal as no industrial dispute had been declared". It was, he said, "a coup plot".[57] Two days later Bank and Zambia State Insurance Company clerks went on strike in Zambia's five major towns, protesting against poor conditions and the beating up, in Lusaka, of one of their officials by "Party militants". Meanwhile, the chairman of the MUZ, David Mwila, began to call for the miners to return to work when the Ministry of Labour and Social Services "clarified" the position of the expelled trade union leaders in that "they continued to hold their leadership position in the respective unions" — on the face of it, rather an incongruous situation! The ZCTU executive then called the eight-day strike off also. It had cost Zambia about K 20 million in foreign exchange.

By the end of April, after an abortive attempt at reconciliation, the government responded favourably to the appeal by the ZCTU to reinstate the leadership to party membership. The ZCTU insisted that the charges against them (involvement in a coup) were false.[58]

The peace was short-lived. At the end of June the government appointed Basil Monze as the new General Manager of Zambia Railways. With the mood of the workers there, already hostile over low salaries and conditions, the appointment of Monze appears to have been quite an unfortunate one. According to a *Times of Zambia* editorial,[59] "Monze was involved in the Mumpanshya Report, has been tainted with the negative aspects of that Report and, for all his virtues, is a misfit". According to the Union, Monze was the architect of "all the trouble in the system and his appointment showed that the effect of the Mumpanshya Report had been absolutely nil".[60] In this explosive situation, both the ZCTU and the government called on the men to return to work, especially in view of the essential services provided by the railways (the most important means of transport in Zambia) and to sort the matter out afterwards.

Before anything could be settled, however, the government suddenly detained Chiluba, Zimba and Sampa, one MUZ senior official and a businessman for allegedly inciting workers to disrupt industrial peace and eventually overthrow the government.[61] The President addressed the nation in order to explain why the government had acted in the way it had and to inform the people that 205 681 man-days had been lost through wildcat strikes since independence, detailing that "this year there had been no fewer than 84 illegal strikes involving 46 399 workers". In the ensuing court proceedings, the same charges that the President had made publicly were laid: the ZCTU had the political objective to topple the government.

It would seem, however, that the government had overreacted as the charges were thrown out by the High Court as being "too general and lacking specificity and, in one aspect, demonstrably incorrect". What Chiluba had said was that, the way the country was going, the President would be "toppled within five years", though he did not say by whom or how. Chiluba and three others were released on October 28 1981, and Zimba on November 10 1981.

There is certainly much speculation in Zambia that Chiluba has presidential ambitions, but under the present constitutional arrangements, it is extremely difficult for an alternative candidate to muster sufficient party support to gain official endorsement for candidacy. It is therefore unlikely that
Chiluba will enter the race in the forthcoming 1983 election. Although 1982
was a relatively peaceful year in industrial relations, miners can soon be expected once more to put the government to the test, as the new International
Monetary Fund deal has necessitated an emergency austerity programme and
a 20 % devaluation in January 1983. This means that in the short-run at least
real wages are more likely to fall than to rise.

Conclusion

Progress toward development and economic reorientation in Zambia is greatly
hindered by an inefficient administration and creeping corruption amongst
some high officials and politicians. Not surprisingly, donor agencies operating
in Zambia frequently try to work around the bureaucracy rather than with it.
Often this is simply not possible. Permits must be granted, licences issues,
goods cleared through customs and transport arranged. Foreign companies
may try to do likewise or may resort to bribery, sometimes merely to speed
up services. The deficient operation of the state's machinery dismays many
Zambians and there is no shortage of criticism. Analysis of the managerial
and administrative problems is adequate and public exposure and discussion
of them is as intense as in Western countries, at least in the short-run. Formal
recommendations to remedy deficiencies are usually on target and legislation
has been passed to deal with corrupt practices.

The problem lies in the frequent nonimplementation of the recommendations by Commissions of Inquiries and of the legislation. In Zambia the way
to Kafka's Castle is paved with good intentions. In fact, it has become a maze
of good intentions. The reasons why measures to counteract inefficiency
and corruption don't have the desired effect are no doubt complex. Lack of
political will is an obvious one but why there is this lack of political will is
not so easily answered. It could hardly be argued that cultural factors preclude
Zambians from being severe on their compatriots. One only has to witness the
sometimes very rough treatment members of the Zambian police force dish
out to suspects – let alone the "justice" administered by angry crowds at
times – to appreciate that this explanation is inadequate. Rather, I suspect,
the lack of political will to implement recommendations effectively or to
prosecute and convict is related to the collective interest of the political
elite or "social bureaucracy", as Professor Turner calls it, as a class. Members

of this class, which Marxists describe as a quasibourgeoisie, tend to cover up one another's misdemeanours in the interests of the class as a whole. A show is made of the wrong-doings but exemptions and loopholes are usually available to excuse the culprits.

Seen in this light, it is highly unlikely that the six plotters, convicted to the mandatory death sentence in January 1983, will in fact be put to death. With a presidential election coming up in October such treatment would be politically undesirable in any case, but even after President Kaunda's almost certain reelection it would be contrary to class interest to carry out the sentence. One might add that to carry it out would also be a waste to the nation because the managerial, entrepreneurial and administrative talents of these convicted men are quite considerable. Their behaviour in 1980 should be seen as a consequence of highly unsatisfactory government practices, which they rightly criticised and from which they deliberately dissociated themselves. Rather than criticising their capitalist orientation it would make more sense to respect their abilities as managers and entrepreneurs and to recognise that they appear to have been motivated primarily by their partiotic concern for the slide in standards and living conditions in Zambia.

The Treason Trial (1981/82) has brought to a head the very precarious internal state of affairs the country is faced with in the early 1980s. One can only hope that the President sees his way clear to productively reintegrate the convicted men into Zambian society rather than to eliminate them – either by death sentence or imprisonment for life.

A secondary conclusion should be that the ZCTU has emerged as a viable *de facto* opposition party. Although in the main still concerned with working conditions and wages, the ZCTU has increasingly pronounced on and often criticised general political matters. Reluctantly, the leaders of the political elite have accepted this new rôle. What remains to be seen of course is whether or not this new dimension of Zambian politics will provide the framework, within UNIP, for reopening negotiations on constitutional change, especially in relation to the Presidency.

Notes

1. *Second Report to the Government of Zambia on Incomes, Wages and Prices in Zambia:* Part I: General Review and Recommendations, I.L.O., Geneva 1978.
2. Op. Cit., pp. 10-11.
3. Op. Cit., p. 1.
4. *Times of Zambia*, 8 February 1981 (hereinafter quoted as *ToZ*).
5. *ToZ*, 6 February 1981.
6. *ToZ*, 18 November 1979.

7. *ToZ*, 3 February 1980.
8. *ToZ*, 3 May 1980.
9. *ToZ*, 6 May 1980.
10. *National Mirror*, November 21-December 4, 1980.
11. Republic of Zambia, *Report of the Commission of Inquiry into the Affairs of Zambia Railways*, Lusaka, March 1978.
12. Op. Cit, pp. 12-12. Zambia Railways Police Commandant Bartholemew Mwale, who was quite unfairly dismissed, was subsequently reinstated and promoted to the rank of Assistant Commissioner in the Zambia Police. He was then instructed to resume his investigations into Zambia Railways but by mid-1981, surprisingly, no formal charges had been laid.
13. Op. Cit., item 169, p. 161.
14. Republic of Zambia, *Report of the Committee on Parastatal Bodies* (for the fifth session of the third National Assembly – appointed on 31 January, 1978), 1978.
15. Republic of Zambia, *Report of the Auditor-General for 1979 on the accounts for the financial year ended 31st December 1979*, Lusaka, 1980.
16. Republic of Zambia, *Report of the Committee on Parastatal Bodies* (for the first session of the fourth National Assembly – appointed on 16 January, 1979), 1980.
17. Op. Cit., item 14.
18. *ToZ*, 18 January 1981.
19. Republic of Zambia, *Report of the Auditor-General on the accounts for the financial year ended 31st December 1979*, Lusaka, 1980.
20. *Sunday Times*, 15 March 1981.
21. *Zambia Daily Mail*, 21 January 1981; *ToZ*, 4 February 1981.
22. *ToZ*, 9 December 1980.
23. Kapelwa Musonda regularly writes a Tuesday column in the *Times of Zambia*. He is believed to be a high party official writing under a nom-de-plume. In 1979 the Zambian publishing house NECZAM published *The Best of Kapelwa Musonda* covering a 10-year period of ridiculing Zambian weaknesses.
24. *ToZ*, 30 November 1980.
25. *ToZ*, 13 March 1981.
26. *ToZ*, 12 April 1980, 23 April 1980, and 19 February 1981.
27. Patu Simoko, "Down TIKA Memory Lane" in *Times Review*, 1 March 1981.
28. Op. Cit.
29. *ToZ*, 4 December 1980.
30. *ToZ*, 12 March 1981.
31. *ToZ*, 24 April 1981.
32. *ToZ*, 21 June 1981.
33. *ToZ*, 8 August 1980.
34. *ToZ*, 8 August 1980.
35. *ToZ*, 28 July 1980.
36. The bizarre case of the Lusaka strangler, who in the first half of 1980 killed 29 young women before he was apprehended, comes to mind. A further display of inefficiency occurred when the Australian journalist Tony Joyce was shot at the Chongwe Bridge whilst in police custody. Although this was an unfortunate accident that the police cannot be blamed for, the subsequent handling of the affair was unsatisfactory and rightly dismayed Australian authorities and Joyce's relatives. The rough treatment meted out to the six UNZA lecturers in April 1982, notably the Dutch philosophy professor, Lolle Nauta, was highly inept also, but in this case at least public apologies were tendered afterwards.

37. *ToZ*, 9 October 1980.
38. *ToZ*, 27 April 1981.
39. *Zambia Daily Mail*, 5 May 1981.
40. *ToZ*, 10 August 1981.
41. *ToZ*, 12 August 1981 – letter by Chamina Mulofwa.
42. Republic of Zambia, *Summary of the Main Recommendations of the Administrative Committee of Inquiry into the Salaries, Salary Structures and Conditions of Service, together with the Party and its Government's Reactions to the Recommendations*, Government Paper No. 3 of 1980.
43. *Summary*, Introduction.
44. *ToZ*, 29 March 1981.
45. *Summary*, Section A.
46. *Zambia Daily Mail*, 20 November 1980 (based on Section 46.4).
47. *Zambia Daily Mail*, 20 November 1980.
48. *ToZ*, 21 April 1980.
49. *ToZ*, 23 April 1980.
50. *ToZ*, 17 October 1980.
51. *Zambia Daily Mail*, 28 October 1980.
52. *ToZ*, 29 May 1981.
53. *ToZ*, 29 September 1980.
54. *ToZ*, 30 September 1980.
55. *Sunday Times*, 2 November 1980.
56. *Zambia Daily Mail*, 17 January 1981.
57. *ToZ*, 22 January 1981.
58. *ToZ*, 25 January 1981.
59. *ToZ*, 20 June 1981.
60. Basil Monze had recently retired as Permanent Secretary of the Lands and Natural Resources Ministry.
61. *ToZ*, 28 July 1981.

Chapter 8
The Rôle of the Press
by Francis Kasoma

Press refers to a section of the mass media that transmits its messages through print. It does not refer to mass media like radio, television and the cinema which inform by the use of electronics. Broadly, *press* includes books, posters and periodicals such as newspapers, magazines and newsletters. In this chapter, *press* takes the narrow meaning of *newspapers*. For reasons of space and coherence, the discussion will only deal with the rôle of the national press in Zambia. It will not cover the role of the press in the country as a whole. There are three sections. The first one is an historical overview. It discusses what has been the rôle of the press in Zambia from its start until 1980. The second section looks at the future rôle of the press in Zambia in the light of past experience. There is a short conclusion.

1. An Historical Overview

From Leopold Moore's *Livingstone Mail* in 1906 right through to the government-owned *Zambia Daily Mail* in 1980, politics has been the mainstay of national newspapers in Zambia. The press in turns has served as the unflinching supporter of the establishment, agitator of political change, pacifier, troubleshooter, king-maker as well as king-destroyer.

Historically, the national press in Zambia reveals three overlapping eras or episodes. These are: the press for White settlers or simply "the White press", the press for Africans, and, the multi-racial press.

The White press started with, W. Tranter's short-lived *Livingstone Pioneer*[1] in 1906 and lasted up to the early 1960s. Newspapers in this era included Moore's *Livingstone Mail* (1906-1968), E.C. Wykerd's and E.B. Hovelmeier's *Copperbelt Times* (1932-1943), F. Mackenzie's *Northern Rhodesian Advertiser* (1935-1956), Roy Welensky's[2] *The Northern News* (1943-1965), and Dr. Alexander Scott's *Central African Post* (1948-1964).

These newspapers exclusively served the interests of White settlers. Editorially, they were their voice. Their editorial "we" very often referred to the White settlers rather than the editors. They defended racial segregation on the principle succinctly expressed by one of them that:

The races can never mix, they are as divided as East is from West.[3]

Whites were superior to Africans. Any pronouncements or policies by the colonial administration which suggested equality were condemned. The reaction of one of the White newspapers to an announcement by the Governor of Nigeria, another British colony, that the administration there was considering lifting the colour bar to "civilized" Africans was typical of the White press:

> No colour bar to civilized Africans says Nigerian Governor! Thank heavens ours are not civilized but it won't be long before the socialist Labour Government forces us to do the same here.[4]

The White press consistently supported perpetuation of White rule, arguing that Africans were uncivilised and incapable of ruling. It was unthinkable that Africans could be elevated to the status of political equality with Whites.

For the White press only Whites made news. The only time Blacks made news was when whatever they did or said affected the well-being of Whites in one way or other. Hence, any references to Africans in the news were nearly always negative.

Naturally, the editors or proprietors of these newspapers were rewarded for championing the White cause by being elected to positions of political leadership by the White electorate. Nearly all of them became members of the Legislative Council or the Federal Parliament, with Welensky assuming the high office of Federal Prime Minister. It cannot be denied that editors or proprietors of the White press used their newspapers as stepping stones for political power.

The African press was started by the colonial government in 1936 with *Mutende* and ended in the early 1960s with the establishment of the *(Central) African Mail.* Newspapers in this era included *Mutende* (1936-1956), *African Eage* (1956-1962), *African Times* (1957-1958) *African Life* (1958-1961) and *African Mail* (1960-1965).

From the ownership point of view, there were three types of African newspapers in Northern Rhodesia. Apart from government-owned, there were also privately-owned and church-owned African newspapers.

Officially the government press like *Mutende* was established to supply Africans, only a few of whom had become barely semiliterate, with reading matter.[5] But this reading matter presented only one viewpoint of the news and features – the administration's view. So biased in favour of the administration was *Mutende* that one of its former editors confessed in the paper's final issue:

> ... Mutende gave news but it was difficult for it to be critical, especially of Government affairs because it was a Government newspaper; it could hardly criticise itself and it is not the function of a Government newspaper to deal with controversial matters.[6]

Even the semigovernment *African Eagle* found it hard to keep its government subsidy and at the same time maintain reasonable objectivity. In the end the newspaper's publishers, Southern Rhodesia-based African Newspapers, were forced to do away with the subsidy rather than "maintain an effective liaison with Government."[7]

Privately-owned newspapers for Africans started with Dr. Alexander Scott's *African Times* in 1957 and ended with David Astor's Central African Mail in 1965. The common role of these newspapers was to support African political advancement which was identified with African nationalism. In this they were diametrically opposed to the White press and the two sides were constantly engaged in a press war, typified by the *Central African Mail* vs. *The Northern News* tussle of the 1960s. During that time the *Mail* persisted in calling on the British government to grant Africans independence while *The Northern News* insisted that Africans were not ready for independence because they were not yet civilised.[8]

Excesses in both opinion and news presentation by the pro-African privately-owned press and the White newspapers, as each tried to out-do the other, brought in a need for the third kind of African newspaper — one whose rôle was to act as referee or peace-maker. The Catholic Church Press filled that rôle with newspapers like *The Leader* (1961-1962) and *The Northern Star* (1963-1964).

However, because these church newspapers were published for the African readership, their peace-maker rôle was very often one-sided. They were more concerned with checking views and opinions of African extremists than they were with checking those of White extremists.

The church press stand of political reconciliation was out of tune with the political climate then prevailing in the country. Welensky's Federation was making its dying kicks and most Africans in Northern Rhodesia were anxious to finish it off as a prelude to independence. At the same time most Whites were desperately trying to prevent the death of the Federation and the coming of independence of Northern Rhodesia. Anybody who preached a course of compromise, like *The Leader* did, was regarded as a political misfit. Any newspaper with such a stand was destined to fail.

The postindependence national press in Zambia first assumed the role of reconstruction.

With the coming of independence in 1964, the various press camps discussed above were forced by circumstances to change their stance. It was realised that in independent Zambia, looking at issues with racial spectacles, would be anathema. So would addressing one's newspaper to one racial group.

The White press had to come to reality and report on Africans fairly and not in derogatory terms. Africans were no longer uncivilised and incapable of ruling. They had to be treated as equals with Whites in all news reports, features and comments. The racial epithets of "African" "native" and "Black" which coloured every news story in which an indigenous person was involved had to disappear from the columns of the White press. Instead the newspapers started reporting and commenting on Zambians as a people, irrespective of their colour.

Similarly, the privately-owned African press too had to adjust its stance and address itself to both Zambians and expatriates. It had to water-down some of its extreme views, accept Whites as part of Zambian society and bury the past.

The change in policy in the two press camps did not come easily. In the case of the White press, it was successfully implemented only after effecting changes in both ownership and staff. With regard to *The Northern News* for instance, the Argus Group and its subsidiary, the Rhodesia Printing and Publishing Company, suddenly sold it to Lonrho in 1963. It was obvious that the two sister companies with headquarters in racially segregated South Africa and Rhodesia, respectively, were embarrassed. They knew that the pro-White record of their newspaper would not be forgotten by the new Zambian Government as well as the Zambian public and that they would inevitably lack credibility.

As a matter of fact, the new Zambian Government did make its feelings about the Argus-owned White press very clear in a lively debate in the Legislative Council early in 1963. The debate had been instigated by a motion by John Roberts, leader of the opposition National Progress Party which represented White interests. Robert's motion to the nationalist coalition government to affirm freedom of the press, came after Kenneth Kaunda the UNIP leader, had reportedly threatened to suppress Northern Rhodesian newspapers if they did not change their attitude. Although both sides eventually agreed on freedom of the press in principle, Kaunda's parliamentary secretary and UNIP publicity chief, Sikota Wina, made the new government's analysis of the White press explicit when he said:

> The history of newspapers in this country right from their establishment has been to serve a minority group, the Europeans, and now that things have changed hands, the so-called wind of change has blown, the newspapers find themselves in a bit of a spot. "How can we change overnight? We still get our advertisement revenue from the European section because the Europeans are still in charge of firms and companies, but at the same time we have now got an African coalition government. How can we commit this change-over without losing our advertisement revenue?"
>
> Therefore you will find, Mr. Speaker, that the press today still suffers from the nostalgia for the past, lives in fear for the present and is completely confused about what to do in future. . . .[9]

The new Black government too was suspicious of foreign White-owned companies publishing national newspapers. This suspicion was the main reason why the government bought the *Central African Mail* in 1965.[10] About the new governmentowned newspaper, President Kaunda pledged:

> It will not be a Government trumpet. I will not allow it to report my every cough. . . We want to establish a paper that will be informative – that will be able to say that I should do a little more at the moment. It will be something with dignity, not designed to mislead the people, something to serve Zambia.[11]

The *Central African Mail,* now renamed *Zambia Mail,* came out with a promise by Minister of Information Lewis Changufu that the intention of the government was to make it a lively, stimulating and readable newspaper. He did not want it to be a dull catalogue of official announcements, locking impact, and ultimately rejected by its reading public.[12]

The *Mail* as a government newspaper started on a low key, avoiding controversy, especially where UNIP was involved.

It should be remembered that this period was one of intense politicking by the country's two main political parties, UNIP and the minority ANC. During this time UNIP was trying to silence ANC politically so as to make Zambia a *de facto* one-party state. The ANC, on the other hand, was busy trying to build up its popularity. Both parties, therefore, were literally at each other's throats, often engaging in sensitive methods of politicking which made controversial and sensational news.

But generally the *Zambia Mail* was unusually critical for a government newspaper. On a number of times it embarrassed the administration by coming out with editorials contradicting or at least differing from official government thinking.

For example, when South African Prime Minister Hendrick Verwoerd was assassinated in September 1966, President Kaunda sent condolences in which he said that although Verwoerd had been one of his bitterest political opponents, he nonetheless mourned his death. But the *Zambia Mail* declared in its editorial: "We cannot join in mourning for Verwoerd who died a death he richly deserved."[12]

The Lonrho-owned *Times of Zambia,* unlike the *Zambia Mail,* did not flinch from criticising the administration and, particularly, UNIP. The *Times* literally went to war against UNIP's card-checking activities in which people were prevented from using public facilities if they did not produce UNIP cards, UNIP's miniskirt campaign in which party youths forcefully lowered girls' hems, and similar excesses.

Indeed, one of the *Times of Zambia* editors, Dunstan Kamano, regarded his role as that of an opposition to the government, since the ANC was so weak it had even ceased to be the official opposition in parliament. He once told members of Kitwe Lions Club that far too few people were prepared to speak their minds in public; that the burden of constructive criticism against the government was being brought to lie squarely on the shoulders of the press; that in a country like Zambia where there were only two (daily) papers, the shoulders of the press might one day prove to be not broad enough to bear the daily pressures thrust upon them from various quarters.[13]

But the administration took exception to the "opposition role" of the press. Early in 1972, President Kaunda called a national mass media seminar at Lusaka's Mulungushi Hall at which he called for a change to a new brand of journalism to suit Zambia. In a long "brutally frank" address, the President called on the journalists:

(a)   Not to conduct themselves as if they were an alternative government;
(b)   To serve Zambian humanism, not capitalism or to live in the colonial past;
(c)   To eschew sensational news; and
(d)   To remember that freedom of the press was based on the right of the people to know, to have access to information.

The aim of the President's address was clearly to prepare the press for its role in the one-party state which was ushered in the following year in August 1973.

Soon after the President's admonition there was a marked change in the content of the two national dailies and the *Sunday Times of Zambia*. Verbatim speeches of important party and government figures became regular features of reporting, hot or sensational stories were often avoided or merely alluded to briefly, and the *Times of Zambia* and *Sunday Times of Zambia* became more docile to the administration. It was during this period that the *Zambia Dail Mail* earned the name "Government Gazette" for being the more docile of the two dailies. It is true that occasionally one read an editorial in either paper attacking one or other sector of the administration or the party but there were no editorials criticising the party as a whole or the government as a whole in both dailies.

The burden of revealing details of many sensational stories as well as criticising the administration now fell on the church press, mainly the *National Mirror*. This 12-page tabloid, published by Multimedia Zambia, a Christian churches-owned organisation, really took on the administration on a number of issues such as the rights to a fair trial for political detainees and the proposed Press Council Bill.

The news format or reporting style in the press, however, was still very much based on the traditional journalism of the West with little or not interpretation of news within the news story and strict adherence to the facts.

The draft of the proposed Press Council Bill which was currently under consideration at the time of writing this chapter in May 1981, was clearly an attempt by the administration to control the press effectively for it to become solely an instrument of the Party.

In the draft Bill, the Press Council was entrusted with the power to ensure that every journalist obeyed the following code of conduct:

(a) Propagate the Philosophy of Humanism and communicate it correctly through mass media and work as a vanguard for the spread of humanist and socialist ideals and other policies of the Party and Government.
(b) Report accurately and objectively on all matters.
(c) Obtain by fair means and by honest methods materials and information for use in mass media.
(d) Behave in public and in private in a manner that would not bring mass media into ridicule or disrepute.
(e) Keep secret all confidential information made available to him or to the mass media.
(f) Report accurately and never distort or misrepresent, or falsify information or documents.
(g) Avoid character assassination and not to act as an agent for the spread of gossip or rumour or information likely to cause tribal, religious or political disunity.
(h) Set an example of loyalty and devotion to duty by observing high standards of good manneriness and behavious; punctuality at all times, sobriety, decent dress, courtesy, tolerance.
(i) Observe the individual's right to privacy.
(j) Avoid taking advantage of the ignorance of persons; organisations or group of people.
(k) Do nothing in news or pictures that would cause pain, embarrassment or humiliation to people, bereaved or distressed persons.
(l) Be fair to all persons in reports and pictures.
(m) Not to accept bribes or favours in return for publishing in mass media stories, features, pictures or reports.
(n) Recognise in particular and abide by the laws of libel, contempt of court, and in general all other laws.
(o) Avoid being influenced in the dissemination of news by religious, tribal or ethnic or any other bias.
(p) Observe restrictions on reporting certain matters as specified by Party and Government or any organisation.
(q) Faithfully interpret, report and comment on major Party and Government pronouncements in a manner which would be easily understood by members of the public without deliberately causing confusion or misunderstanding.
(r) Educate the masses to guide against such evils to society, as drunkeness, crime, indecency, the erosion of Zambian morals and cultures.

2. The Rôle of the Press in the 1980s

Traditionally, the press anywhere in the world has six main roles. It 1. informs people of news and events, 2. interprets news and events, 3. educates, 4. advertises, 5. entertains and 6. transmits cultural heritage. Interpretations of these six functions of newspapers, however, are not necessarily the same from one part of the world to another. They particularly differ between Eastern and Western countries.

The role of the Press to carry news is subject to the understanding of what makes news, how it should be obtained and how it should be reported. In the West, news is any information that journalists think readers have a right to know. It is gathered by journalists from both official and unofficial sources and is published in full while it is still fresh. On the other hand, for Eastern countries, particularly the Soviet Union, news must have one purpose – to propagate the struggle of the proletariat to defeat capitalism. Any information which does not contribute even indirectly to the eventual victory of communism over capitalism is not news and should be underplayed, or better still, left out entirely from the press.

Historically, as we have just seen, the news-reporting function of the Zambian press has been patterned on that of the West. This is not surprising since the journalists themselves have been trained in Western journalistic traditions. Calls by the administration on Zambian journalists to abandon Western or capitalist journalistic practices can only be heeded if a new journalistic tradition was introduced in the training of journalists. Such training requires careful research, planning as well as selection of lecturers in journalism-training institutions.

It is, therefore, not unreasonable to predict that the Western-orientated news-reporting tradition of the Zambian press will remain unchanged throughout the 1980s. No amount of coercion would change the style.

Too much coercion by the administration on Western-trained journalists to change from their well-beaten path is likely to result in these journalists getting frustrated and either resigning or "sticking around" for the sake of earning a living. Those who stay would be preoccupied with trying to please the authorities in order to keep their jobs. At this stage, journalists would become merely public relations officers for the administration and would cease to be go-betweens of the administration on the one hand and the public on the other. They would lack dedication and commitment. Above all, they would lack credibility from the readers who, also having been brought up to read Western-style newspapers, would feel they have been betrayed.

What is likely to modify the content of Zambian newspapers during the decade is the probable shift from what may be termed "hot news journalism" to a misconception of "development journalism". In "hot news journalism" the most newsy stories get the biggest headlines. In misconceived "development journalism," however, the aim is to mobilize the people for economic development by merely explaining government policies and reporting on progress made in implementing these policies. In this type of journalism newsy stories, particularly if they are not development orientated, do not often get the biggest headlines, instead what the leaders are saying forms the bulk of the news, with stories classified according to the leadership hierarchy. Zambia is likely to see a lot of this type of so-called development journalism in the 1980s. In fact, at the time of writing this chapter, signs of it were already noticeable in the press.

The impartiality of an administration-owned press is questionable anywhere in the world, not only in Zambia. It would seem, from the general tone of the proposed Press Council Bill, that there will be a deliberate attempt by the administration to have only official newspapers in Zambia. If this attempt succeeds, then the public would be deprived of that "other voice" which the church press has hitherto provided.

This "other voice" has been particularly noticeable in the interpreting or editorialising role of the Press. It is very unlikely that the official press would even exercise its participatory democratic rights to the full by criticising the administration *per se*. What is likely is that the official press may continue to point fingers at one or other institution or person in the administration while continuing to shower praise on the administration as a whole even where such praise is not due. This kind of journalism is likely to result in the public, or at least the readers, taking a negative attitude towards the administration.

A critical Press can and does play an inspectorate role towards a government, particularly in a developing country like Zambia. It can serve as a constant reminder to the administration to complete unifished projects as well as fulfill those unfulfilled promises. It can force government to abandon bad economic policies and practices by both exposing and criticising these policies and thereby make government answerable to the people. Such constructive criticism should form the basis of real "development journalism."

The Zambian press is likely to continue its educative function in the 1980s. Many more Zambians will become newspaper readers as the population becomes more literate. But this educating role will still be very much concentrated in towns. There will be very little of it in rural areas where it is needed most. Newly literate and semiliterate people in rural areas do not have reading material to maintain their literacy, as libraries are extremely rare. Consequently, the once literate become illiterate for lack of reading material. Newspapers would go a long way in providing this reading material if only they were available to many rural people. Unless the current newspaper distribution system changes drastically and unless the circulation of newspapers increases substantially, there is little or no prospect for many people in rural Zambia to read the national press in the 1980s.

The advertising role of the press is derived from the Western premise that newspaper publication is a business like any other. It must make money of fold up. In the West, newspapers get most of their revenue from advertising. Just like news, almost any advertisement can be published in Western newspapers. There are very few legal restrictions regarding what one cannot advertise.

There are, certainly, no official or political restrictions. The situation is not the same with regard to advertising in Soviet newspapers. Because Soviet newspapers are not business enterprises but state-owned service wings of the Soviet political system, there is less preoccupation on making a profit. The Soviet administration regards advertising not so much as a source of revenue but as a cog in the propaganda machinery. Consequently there are greater restrictions to information that can be advertised in the Soviet press than there are in the Western press, like that of the United States of America.

As in news reporting, the advertising tradition of the press in Zambia stems from the West. Yet the newspaper institutions, inasfar as official ownership is concerned, lean towards the East. It will be interesting to see what role advertising in Zambian newspapers will perform in the 1980s – continue with the Western role, adopt that of the East, or develop its own?

It should be pointed out here that, unlike the West, Zambia does have a few official (as opposed to legal) restrictions on advertising such as advertisements on beer and cigarettes. Whether or not such official restrictions would increase in the 1980s is anybody's guess.

Entertainment columns in the Zambian press have also been modelled on those of the Western press. Political and social gossip columns, as well as music, theatre, art, book, and cinema reviews are mostly imitations of similar entertainment columns in the Western press. One can see a need by the administration to make these columns Zambian in content, though not so Zambian in style of writing, by encouraging Zambian journalists to write on Zambian topics.

The role of the Zambian press in propagating and transmitting the country's cultural heritage would, itself, depend on how well the Zambian press reflects Zambian society not only in its entertainment columns but also in its news, features and advertising columns. A newspaper in a faithful recorder of a people's history which reflects their cultural heritage. One learns a lot about the way of life of early White settlers in Zambia through the columns of the *Livingstone Mail*, for example.

However, because of the presence of a small but influential expatriate clientele (both Black and White) which the Zambian press also, and perhaps mainly, caters for, it is easy for the newspapers to misrepresent foreign culture as Zambian culture. There is also a danger of underrepresenting Zambian culture by neglecting those aspects of it that have been moulded as a result of the clash between foreign and traditional Zambian culture, particularly in the spheres of music and dance. Such are the pit-falls which the press in Zambia will have to watch as it grapples with the task of transmitting Zambian cultural heritage from the generation of the 1980s to that of the 1990s.

3. Conclusion

The press reflects the spirit of its time. The people in the Zambia of 1980s are not primarily concerned about party politics. What is likely to worry them is what to eat, dress and live in as the country's economy fluctuates. They want economic progress.

It does seem, therefore, that the role of the press in Zambia will shift from that of king-maker to that of development agitator. How well this development agitation is performed will depend upon how much freedom the administration gives to what is expected to be a totally official national press.

Postscript

Since completing this chapter in May 1981, there has been little progress with the proposed legislation. By the time this book went to press, in December 1983, the controversial Press Council Bill had still not been tabled before parliament. This is a strong indication that the Bill – if, indeed, it is ever brought before the House – is likely to be amended substantially.

Notes

1. *Livingstone Pioneer* is believed to be the first newspaper in the country.
2. Roy Welensky was the sole owner of *The Northern News* from 1944 until the end of 1950 when he sold the paper to the Southern Rhodesia-based Rhodesia Printing and Publishing Company (4,000 shares) and its parent company, the South Africanbased Argus Group (3,500 shares).
3. *The Livingstone Mail,* 24 October 1947, editorial.
4. Ibid. 3 April 1947, editorial.
5. *Mutende,* January 1936, editorial.
6. W.V. Brelford "Director of Information's message of Farewell." *Mutende,* 30 December, 1952.
7. Federation of Rhodesia and Nyasaland, Auditor-General Report for Northern Rhodesia, Financial Year 1957-58, p. 4.
8. *Central African Mail* and *The Northern News* editorials of 13 February 1962.
9. Northern Rhodesia Legislative Council Debates Vol. 106-7 (January 1963), pp. 432-435.
10. Although the *Central African Mail* had supported African independence and its owner David Astor was a friend of the African nationalists, Lonrho had made overtures to buy this newspaper too and the Zambian Government had to a step in and prevent the deal which would have meant the total ownership of the national

press by Lonrho since they (Lonrho) already owned the *Northern News* and *Sunday News.*
11. *The Northern News,* 19 February 1965, editorial.
12. *Zambia Mail,* 9 September 1961, editorial.
13. *Times of Zambia,* 17 March 1972, editorial.

Selected Bibliography

Ainslie, Rosalynde. *The Press in Africa.* London: Victor Gollanoz Ltd., 1966.

Busek, Anthony. *How the Communist Press Works.* London: Pall Mall Press, 1964.

Hachten, William. *Muffled Drums.* The Iowa State University Press, 1971.

Kasoma, Francis. *The Development, Role and Control of National Newspapers in Zambia 1906-1975.* Ann Arbor: University Microfilms International, 1980.

Kitchen, Helen. *The Press in Africa.* Washington D.C.: Ruth, Ruth Sloan Associates, Inc., 1956.

Potter, Elaine. *The Press as Opposition.* London: Chatto and Windus Ltd., 1975.

Schramm, Wilbur. *Mass Media and National Development.* Standord: University Press, 1964.

Sommerlad, Llyod E. *The Press in Developing Countries.* Sydney: Sydney University Press, 1966.

UNESCO. Reports and Papers on Mass Communication No. 69. *Mass Media in an African Contex:* An Evaluation of Senegal's Pilot Project, 1974.

UNESCO. Reports and Papers on Mass Communication No. 76: *Towards Realistic Communication Policies:* Recent Trends and Ideas compiled and Analysed, 1976.

UNESCO. Reports and Papers on Mass Communication No. 74. *National Communication Systems:* Some Policy Issues and Options, 1978.

UNESCO. Reports and Papers on Mass Communication No. 83. *National Communication Policy Councils:* Principles and Experiences, 1979.

UNESCO. *Intergovernmental Conference on Communication Policies in Africa Final Report.* Yaounde (cameroun) 22-31 July 1980.

UNESCO. *Many Voices, One World.* Report by the International Commission for the Study of Communication Problems, 1980.

UNESCO. *New Communication Order 4:* Protection of Journalists.

Wilcox, Dennis L. *Mass Media in Black Africa, Philosophy and Control.* New York: Praeger Publishers, 1975.

Chapter 9
A. External Aid Agencies
by Fred Roos

According to the latest UNDP report on development assistance to Zambia, the total technical assistance given to that state during 1979 amounted to the equivalent of US$ 102.7 m. The same document reports that, during the same period, US$ 147.7 m had been made available for commodity aid and US$ 224.9 m for capital assistance.

This report was based on information from 17 UN organisations and agencies, including the World Bank and the IMF, 5 other multilateral and 27 bilateral donors and 15 nongovernmental organisations.

Although all assistance recorded by UNDP for 1979 might not have actually been disbursed during the same year, it is clear from Table 1 that external aid is becoming an increasingly important factor in Zambia; indeed, even if we restrict ourselves to technical assistance, it has grown from something like 5.3 % of the government's budget in 1975 to 8.5 % in 1979.

Although it is the financial rather than the technical forms of assistance that appear to have been the more sizeable, we will restrict ourselves, in this chapter, to the technical. This does not mean that financial assistance should be considered an uninteresting subject; quite the contrary. Improvements involving technical co-operation, however, seem to present a more promising opportunity, since, where financial co-operation is concerned, aid is usually tied to purchases from the donor country. In some cases, in fact, finance appears to be available solely to ensure that specific commercial transactions can take place. As, in most of such cases, there exists no alternative supplier offering the same financial package to the recipient country, it is hardly interesting to discuss this type of external aid in exploring possibilities for improvement.

Presently, most donor countries offering financial assistance are not interested in changing current practices, as they are often more advantageous to the donors' industries than to the recipient. That, apparently, is well understood both by industries in donor countries and by involved government officials in recipient countries. The consequence, however, will be that, in the coming years, Zambia (and many other developing countries) will continue to be confronted with fleets of irreparable trucks and tractors of all possible makes, nonoperational or unfinished manufacturing plants, promised plants that have never even been built, and so on. This form of cooperation clearly constitutes a considerable waste of opportunities for developing countries. In this respect, then, donor and developing countries should consider gradually changing their policies.

Development of Technical Assistance

Table 1 indicates that, in the technical assistance given by external aid agencies, there was a remarkable increase in assistance to agriculture (from 14 % in 1975 to 35.1 % in 1979), while in the same period that received by the educational sector declined (from 34 % to 12.7 %).

Despite the development of the budget of Zambia's Ministry for Agriculture and Water Development, the interest of donors in agriculture showed an even more rapid growth. Even though UNDP data include the costs of expatriate personnel under aid programmes (which are very often a considerable proportion of total assistance costs and which are usually not reflected in the government's budget), the growth of inputs by external aid agencies into Zambian agricultural development is remarkable, and, in recent years, tends to be greater than that of Zambia's own inputs. For 1981, for example, the budget estimates indicate that, out of the total of capital and recurrent expenditure for the Ministry of Agriculture and Water Development, 65 % was being met by external aid; for the capital budget alone, the percentage amounts to 74.

The development of external aid overall to Zambia shows a similar trend: external aid is growing faster than the Zambian government budget. The estimates for 1981 indicate that, out of a total capital budget of K 225.8 m, 61 % was expected to be financed by external aid agencies.

Foreign Experts

If external aid is a factor of increasing importance in financing Zambia's development programmes, it would be interesting to know what benefits Zambia derives from this assistance.

One should look first at the form the assistance usually takes, i.e., expert personnel and consultancy services. Although exact data are not easily available, the UNDP reports again provide some useful indications: during

1979, for the sector "general development issues, policy and planning", 130 experts were provided, while the agricultural sector alone received the services of over 200 experts and consultants. It can safely be assumed that the total number of externally funded experts is well over a thousand per year.

	1975 US$ mln	%	1977 US$ mln	%	1979 US$ mln	%	1980 US$ mln	1981 US$ mlnn %
TOTAL TECHNICAL ASSISTANCE	35.0	100	40.5	100	102.7	100		
Of which multilateral	N/A		8.3	20.5	8.8	8.6		
bilateral	N/A		32.1	79.3	81.1	80		
Of which agriculture	4.9	14	13.2	32.6	36.1	35.1		
education	11.9	34	7.8	19.2	13.4	12.7		
transport & communication	3.5	10	2.1	5.1	7.5	7.3		
planning	3.7	10.5	4.3	10.7	5.4	5.3		
TOTAL GOVERNMENT BUDGET in Kw mln.	855.1		821		796.9		1301.5	1183.0
TOTAL TECHNICAL ASSISTANCE IN % OF GOVERNMENT BUDGET	5.0		4.4		9.6			
Government Capital Budget	245.6		160.3		149.8		194.0	225.8
TOTAL TECHNICAL ASSISTANCE IN % OF GOVERNMENT CAPITAL BUDGET	17.4		22.6		50.8			

Table 1

External Technical Aid in Zambia: 1975-1981.

Fortunately for Zambia, not all these experts require Zambian counterparts. Many are supplied simply to fill established posts in the public and parastatal sector for which no adequately experienced Zambian staff are yet available. The most important fields, in this respect, are health and education. In 1979, for example, the United Kingdom alone, through various supplementation schemes provided well over 300 staff – from secondary school teachers to medical superintendents.

But even when such expatriate personnel are excluded, there are still more experts than Zambia could provide counterparts for, to be trained to carry on the projects after the experts depart. Experts, in fact, can be of use only for the period of their assignment, unless the relevant project changes from implementation to continuation, requiring only locally available inputs.

A growing number of external aid agencies have therefore concluded that the projects they support should train counterparts who will eventually take over, and that, if their activities are to bear fruit in the long run, they should support them over a longer period than has been usual. This would enable the projects really to prove their viability and at the same time allow sufficient time for Zambian counterparts to be trained and to gain experience in managing the project.

The real value of technical assistance, of course, mainly depends on the quality of the expert and of the donor organisation. It is here that several matters should be raised. First, one of the more frequently occurring problems: too many experts[1] are working well below their capacity. In many cases there may be very reasonable explanations; for example, the qualifications sought for a certain job often indeed tend to be too high; the job description might have been vague or might not have exactly specified the duties that the expert in fact was supposed to carry out; the expert might have arrived in Zambia well before project preparations had been finalised.

In all such cases, expert capacities can be, and often are, underutilized, even to the extent that the duties experts perform could just as well have been undertaken by available Zambian staff. This readily leads to personal frustrations, with a negative influence on the expert's performance. Above all, however, is a waste of resources that are supposed to be scarce, either by the very nature of the specific expertise or because the expertise is being paid for with foreign currency which is itself a scarce resource. Unfortunately, neither Zambia nor the external aid agencies seem to be constantly aware of these scarcities and tend to be slow or reluctant to take corrective measures.

The above is written under the assumption that the experts Zambia is sent really are experts in their particular field. Unfortunately, it is not always so. Some are not only not outstanding in their field, but even below average. As well as the lack of awareness of resource scarcity, the fact that quite a number of experts fail to perform their duties could indicate a cultural arrogance in external aid agencies.

Although the individual incidences of experts being either too highly qualified or working below standard may be understandable, such situations should not, in general, be tolerated. There is a clear need for both donor nations and Zambia constantly and critically to monitor "expert" performance and, where necessary, to take corrective measures. Considerable improvements are possible here. One possibility is for there to be more openness among donors about their plans and programmes, with an exchange of descriptions for the jobs concerned. There is no harm in the Dutch aid programme recruiting through USAID the expertise they need, if such expertise is in short supply in their own country. On the contrary, it could (through widening the market) lead to quicker and better results. Currently, many posts in projects and programmes remain unfilled for such a long period that it almost seems that both donor and Zambia have altogether forgotten the very existence of the vacancies.

A further step could be to establish an information system among external aid agencies. This could be supplied with all data relevant to the vacancies in those projects and programmes for which one of them is providing finance. Potential candidates should have easy access to this data bank.

Co-ordination of External Aid

In practice, however, the activities of donor agencies in Zambia do not appear to be co-ordinated in any way. Several reasons for this phenomenon can be imagined, of which the most important seem to be the following:

A. *Ineffective co-ordination in the executiion of Zambia's development policy by the government itself, and poor national planning in general.*[2]

Planning units within most ministries are usually grossly understaffed, both in quality and quantity. The same can be said about the National Commission for Development Planning (NCDP), which is responsible for planning and co-ordination of Zambia's development at the national level. A stronger NCDP and stronger planning units within the ministries could contribute considerably to better performance of Zambia's own projects as well as of those financed by external aid agencies. The lack of coherent planning, monitoring and evaluation results in too many projects failing to reach projected goals within the originally planned period, and this again means that scarce resources (foreign exchange and expertise) have not been optimally used. At present, the failure rate of projects, as well as the level of tolerance for failure, is unacceptably high. Yet there are exceptions which, as such, demonstrate that change is possible.

In most cases, however, external aid agencies tend to be understanding and to agree to extensions and further allocation of funds. Sometimes the possibility is overlooked or not considered seriously enough that the original conception of the plan might not have been as good as initially thought. After all, they are aware of co-operating with a country that is in the process of development, and they would not expect everything always to go smoothly and according to plan. Basically, however, this attitude could be wrong, since too-easily-agreed-upon project extensions and further allocations of funds could strengthen the false impression that the mere availability of money is the solution for all problems. This creates expectations which the government could later probably not meet, and leaves the country with a bad project – a more permanent contribution to underdevelopment.

B. Lack of co-ordination and consultation by the external aid agencies

There seems to be a general understanding among external aid organis-ations that co-ordination should be avoided. One reason for this peculiar attitude could be the competition among donors for attractive projects. Another explanation might be that there is a general feeling among donors that the others have an inferior perception of Zambia's development needs and that therefore co-ordination or co-operation would be less desirable in order not to run the risk of lowering the quality of one's own program-mes. A third (alternative) explanation might be a general fear in some donors of (justifiable) criticism by the others of the quality of their activ-ities, once real insight into them is made possible.

Whatever the reason, lack of co-ordination results in continual dupli-cations and overlapping activities where co-operation could have achieved improved results. Remarkably enough, the multilateral institutions that, *qua* multilaterals, should have a high propensity towards co-ordination, are notorious for their abundance of studies and advisory missions that overlap not only the activities of bilateral agencies, but even those of organisations within their own multilateral family. With the proliferation of multilateral organisations, this should not be surprising; it is nevertheless annoying, since the rationale of having the multilateral institutions was that the pooling of resources and know-how would lead to better results. At present, however, most of the institutions do not appear to operate in any way different from the bilateral agencies; nor do they seem to be considered by those agencies or recipient countries as an extremely valu-able source of expertise.

It is therefore understandable, though disappointing, that the multila-terals do not fulfill a useful role in the co-ordination of external aid activities. Yet they could create a platform on which donors and the government could regularly meet, exchange views and possibly discuss how each could best contribute towards the solution of specific problems. This could also be a useful neutral forum for discussion and growth towards long-term plans. The main problem that might arise here is, again, the lack of appreciation among external aid agencies of each other's activities. A more regular contact at working level, however, would probably contribute to better appreciation of each other's activities. Further improvements might be expected from a form of co-operation in which agencies participate in evaluating each other's projects. This would allow donors to appreciate that problems which confront other donors are often similar to their own. In addition, a participating donor may benefit from the experience and possibly also from the solutions that an evaluating donor agency has itself found effective.

Whatever form the co-ordination of external aid activities takes, it should lead to an improvement in the present situation wherein some 65 different agencies, each with its own criteria, procedures, consultative sessions etc, constitute, for the Zambian administration, a burden with which it is, in fact, unable to cope. If a consultative group for Zambia, under the aegis of the World Bank, does not prove to be feasible (as past experience seems to indicate), and if, because of insufficient staff, the NCDP (the responsible body for these matters) is unable to take up this task, perhaps the lead should be taken by some other organisation, possibly UNDP, as the main UN development institution or FAO, since it is in the field of agriculture that the need for co-ordination seems to be the most urgent.

Quality of External Aid

A donor platform such as suggested should also prove to be a useful instrument for external aid agencies and Zambia to jointly and regularly assess the possibilities of reaching the goals set in Zambia's Development Plans. If, in the process, it is concluded that certain targets should be reconsidered or certain policies reformulated, opportunity should be given to the agencies concerned to contribute their views. The history of consultation groups seems to indicate that the involvement of donor agencies in discussions preparatory to policy formulation, might, in turn, increase the chances of obtaining funds.

It is not being suggested here that Zambian development-policy formulation be put under the control of an international institution or a group of donor countries. Zambia is, and should continue to be, the sole responsible authority for its own policies. What is suggested is that regular consultation with and among external aid agencies could improve policy formulation and avoid situations wherein donors are requested to take part in financing programmes that they consider to be ill-conceived or badly planned. Such situations do no good to the relationships between Zambia and the external aid agencies, and are not likely to create an atmosphere in which open and critical discussion can fruitfully occur. Most importantly, however, they are not in the best interests of project beneficiaries.

Even without any co-ordination of donor activities (as at present), there is considerable room for improved performance through the introduction of a system whereby all ongoing activities are continually monitored and evaluated. The current attitude seems to be that ongoing projects are *per se* good projects and, in many cases, neither the responsible Zambian government institutions nor the external aid agencies seem to monitor their projects in such a way that unsatisfactory performance is identified and remedied in an early stage. As a result, quite a number of projects fail to deliver the results they are supposed to do. This again strengthens the false understanding that certain resources are not as scarce as they are said to be.

A good monitoring and evaluation system is one suggestion that could lead to improved performance. In an earlier phase of the project cycle, further improvement is possible, with project preparation as probably one of the most promising fields.

Although the policy of the Zambian government to request donor-country assistance, especially for fields in which those countries have been very successful at home, seems to be a wise one, it does not automatically guarantee that these donors will actually achieve the outcomes that are so hopefully expected. Circumstances in Zambia may in fact be, and often are, too different; an approach that works well in the donor country, or even in projects funded by that donor in other developing countries, may be a total failure in the Zambian context. Too often, it seems that projects are set up on the assumption that they *should* work, without a careful analysis of the circumstances under which they *could.* Very basic factors such as soil conditions, climate, attitude and motivation (including that of local staff) tend to be easily overlooked. Examples of such careless project preparations are numerous: wheat production on unsuitable soils; the attempt to produce seed that needs a temperate climate; top-down promotion of a co-operative movement where people are not really motivated to form and maintain their own primary societies, and so on. Further, the introduction of agricultural technologies that are too far removed from the traditional production patterns of the farmers involved; the promotion of projects that lack the active support of local populations; and project inputs that far exceed what the people concerned could ever afford to invest themselves, and which therefore alienate them from their own realities. Both Zambia and the agencies should be expected to be more realistic in their preparation, and should be continuously aware that the negative effects of project failure may have a greater impact than the positive effects of success.

The need for improvement in project preparation and appraisal is not the concern of aid agencies only; the relevant Zambian government departments also have an important role to play, for development co-operation implies the responsibility of both donor and recipient for the quality of their co-operation. Indeed, it is the especial government responsibility to ensure that activities, once started, will continue when the donor's contribution has come to an end.

A recent World Bank study into the development of the agricultural sector indicates that, in that sector, recurrent cost financing has become a real problem. Implicitly, this study indicates that, under present circumstances, Zambia has reached its ceiling of absorptive capacity for external aid, unless donors consider financing recurrent cost as a part of their projects. This is one of the World Bank recommendations.

From the same study, it could be concluded that both Zambia and the external aid agencies should be more critical in selecting capital developments or projects to be financed, and that, in the decision-making process, more attention should be paid to the longer-term consequences for recurrent budget requirements.

At times, it would appear that projects are regarded as instruments for obtaining the external aid rather than the aid being thought an instrument for getting valuable developments moving.

Both donor agencies and Zambia, it would seem, have a responsibility to ensure that the available funds are being used to the best possible advantage for Zambia, in both the short and long terms. Generally speaking, however, external aid agencies, especially the larger ones, are handicapped, since they need to be biassed towards projects for which considerable amounts of money can be allocated. The consequences of such projects for the recurrent budget are very often difficult to estimate, and this, in turn, makes it difficult properly to compare the costs of the inputs (often scarce foreign exchange) with the value of the output (in terms of, for example, increased production). For many externally funded projects, such a cost-benefit analysis would lead to unfavourable conclusions. It should, therefore, be no surprise if, after the withdrawal of external assistance, the Zambian government's interest in a project gradually disappears as well.

From the above, it could be concluded that, if it is not clear from the start that funds for recurrent expenditures will be available, then developments that would require a continuous input of recurrent expenditure should not be promoted.

The number of such projects is limited and is unlikely to increase. Under current arrangements with IMF, it has been agreed to concentrate on: redirecting resources towards the productive sectors, especially agriculture; rehabilitating past investment; and promoting new investment in "quick-yielding projects". Expenditure of a consumptive nature, for both public and private sectors, would be restrained. It may therefore be expected that projects which merely provide services to the people without having direct impact on production levels may not, in the coming years, expect much government support in terms of budgetary allocations for recurrent expenditures. In their negotiations with the government, external aid agencies should be aware of this. They should, indeed, have long ago adopted a similar policy. Probably the best form of assistance external aid agencies could provide would be aimed at stimulating income-generating, agriculture-related production, especially for those strata of the Zambian society that, under present circumstances, have an unsatisfactory nutritional status and no wage-earning opportunities.

Influence of External Aid Agencies on Development Policies

Because of the size of the funds controlled by external aid agencies (in some cases allocations are larger than the budgets of some government ministries), a situation could occur wherein the Zambian authorities no longer command the direction of their national development.

Such a situation might more easily develop where (as at present) national and ministerial planning organisations are rather weak. In that case, they would not be in the best position to counterpoise donor agencies that might want to develop projects or programmes that may not be suited to Zambian conditions or in line with Zambia's declared policies. (One's judgement of whether such a situation has already developed depends greatly, of course, on one's judgement of present policies, projects and programmes.)

In the author's opinion, the present picture would not look very different if the Zambian planning mechanism had been better developed, even to the stage where most key positions were not manned by external aid experts at all, but by Zambia's own experts. There is no evidence to conclude that, because of the presence of many external aid agencies and foreign experts, Zambia is not in control of its national development policies. If one considers the number of donor-funded activities that are not contributing to national development, however, it is clear that this conclusion has to be qualified. Many projects are only very remotely controlled and do not form a meaningful and integral part of planned development.

More important, it seems, would be a national planning mechanism that could develop a policy for the application of all available inputs in such a way that the outcome could be considered optimal, from a national perspective, and therefore socially justified. Whether this is presently the case is also doubtful, as seems to be indicated by recent research into the funding of agricultural development since independence. This research concludes that finance for developments that are relevant for the population (in areas other than the line of rail) has been coming mainly from external aid.

It would, nevertheless, be unfair to conclude that, because of this bias in the allocation of national resources, national policy planning should be condemned. It is considerably more difficult to develop policies that would lead to development for groups of people or regions for which only sparse information is available than it is for areas that are already better developed and therefore better known. Development is a learning situation and is therefore dynamic. Information seems to be an essential prerequistic for any successful development activity. Consequently, an information system that provides planning institutions with relevant data is imperative. Donor agencies could contribute considerably to the development of such a system, both by helping to establish a data base that is more adquate from a statistical point of view, and by ensuring that social science research is translated into recommendations and policies that are not only relevant but also practical for planning purposes.

As experience of many past national aid development efforts has proved, many programmes that could have been beneficial for the development of rural areas, failed because the real needs of people were not understood. This resulted in the discouragement of project participants. Planning should be based on the needs of people rather than aim at achieving abstract national goals such as growth percentage of national income or national self-sufficiency in food.

The most important factor, however, would seem to be a genuine interest in the well-being of the people for whom the development programmes are devised — an interest one should be able to expect from both the planners of those programmes and the officers responsible for their proper execution. There is little that external aid agencies can do in this respect, apart from supplying experts that show such an interest and are prepared to work with the people, rather than for them.

Notes

1. "Experts" is a term we use for all staff funded by external aid agencies.
2. See President Dr K.D. Kaunda in his foreword to the *Third National Development Plan, 1979-1983*.

B. Aspects of Zambia's Foreign Policy in the Context of Southern Africa
by Klaas Woldring

Zambia is one of fourteen land-locked countries in Africa,[1] a circumstance that places her in special category from the outset. She is moreover, situated in southern Central Africa far removed from ports and has to rely on long supply routes through neighbouring transit states of which there are no fewer than eight. Ever since her independence in 1964, almost all of these countries have been at one time or another in a state of war. This has played havoc not only with Zambia's import and export routes but also with her air traffic and post and telecommunications, affected her considerable tourism potential adversely and jeopardised her economic development.

Furthermore, Zambia has been a leading actor in Black Africa's confrontation with the white-dominated south. As a state she has paid a "high price of principles"[2] and has probably suffered as much as, if not more than, Zimbabwe on account of UN sanctions against that country. With the landslide victory of Mr Robert Mugabe's ZANU-PF in Zimbabwe, 16 years of hazardous existence appeared to draw to a close. In the process the Zambian political system was transformed – partly be design and partly of necessity perhaps – into what is held to be a one-party state but is in fact a benevolent monocracy. It is remarkable that in spite of recurring economic hardship, especially from the mid-seventies onwards, as well as a measure of corruption and inefficiency, political stability has been maintained. President Kaunda's diplomacy in relation to Southern Africa has been interpreted in many conflicting ways. There are contradictory and controversial aspects but a thread does run through it all as it seems unified by a Christian-based, pacifist attitude which has found expression in his philosophy of "Humanism" stressing the dignity of man.

This chapter will look at the development of the foreign policy of Zambia primarily in the context of the Southern African region with emphasis on events in the seventies. There will be two sections: (a) An assessment of Zambia's geopolitical position, and the disengagement from the south; (b) Zambia's involvement in the liberation struggle.

Zambia's Geopolitical Position: Disengagement from the south

There are three important geopolitical aspects which influence Zambian foreign policy:

(1) Political turmoil in neighbouring countries;
(2) Zambia as a host country for guerillas;
(3) The problem of supply routes.

Political turmoil includes the liberation wars in Mozambique and Angola, Zimbabwe, Namibia and South Africa, as well as the civil wars in Angola (since 1975) and in Zaire (in 1964, and again in 1978 in Shaba Province). In most cases Zambia has been involved to a lesser or greater extent as a partisan power, as a transit state or as a haven for refugees. Zambia borders on several guerila war theatres such as the Tete Province of Mozambique, the Zambezi Valley, the Caprivi Strip in Namibia, Eastern Angola and Shaba Province. Since independence she has accommodated large numbers of refugees from Zaire, Angola and Zimbabwe as well as South Africa. Several liberation movements have had and still have offices in Lusaka. These include ZAPU, ZANU (until the murder of Herbert Chitepo in 1975),[3] SWAPO (which is also associated with the UN Namibia Institute established in 1975), ANC (South Africa) and previously MPLA and UNITA of Angola. This has made Zambia extremely vulnerable to attacks by the white minority regimes, as was experienced particularly throughout 1978 and 1979. A ZIRIC brochure gives the following details of Rhodesian attacks on refugee camps during October-November 1978:[4]

> ... an attack on Freedom Refugee Camp at Chikumbe, 20 kms north of Lusaka, where 225 refugees were killed and 629 seriously injured. The camp itself which catered for 2948 non-combatants was completely destroyed. Independent observers, including the UN and the Red Cross confirmed that this was a genuine refugee camp ... [Secondly] the massacre of Mkushi Refugee Camp, 150 kms north of Lusaka, on 19th October, 1978. This camp housed 1589 young girls and 36 men. Little military hardware was present – the girls were trained to take up civil service positions in an independent Zimbabwe. 100 girls died and 90 were wounded. Survivors described the raid as extremely callous. An attempt was made to make the head girl shoot all the others (she refused and was shot) ... a third raid was on a Workshop Camp, 12 kms from Lusaka, on 2nd November, 1978. 10 were killed and 40 injured.

In November 1979, in the final stages of the Lancaster House Conference and in an apparent attempt to put pressure on the Front Line States and the Patriotic Front, Rhodesian security forces blew up twelve key bridges in Eastern and Southern Zambia, thereby cutting most major supply routes. More recently South African forces have been involved in "hot pursuit" actions from the Caprivi Strip and have bombed villages in Zambia's Sesheke

District. These attacks have forced Zambia to abandon her relatively low-key military posture and to strengthen her very modest army and air force for defence purposes.[5] When the bridges were blown up, the then British Ambassador, Sir Len Allison, expressed the opinion that Britain could not be held responsible for the damage. This naturally infuriated Kaunda and sparked off student demonstrations against the British Embassy, after which Sir Leonard was recalled and replaced.[6]

As regards the supply routes, it should be remembered that the boundaries of Zambia's butterfly shape were settled by British prospecting and farming colonists moving up north from South Africa early in this century. This historical fact set the pattern for colonial development from the South and dependency on the white-controlled southern region not only financially but also in terms of communications. After 1909 the most important rail routes were through Rhodesia to the port of Beira in Mozambique and via Bulawayo and Francistown (Botswana) to South African ports and, recently, even to Maputo (formerly Lourenco Marques).

In 1931 another major rail link was established, to Lobito in Angola, to facilitate the export of copper which has been exploited commercially since 1925. A (gravel) roadlink to Dar es Salaam was opened in 1940, but this route became significant commercially only after independence and the subsequent disengagement from the south. There are other less important routes such as road-rail connection to Nacala (Mozambique, via Malawi), Francistown (via Kazangula) and Beira (via Moatize, Blaka or Blantyre)but these have many constraints for commercial purposes. At best they are emergency routes. The new rail link to Dar es Salaam will be discussed below.

The decision to disengage from the south was taken by Kaunda at the time of UDI when he urged the nation and the business community to "use this tragedy to sever our links with the racialist south".[7] In 1973 the Smith regime closed the border with Zambia – a retaliatory action which was soon recognised as a blunder – and Kaunda decided to keep the Zambian side of the border closed after the Rhodesians had reopened theirs. This display of independence anticipated rapid progress with the TAZARA Railway project, linking Zambia to Dar es Salaam, then under construction. Imports from Rhodesia dropped to nil whilst imports from South Africa declined to a level of approximately 7 per cent of total imports in 1974 and remained at that level until 1979.

Zambia's trade has been reoriented towards the EEC and Far East countries. New and improved links with Dar, e.g., an oil pipeline, a tarred road and the TAZARA Railway, officially opened in 1976, have contributed substantially to the diversification of trade routes and reduced the dependence on the south. Unfortunately, the Benguela Railway to Lobito could not be used after mid-1975 on account of the Angolan civil war. This route

Table 1[8] Zambian Exports and Imports by Route (Thousands of tonnes)

Year	Tanzania Rail	Tanzania Road	Tanzania Total	Lobito	Mozambique via Rhodesia	Mozambique via Malawi	Mozambique Direct Route	Mozambique Total	Kenya Mombasa	Botswana Kazungula	Air	Total
EXPORTS												
1970	–	253	253	187	398	6	–	404	–	–	4	848
1971	–	221	221	176	390	9	–	399	–	–	2	798
1972	–	210	210	170	467	7	–	474	45	–	–	854
1973	–	284	284	438	5(a)	41	–	46	86	–	–	813
1974	–	319	319	509	–	10	–	10	2	–	–	924
1975	46	349	395	309(b)	–	66	10	76	12	–	–	782
1976	349(c)	323	672	–	–	48	35	83	1(d)	–	–	767
1977	524	181	705	–	–	34	–	34	–	–	–	740
IMPORTS(e)												
1970	–	248	248	118	1293	18	–	1311	–	–	4	1681
1971	–	295	295	269	1048	29	–	1077	–	–	7	1648
1972	202	202	114	864	39		–	903	–	–	8	1257
1973	200	200	200	418	35(a)	109	–	144	68	4	25	859
1974	18(f)	271	289	438	–	125	–	125	86	15	29	982
1975	69	311	380	257(b)	–	129	30	159	86	41	20	879
1976	326(c)	248	574	–	–	71	58	129	22	9	21	755
1977	413	156	569	–	–	25	9	34	3(d)	47	18	671

took up to 45 per cent of copper exports at one stage. Moreover, the port at Dar is often congested and TAZARA has been flooded in places for up to two months of the year.

Yet TAZARA's performance has not been up to expectations. It has failed to achieve its projected capacity of 80,000 tonnes per month in either direction. Apart from the reasons stated above, an inadequate supply of rolling stock and inefficient management are blamed for this state of affairs. When a crisis arose in October 1978 over the speedy transport of much needed fertilizer, waiting in Beira and Maputo ports for shipment to Zambia, the government decided to reopen the southern railway route for that purpose and for other essential imports and exports – a painful but apparently unavoidable decision.[9]

The cost of disengagement to this nation of nearly five million inhabitants is hard to quantify but some attempts have been made. Anglin and Shaw, in their most comprehensive and authoritative text on Zambian foreign policy quote a UN source:

> The latest annual estimate of the Coordinator of UN assistance to Zambia of the direct financial outlay is 'well in excess of US$ 800 m'. If exceptional transport costs are included Zambian figures run as high as $ 1250 m. Yet even these huge sums fail to take adequate account of the real costs resulting from aggravated inflation, distorted development, and resort to alternative sources of supply, and other contingency planning expenses.[10]

The history behind the TAZARA line, which was built in record time by Chinese engineers and Chinese and local labour, is fascinating.[11] Several Western countries as well as the World Bank had earlier rejected requests for funding either for political or for economic reasons or both. To be sure, the railway was politically inspired. It was the most important ingredient in Zambia's strategy to disentangle herself from the south and thereby enhance her effectiveness as a Front Line State in the liberation struggle. In spite of all scepticism and Western reluctance, the project was completed well before the scheduled time and certainly helped to redirect trade, as can be seen from Table 1.

Former Foreign Minister Wilson Chakulya estimated the cost of the closure of the border with Rhodesia alone at over K1,000 and UNIP's Central Committee Member Mr Elija Mudenda told Parliament that "the cost of reconstructing the ravages of the libration war would exceed K600 m".[11] Zambia also claims K2,500 damages from 17 British oil companies caused by their sanctions-busting operations. According to Zambia the companies were in a conspiracy with the Smith regime just prior to and after UDI and thereby deprived Zambia of substantial quantities of oil.[12]

Disengagement with the south has been accompanied by integration of a voluntary nature amongst the Front Line States. Although Zambia was not overly interested in becoming an Associate Member of the now defunct East African Community[13] – contrary to initiall high expectations – cooperation and coordination takes place at Heads of State, government and societal levels as has been demonstrated by transaction analysis.[14] There are important emotional, ideological, ethnic, and historical bonds which naturally facilitate such integration. However, trade between these countries is still at a low level; although it is possible that the independence of Zimbabwe will now boost intraregional trade considerably.

It should not be thought however that the "high cost of principles" in Zambian foreign policy has greatly affected the lifestyle of Zambia's emerging national bourgeoisie. Since independence there has been a steady growth of inequalities in income, education, housing and lifestyle generally. This is not the place to delve deeply into the vexed question as to whether the national bourgeoisie is a comprador class or not, as some class analysts claim,[15] but some comments will be offered.

The Zambian bureaucratic elite, which includes politicians, senior officials in government, senior officials in the parastatals and party officials, is not as yet a homogenous group. There is also a continuous debate on ideology which, it is argued, should be more socialist and less capitalist – contrary to actual practice. Zambia's economy is in fact best described as a mixture of state and private capitalism.[16] The bourgeoisie in the private sector, part of which is expatriate, could perhaps be characterized as comprador-oriented. This subclass has been kept in check, however, and has at least complied with the disengagement from the south. The greatest risk to the bureaucratic elite was political instability, and this been well contained. Kaunda's most formidable rival, his former vice-President Kapwepwe – who wanted trade with the south – was neutralised first by imprisonment and later by disqualification from standing for the presidency following a hasty amendment to UNIP's constitution in 1978. This Bemba leader died early in 1980. Although soon afterwards new pretenders to the throne emerged – all challengers from the right rather than the left – they have been contained fairly comfortably.

In practice much of Kaunda's political manoeuvring is aimed at promoting unity. He has been relatively successful in counterbalancing tribal rivalries and has ensured reasonably fair representation on a provincial and tribal basis in party and government. However, remnants of the former opposition party, the African National Congress, which was banned in 1972, remain active in Southern Province and Kapwepwe's former party, the United Progress Part, still has members in jail since its banning also in 1972. At Kapwepwe's funeral Kaunda wept for his former schoolfriend and colleague – he is always armed with an oversized white handkerchief on public occasions – but the mourners did not forget to remind him of the political detainees. It seems that Kaunda's main political problem is that he is in danger of becoming incarcerated in a system of which he himself increasingly disapproves. It could be argued that in spite of his considerable power over individual leaders of the establishment the system is actually using him and his popularity to perpetuate itself.

Involvement in the Liberations Struggle

Zambia's foreign policy is claimed to be built upon a number of commitments. These are panafricanism, nonalignment, common interests of the Front Line States, humanism and the Lusaka Manifesto of 1969.[17]

Panafricanism has been demonstrated in President Kaunda's strong commitment to the ideals of the OAU of which he was chairman in 1970–1. Commitment to the Nonalignment Movement is connected with the philosophy of humanism in that it projects a concern for the dignity of man at the international level. A dislike of being dependent on either of the superpowers further explains this stance. Moreover, Zambia plays her role in the quest for a New International Economic Order and the elimination of all forms of colonialism and imperialism. She is a party to the 1975 and 1979 Lome Conventions, the North-South Dialogue in Paris (1975–77) and UNCTAD's Group of 77. The result of these activities has not been very rewarding for Zambia thus far. She is a member of the Council for Namibia which she has chaired for some time now.[18] Humanism is an eclectic moral philosophy which draws on social norms and values of the traditional tribal society rather than an economic theory or Western ideology. Basic to it is the dignity of man and cooperative enterprise but this does not necessarily imply socialism. It is pragmatic in that regard and, therefore, a measure of local private enterprise is acceptable and even desirable in Zambia under humanism. There is certainly considerable ambiguity in this moral philosophy, however, and it is open to a variety of interpretations.

The basis for Zambia's policy towards Southern Africa is set out in the Lusaka Manifesto which was agreed upon at the Fifth Summit Conference of East and Central African States. The objectives for Southern Africa were "the achievement of human equality and national self-determination". The tone of the Manifesto was still pacifist in nature, indicating a strong preference for negotiation rather than violence and destruction. A year later, however, following South Africa's "dialogue" offensive, this group of states adopted an amended policy position (at Mogadishu) which accepted the necessity of violence. In 1974 President Kaunda mediated between Frelimo and the new Portuguese government preceding Mozambique's independence. The concept of "Front Line State" then came into existence, and in the following year he saw the Lusaka Manifesto's principles reiterated in the Dar es Salaam Declaration on Southern Africa. Kaunda's positive role in the Commonwealth was highlighted when Zambia successfully hosted the Heads of Government Meeting in Lusaka in August 1979. It was at this meeting that agreement was reached making possible the Lancaster House Constitutional Conference on Zimbabwe. Kaunda has acknowledged the important contribution made by the Australian Prime Minister, Malcolm Fraser and the then Australian Foreign Minister, Andrew Peacock towards that end.

Foreign policy-making in Zambia is virtually the prerogative of the President. Since the inauguration of the one-party state in December 1972 and the disappearance of a number of colourful and indepedent-minded Foreign Ministers as well as other Cabinet members, at least the general direction of foreign policy is determined by Kaunda. The exercise of participatory democracy in the party and in government and industry has not been a success. It is not too far-fetched to describe in Zambian polity now as a benevolent monocracy. The input of the Foreign Affairs Ministry is relatively small, although it has asserted itself *vis-à-vis* other departments successfully in recent years at the administrative level. At the same time repeated calls are heard in Parliament to curb Zambia's foreign representation and commitments abroad in view of the poor state of the economy.[19] In practice the stronger advisory input comes from the Central Committee of UNIP rather than from the Cabinet but it too operates largely as a sounding board for the President's ideas. Kaunda's sincerity in respect of the liberation struggle has been tested on four occasions. Particularly his stand on Angola — when he favoured a government of National Unity over the MPLA — caused great concern, domestically[20] and externally.

The first occasion was when secret correspondence between the South African Prime Minister Vorster and Kaunda during 1968 and 1969 was exposed by the former in the South African Parliament in 1971 in an obvious attempt to discredit the latter.[21] As a gesture of goodwill Kaunda had initially offered to establish diplomatic relations with South Africa in 1964 but the (informal) offer was then ignored. As part of Vorster's Africa policy designs — an apparent about-face — Pretoria wanted to entice Zambia to enter into a friendly relationship (styled "goodneighbourliness") with the principal aim of neutralising her as a base for guerrilla fighters. These approaches were at first ignored by Zambia but Kaunda later wanted to explore the possibility of a negotiated settlement over Rhodesia. His precondition for any form of suggested cooperation between South Africa and Zambia was that Apartheid was to be dismantled. This proved to be unacceptable and was rejected as unwarranted interference in South Africa's domestic affairs. What the correspondence showed, when it was published by Kaunda,[22] was not his lack of integrity or commitment but his naiveté about the essential nature of Apartheid and the very aims of the Africa policy and "dialogue" which were designed to protect and to perpetuate that exploitative system, even with the connivance of African elites.

A second period of contact with Mr Vorster, during 1974 and 1975, described as a "détente" by the South African and conservative Western press, followed in the wake of Portugal's decolonisation and Pretoria's reluctant acceptance that Rhodesia would have a black government in the foreseeable future. The aim was now to establish a "moderate" black government in Zimbabwe, an aim that was less unrealistic at the time than the "good neighbourliness" policy had been, but which was thwarted by Mr Smith's intransigence. As a result the crucial talks in a railway carriage on the Victoria Bridge, in August 1975, failed. Kaunda felt betrayed by Vorster, arguing that he had not put enough pressure on Smith to accept the proposed constitutional deal.

The third involvement which incurred for Kaunda the wrath of some Marxist-oriented groups as well as students of the University of Zambia was his ambiguous and apparently suspect position in respect to Angola. In this instance Kaunda was accused of favouring UNITA over MPLA and worse still of collaboration with South Africa's abortive intervention. Anglin and Shaw base their assessment of the Zambian involvement on "the underlying assumption of Zambian policy that Soviet intervention came first, and that the Americans and even the South Africans, were merely reacting to it".[23]

Although the suspicion was reinforced by Zambia's refusal – until April 1976 – to recognise the MPLA Government, these authors argue that there is no substance in the allegiations. During the early years of armed resistance by the MPLA, i.e. from the mid-sixties to the early seventies, Zambia afforded host-state support to that movement. This not only resulted in Portuguese attacks on Zambian soil and in loss of life but also led the Portuguese authorities to apply sanctions against Zambia by denying her port facilities in Lobito and Beira. In 1972, following a split in the MPLA in Zambia – whereby Kaunda was accused of siding with Neto's opponent (Chipenda) – the relationship with the subsequently victorious faction deteriorated. The split weakened the MPLA and indirectly strengthened the other two movements, UNITA under Savimbi and FNLA under Holden Roberto. All three movements were recognised by the OAU and President Kaunda's and UNIP's main concern seems to have been to promote the maximum of unity within and amongst them in order to successfully dislodge the Portuguese and to install a government of National Unity. The late recognition, so these authors argue further, is explained by the fear that the MPLA would have to remain dependent on Cuban and Russian support and the independence of Angola would thus be jeopardised.

Critics in the liberation movement have observed that in these three instances, and also in relation to the ZAPU-ZANU ideological differences, Zambia appears to have shown a preference for the soft option of a neocolonial solution. Whilst there is some evidence for this it cannot be fairly deduced from the Angola situation, since there were three parties and MPLA did not have majority support at the time. Moreover Zambia was very concerned to safeguard the important rail route to Lobito which, in the case of a civil war, might be endangered. This is exactly what happened subsequently. Furthermore, the preference for a government of National Unity was widespread in the OAU and embraced Tanzania and Nigeria. Kaunda's friendship of long standing with Nyerere also suggests otherwise, as does his attempted, though unsuccessful, emulation of Tanzania's rural policies and the — ineffective — leadership code. All one can say is that Kaunda prefers peace to socialist ideology and is perhaps somewhat gullibly pragmatic as to how this could best be achieved in the prevailing neocolonial situations. The fact remains that he has contributed very substantially towards the liberation of Southern Africa and that the internecine fights and self-destructive tendencies peculiar to all liberation movements have not made this task any easier.

The fourth time Kaunda's commitment was tested was in April 1982 when the President had "frank and useful talks" with the present South African Prime Minister, P. W. Botha. These talks took place in a mobile trailer positioned on the South African-Botswana border on 30th April. Before the meeting Kaunda stated that he hoped to be able to reassure Botha that a victory by SWAPO in the proposed election in an independent Namibia would not necessarily be inimical to South Africa's interests.[24] At the time the Contact Group of Five, through the October 1981 initiative of President Reagan's Assistant Secretary of State for African Affairs, Dr. Chester Crocker, was trying to modify the UN Independence Plan for Namibia which is contained in the Security Council Resolution 435 (1978). The modification involved three aspects (referred to as "phases") of which the first one was gaining acceptance for a two-vote electoral system to elect the Constituent Assembly. SWAPO rejected this system, as did most Front Line State leaders, on the grounds that it favoured the several tiny political parties operating in Namibia and regarded as so-called moderates by Pretoria. This reading was no doubt correct and showed Crocker up as an Africanist who is a novice when it comes to understanding the commitment of African leaders to liberate Southern Africa. Botha presumably used the occasion to persuade Kaunda to lean on SWAPO to accept the first phase. It was also reported that Kaunda used the occasion to urge Botha to release the ANC leader Nelson Mandela who has been imprisoned on Robben Island since 1964 (Mandela was moved to the mainland later in the year but not released).

The Zambian President entered this discussion on his own behalf however which suggests strongly that there was an ulterior motive. The initiative had little support from FLS leaders except from the Angolan President Edouardo dos Santos whom he met in May 1982 to pursue the Namibian independence issue further. The subsequent conference at the Cape Verde Islands between South African senior officials and Angolan leaders was rejected by SWAPO however. Crocker and other American officials quite erroneously engineered a climate of euphoria regarding the progress of the talks but Sam Nujoma, merely confirming his earlier position, did not attend and this seemed to signal the end of the ill-conceived US modification attempts. It should be noted however that the main stumbling block proved to be South African insistence that the Cuban troops depart. Did Kaunda compromise himself and the liberation movement? No full account of what was said is available but the fact is that Zambia has become increasingly dependent on South Africa during the period 1979–1982 in spite of Zimbabwe's independence. During 1980 and 1981 imports from South Africa rose steeply and by July 1982 – as a result of recurring problems with alternative transport routes – about 60% of Zambia's external trade went through South African ports. This, for Zambia, most unpalatable situation hardly placed President Kaunda in a position of strength in his meeting with Botha. In August 1982 the South African journalist Al Venter approached Kaunda about this contact with the Afrikaner Prime Minister and he was then informed that a further meeting with Botha was regarded as desirable in order to persuade South Africans "that time was running out for them".[25] It is well-known however that this kind of message has never moved any Afrikaner political leader although it could be argued that times are changing somewhat perhaps. The split in the National Party in South Africa suggests that FLS leaders are beginning to play a rôle in the South African electorate and presumably Kaunda is banking on being able to exploit that situation. Zambian domestic circumstances are the main factor why the President has cast himself in the rôle of intermediary. Apart from the serious economic problems and the scarcity of effective alternative transport routes, potential political instability, ever since the attempted coup in October 1980, have forced the President increasingly to accept South African assistance in one form or another and to make concessions. Since the April 1982 meeting, South Africa is no longer referred to as "racist", which was common practice in official language ever since 1964. It is not surprising therefore that Zambia is seeking relief from as many other quarters as is possible and that it has promoted the newly established Southern African Development Coordination Conference (SADCC) and the Lusaka-based

Preferential Trade Area (PTA), described below, to the full extent possible. In the meantime, the rehabilitation of the TAZARA Line, with Chinese and Western help, emerged as a high priority project during 1981-1982 and can be expected to be undertaken in 1983.

It can hardly be argued that the forced reengagement with South Africa means that Kaunda has capitulated or is employing double standards. The President has no other options at present if he wants to survive politically and economically except moving sharply to the left. Whilst this may be desirable for Zambia in the long run, Kaunda would probably commit political suicide in the process – the system would not allow this to happen. The consequences of such a turn of events would be quite chaotic since the Zambian socialists are in fact few in number and their organisation rudimentary.

New Forms of Regional Organisation

After the independence of Zimbabwe was secured, the FLS began to consider new forms of cooperation amongst themselves as well as joint approaches to development aid donors and projects. This new direction was greatly stimulated by the neocolonial initiative of the South African Prime Minister, termed "A Constellation of States", a mysterious concept explained in a number of contradictory ways but which would in any case bring the fruits of capitalist development to all Southern African states – on white South Africa's terms of course. Since the fruits of this kind of development have proved to be so sour for blacks all over Southern Africa ever since 1652, one must wonder how P. W. Botha expected acceptance for this idea amongst FLS leaders. Presumably, the reasoning behind it was that anything and everything is in the end for sale – quite a miscalculation when it comes to the struggle for freedom as the Afrikaners should remember!

Kaunda first coined the term "Anti-Constellation of States" to indicate the main thrust of the new regional grouping. When opening the new Parliament in January 1980 he outlined this idea as follows:

Co-operation between Zambia and neighbouring states grew in scope, intensity and magnitude. Frontline States have virtually become an institution during this period (the seventies), thereby laying the foundation stone for the future transcontinental belt of countries which must form an economic power bloc. Such a powerful bloc will guarantee peace and stability in the entire region. We have Joint Permanent Commissions with almost all our independent neighbours with the task of co-ordinating economic and technical co-operation and trade. In future, while maintaining our strong spirit of internationalism and solidarity with the underprivileged and the oppressed, the cornerstone of Zambia's foreign policy will be to make the new transcontinental belt a viable reality, vibrant and powerful.[26]

The very first meeting of what became known as the Southern African Development Co-ordination Conference (SADCC) was in fact held in Arusha, Tanzania in July 1979 – before Zimbabwe's independence but in anticipation of it. The emphasis from the start was on regional economic self-reliance. The major initial statement, the Lusaka Declaration "Southern Africa: Toward Economic Liberation", embodies the general philosophy of the Non-aligned Movement in a specific context. In April 1980 nine majority-ruled Southern African countries met in the Mulungushi Hall in Lusaka to agree on an outline of the objectives and structure of the new grouping. Apart from the FLS Lesotho, Swaziland, Malawi and Zimbabwe attended. The development objectives were defined as follows:

1. the reduction of economic dependence, particularly, but not only, on the Republic of South Africa;
2. the forging of links to create a genuine and equitable regional integration;
3. the mobilisation of resources to promote the implementation of national, interstate and regional policies;
4. concerted action to secure international cooperation within the framework of our strategy for economic liberation.[27]

The Conference identified transport and communications as being the key to the implementation of these objectives. The programme of action adopted in Lusaka listed the following tasks:

* the creation of a Southern African Transport and Communications Commission (SATCC) based in Maputo;
* measures to control foot and mouth disease in cattle throughout the region;
* the establishment of a Regional Agricultural Research centre specialising in drought-prone areas;
* the preparation of a food security plan for the region;
* plan for harmonisation of industrialisation and energy policies;
* sharing of national training facilities within the region;
* studies leading to proposals for the establishment of a Southern African Development Fund.[2b]

Various tasks were allotted to specific countries, a division of labor ratified by the Lusaka Nine's ministerial meeting in September 1980. For example Mozambique was assigned the task of coordinating transport and communications; Botswana to handle foot and mouth disease; also agricultural research on semi-arid tropics; and Zimbabwe to prepare a food security programme. Tanzania was given the job of preparing a strategy for harmonisation of industries; Zambia that of establishing a Southern African Development Fund; and Swaziland, that of reviewing existing training facilities. Angola heads the Commission, studying alternative energy sources for the region and related environmental programmes.

In November 1980 the first major donors' conference was held in Maputo, Mozambique, also referred to as SADCC 2. The main purpose of ṢADCC 2 was to secure financial and technical support for the projects of regional cooperation which the Nine had agreed upon. Some $ 2,000 million aid was sought on that occasion. Encouragingly, $ 650 million was pledged by 10 countries or institutions. Apart from the Nine, 30 countries and 18 international organisations were represented.[29] Although well below the target, there were a further 12 countries or institutions which promised to support SADCC without specifying amounts however.

Table 2 SADCC 2 Pledges of Support[30]

Country/Institutions	M. US dollars
African Development Bank	380
European Economic Community	100
Italy	50
UNDP	15-20
USA	50
Belgium	8.5
Netherlands	15
Norway	6
Finland	6
Denmark	10
Total	640.5-645.5

Unspecified pledges: Austria, Australia, G. D. R., France, U. K., Brazil, Japan, Canada, Ireland. OPEC Fund, Kuwait Development Fund and Venezuela.

A subsequent summit meeting was held in Herare in July 1981 when it was decided that a permanent secretariat was to be based in Botswana. This was followed by a second donors' meeting in Blantyre in November 1981 which dealt mainly with the improvements to be made to the Beira and Tazara railways, matters of utmost concern to Zambia. Some problems emerged here for the Zambian government. First, it found itself in competition with Zimbabwe as to the establishment and location of a Veterinary School. Secondly, it had its report for an African Development Fund rejected for a second time and was urged to do further and more thorough work on it. The Nine decided furthermore that only an independent Namibia would be allowed to join the SADCC. Interest in joining, expressed by Zaire, Burundi and Kenya was discouraged by the meeting.

By June 1982, according to a communiqué issued after a ministerial SADCC meeting on energy in Luanda (and representing eight countries, Lesotho being absent),[31] of the 106 projects agreed to since 1980, three had been completed, 48 were in progress and 20 were being discussed with possible funding organisation. Clearly, following the encouraging first response by donor countries and lending organisations, SADCC has moved fast to establish itself as an enterprising regional development coordinating agency. It being such a new body no full assessment of its contribution can be made here but its initial success may explain why the South African concept, "Constellation of States", soon faded from memory as yet another attempt to promote a kind of Greater South Africa that is totally inimical to the objectives of the liberation movement. Zambia's foundation membership in it should pay handsome dividends in times to come provided the organisation remains flexible and, as was intended from the outset, keeps its bureaucracy small and efficient.

Apart from SADCC, Zambia is also a founder member of the Lusaka-based Preferential Trade Area (PTA) for Eastern and Southern African states, established in December 1981. By June 1982 PTA already had 12 members: Kenya, Uganda, Somalia, Malawi, Zambia, Zimbabwe, Mauritius, Djibouti, the Comoro Islands, Lesotho, Ethiopia and Swaziland. In addition to easing trade restrictions in all possible ways, including lowering tariffs, PTA aims to relax customs and immigration regulations between African countries. Anybody who has experience in traveling from one African country to another, in whatever capacity, must welcome these aims. Other states invited to join, or interested in membership, are Angola, Madagascar, Mozambique, the Seychelles, Tanzania, Rwanda and Burundi.[32]

Conclusion

In the final analysis it must be concluded that such neocolonialist tendencies as do exist in Zambia and find expression in foreign policy attitudes of the national bourgeoisie have not have a great impact on President Kaunda's commitment to the liberation of Southern Africa. To the contrary, the success of the costly disengagement policy is reflected in the independence of Zimbabwe. It would be reasonable to argue that this success might not have been achieved with a multi-party system in Zambia. It would have been easier for foreign interests to strengthen the incipient comprador class in such a system, either directly or indirectly, especially in view of the powerlessness of the peasantry. By the time Zimbabwe became independent there was noticeably a certain fatigue in Zambia after sixteen years of heavy involvement in guerilla support and economic hardship. Although there are many urgent domestic problems now, such as very high urban unemployment, widespread criminality, corruption and administrative inefficiency, the state has held together under severe strains. It is true that expenditure for defence purposes has gone up in recent years somewhat, but there has not been a resort to military rule as in many other African states.

For the eighties three main tasks still lie ahead in the regional context: the liberation of Namibia; the liberation of South Africa; and national economic recovery within the context of and with assistance from SADCC. These are related objectives. The ousting of the Pretoria regime and the achievement of fully-fledged majority rule in a future Azania remains the central issue. The continuous attempts at undermining majority-ruled Southern African states by South Africa (witness Mozambique, Angola, Zimbabwe, Lesotho, Swaziland and to a lesser extent Botswana and Zambia itself) greatly frustrates rapid development efforts. Pretoria's continued colonialism in Namibia demands that African energies and lives are to be spent on the liberation of that territory rather than on developing the land, the mineral potential and the education of the young to live a life in liberty and prosperity.

As compared to many other Southern African countries Zambia has made very great economic sacrifices in the struggle for the dignity of man in Southern Africa. The future should reward them.

Notes

1. Zdenek Cervenka (ed.), *Land-locked Countries of Africa* (The Scandinavian Institute of African Studies, Uppsala, 1973), Ch. 1.
2. Richard Hall, *The High Price of Principles* (Praeger, New York, 1970).
3. Republic of Zambia, *Report of the International Commission on the Assassination of Herbert Wiltshire Chitepo* (Government Printer, Lusaka, March 1976).
4. ZIRIC (ZAPU Research and Information Centre) *Massacre of Zimbabwean Refugees in Refugee Camps in Zambia* (Lusaka, 1979).
5. *Times of Zambia,* 21 November 1979. Leader: 'It is Full War' address by the President. All army leave was cancelled and reservists were called up. The University was closed indefinitely (reopened on 17 March). The President announced that Zambia would strengthen her defence forces and start with the production of arms. *Times of Zambia,* 7 February 1980. The front page leader stated that Zambia had bought K 70 m. worth of arms from Russia, including 16 MIGs. Some 200 air and ground crew had been sent to Russia for training. The report, although coming from "a government spokesman" and published in a government-owned newspaper, was publicly rejected two days later as "wild allegations" by the chairman of the Defence and Security Committee, Mr Grey Zulu.
6. *Times of Zambia,* 24 November, 1979. President Kaunda in an address to students said that Sir Len had become "irrelevent", a man who "could not operate here anymore".
7. Richard Hall, 'Zambia and Rhodesia – Links and Fetters', *Africa Report,* January 1966.
8. Source: UN Secretary General's Report to ECOSOC. E/1978/114, 5th July, 1978.

(a) For the first fourteen days before the border closure with Rhodesia in January, 1973.

(b) Lobito route severed in August, 1975, following outbreak of civil war in Angola.

(c) First full year of operations of TAZARA from August, 1976.

(d) Route severed following border closure between Tanzania and Kenya.

(e) Excludes crude oil.

(f) To Mwenzo (before the line reached new Kapiri Mposhi).

9. Republic of Zambia, Contingency Planning Secretariat Cabinet Office, Lusaka *Why Zambia Re-Opened the Southern Railway Route* (Government Printer, Lusaka, 1979).

10. C. D. Anglin & T. Shaw, *Zambia's Foreign Policy: Studies in Diplomacy and Dependence* (Westview Special Studies, 1979, p. 17.

11. *Times of Zambia*, 6 March 1980.

12. *Times of Zambia*, 27 November 1979. The intention is to prosecute the twelve non-Zambia based companies in the High Court of Zambia, to enter judgment in their expected absence, have the verdict registered in the countries of origin of the companies and ask their governments to prosecute them. If successful, this would probably be a precedent in international litigation.

13. Frank Ballance, *Zambia and the East African Community* (Maxwell School, Syracuse University, New York, 1971).

14. Anglin & Shaw, *op. cit.,* Ch. 5.

15. Karin Eriksen, "Zambia: Class Formation and Detente", *Review of African Political Economy*, No. 9 (May-August, 1978); also
Robert Molteno and William Tordoff, "Independent Zambia: Achievements and Prospects", in W. Tordoff (ed.), *Politics in Zambia* (Manchester University Press, 1974).

16. Ben Turok, "The Penalties of Zambia's Mixed Economy", in Turok (ed.), *op. cit.*

17. Republic of Zambia, *Manifesto on Southern Africa* (Government Printer, Lusaka, 1969).

18. At present Mr Paul Lusaka, Zambia's representative at the UN; previously Mrs Gwendolyn Konie, now Minister for Tourism.

19. *Times of Zambia*, 22 February 1980.

20. Reflected in demonstrations at the University of Zambia on 15 January 1976, which led to a witch-hunt for Marxist pro-MPLA staff, the closure of the University and the arrest and subsequent deportation of two highly regarded expatriate political science lecturers.

21. Republic of South Africa, House of Assembly, *Parliament Debates*, 21 April 1971, Cols. 4928-40.

22. Zambian Information Services, *Dear Mr Vorster . . . ; Details of exchanges between President Kaunda of Zambia and Prime Minister Vorster of South Africa* (Lusaka, April 1971).

23. Anglin & Shaw, *op. cit.* p. 313.

24. *The Guardian*, 1 May 1982.

25 *The Guardian*, 15 July 1982.

26 Republic of Zambia, *His Excellency the President's Address to Parliament on the Opening of the Second Session of the Fourth National Assembly*, 11th January 1980 (Government Printer, Lusaka), p. 1.

27. *Southern Africa: Toward Economic Liberation.* A Declaration made by the Governments of Independent States of Southern Africa, made at Lusaka on 1st April 1980 (Z. I. S.).

28. SADCC Communique, Press Release Z. I. S., No. 4/1980.
29. Information supplied by Mr. Francis Walusiku, Deputy Secretary (Finance) to the Zambian Cabinet 15th March 1981 on the request of the author.
30. Source: AIM Information Bulletin (Maputo), No. 53, November 1980 – quoted by Peter Meyns in "Non-Alignment and Regional Co-operation in Southern Africa", a paper read at the Fourth Bi-Annual Conference on Liberation and Development of the African Association of Political Science, Harare, May 23-27, 1981.
31. *Daily News* (Tanzania), 28 June 1982.
32. *Daily News* (Tanzania), 21 June 1982.

Conclusion
by Klaas Woldring

One conclusion of the chapters comprising this volume must be that *Zambia is in a greater state of economic dependency than at any other time since October 1964*. Zambian society is divided not, in the main, along tribal lines but, instead, along class lines. Zambia's new elite, the political and managerial class, is far from productive, far from honest and is sadly lacking in managerial skills. The tremendously vibrant nationalist spirit, which characterized this emerging elite in the early sixties, has gone virtually completely. Only the President and a few able and trusted senior aides are keeping the flame alive. Even though it may be argued that the President has in fact become the prisoner of an inefficient, partly corrupt system, his dedication, energy and persistence continue to be a shining example of leadership.

The integration of Zambia into the finance imperialist system is beyond question. Zambia cannot disentangle herself from this system in the foreseeable future. Those bright and clever men who wanted to overthrow the government in October 1980 and were sentenced to death in January 1983 probably wanted to integrate Zambia more actively as an agent of finance imperialism, either for greater personal gain or, they may believe, for the benefit of all Zambians, or both. This is deplorable but it would be ludicrous if these men were to die. They represent a force in Zambian society which will not die with their execution. Their skills and dedication to improve Zambia's miserable economic conditions should not be wasted. Nor should they be made to languish in a prison for long. If put to death or made to suffer a long prison sentence, it is Zambia that will be the loser and the government's popularity is likely to suffer further. These men should be freed soon and reintegrated to the benefit of society as a whole. This is not impossible, nor should it harm the government. I have come to this conclusion not because I approve of the plot that they hatched to overthrow the government or of their political leanings. Messrs Musakanya and Shamwana and the others should be seen primarily as victims of the serious stresses and inadequacies of the present political and economic system prevailing at present. It would make more sense to call on these men to assist the President to reform the polity.

There is a great deal of ideological confusion in Zambia flowing from President Kaunda's philosophy of Humanism. This philosophy, not given much prominence in this text in order to avoid repeating that confusion, cannot be a substitute for effective management. Yet, in government circles frequent reference is made to the state philosophy in preference to effective action. It seems to be used more by incapable leaders as a justification for nonaction. This is not to argue that Humanism lacks a moral basis or that it is a hodge-podge of ideas. Humanism does contain a logical set of moral precepts and as a system of ideas and ideals is grounded upon important traditional values and culture which the President has tried to link primarily to socialist aims. On occasions he has also argued however that Humanist principles can be fruitfully associated with capitalism. It is this kind of dualistic thinking that has led to the ideological confusion which has effected development adversely. It has also led to what could be regarded as an incipient management revolution.

What the plotters want most of all is effective management and that applies equally to the trade union leadership. They should be made to contribute to that on social terms. The solution to the ideological confusion is not to try to refine Humanism or replace it by either socialism or capitalism but to relegate the debate on "isms" to the backseat – at least in the short run. Zambia cannot be rescued from her present several predicaments by any ideology.

To my mind there is no need either, as the President has convincingly demonstrated himself, to change Zambia to a multi-part state so as to provide opportunity for peaceful change of government. Violent overthrows occur as frequently in multi-party systems as in one-party systems. But the 1978 change of the constitution, a hasty move aimed to frustrate a particular alternative candidate for the Presidency, should be repealed. The possibility of peaceful change may be provided quite easily within the existing one-party constitution; and it can be achieved at very short notice if need be. If the 1980s are going to herald a better managed Zambia and achieve self-sufficiency in food production, there can be little doubt about the need for quite drastic reforms in the Civil Service. Since the Report of the Inquiry into the Civil Service has not yet been published no comment on that project can be offered here. One must hope that it will be a far-reaching document and that the recommendations will be acted upon as soon as practicable. There have been many public inquiries and sensible recommendations but remarkable little inclination by the government to act on those inquiries and recommendations. The Zambian government cannot afford to wait any longer if it wants to survive, restore domestic and international confidence, and make a success of Operation Food Production.